The Pantry Gourmet

Over 250 recipes for mustards, vinegars, relishes, pâtés, cheeses, breads, preserves, and meats to stock your pantry, freezer, and refrigerator.

by Jane Doerfer

 Rodale Press, Emmaus, Pennsylvania

Some of the recipes in this book appeared in slightly different form in *Horticulture* magazine.

The recipe, Chili Oil, on page 22 is copyright © 1982 by Nina Simonds, reprinted by permission of Houghton Mifflin Company.

Printed in the United States of America on recycled paper, containing a high percentage of de-inked fiber.

Library of Congress Cataloging in Publication Data

Doerfer, Jane A.
    The pantry gourmet.

    Includes index.
    1. Cookery. 2. Food—Preservation. I. Title.
TX715.D655 1984   641.5   84-8365
ISBN 0-87857-506-5   hardcover
ISBN 0-87857-520-0   paperback

2 4 6 8 10 9 7 5 3 1 hardcover
2 4 6 8 10 9 7 5 3 1 paperback

Contents

About the Author

Jane Doerfer is an editor, former TV producer, cooking teacher, backyard gardener, and, above all, an accomplished cook. She is editor of *MassBay Antiques* newspaper, food columnist for *Horticulture* magazine, and author of many articles about food and restaurants. She collaborated with Marian Morash on *The Victory Garden Cookbook.* Jane lives with her husband and two children in Boston.

Acknowledgments

Many people shared their knowledge of pantry food cooking with me for this book. I am especially grateful to Nina Simonds, Susan Harnett, Ingrid Lysgaard Motsis, Daphne Derven, Patricia and Nitzi Rabin, Robert Carroll, and Alice Senturia for contributing their recipes and special expertise.

My husband, Gordon, and our children, Andrew and Joanna, willingly ate their way through many a success (and failure), as did my neighbors, Loretta and George Slover.

From the first time I visited the Rodale Test Kitchen in Emmaus, Pennsylvania, almost two years ago, I knew I was going to enjoy working with the staff, and that we shared a desire to create delicious and tempting "gourmet" food that was also healthful.

I appreciate the help of Susan Burwell and Susan Pearson who tested recipes, and am especially grateful to Debra Deis and Marie Harrington who not only tested recipes but also contributed their suggestions to the text. Linda Gilbert coordinated and supervised the testing and was always helpful about suggesting further information and food tips.

Once my part of the book was done, the Rodale production team took over. Tom Chinnici designed the book, Pam Carroll did the line drawings, and Louise Doucette provided her skills at copy editing.

Throughout the whole process, I was fortunate to have Carol Hupping as my editor. Carol is a talented and sensitive editor who has always been supportive and encouraging.

To all of these people, my sincere thanks.

Introduction

The word *pantry* evokes images of a room lined with preserves, relishes, and other canned goods, with smoked meats hanging from the ceiling, freshly churned butter mounded in an earthenware bowl, sauerkraut and pickles fermenting in crocks, and a week's worth of breads stored in tins. This type of pantry was common in the 19th century, when ice was the only form of cold storage and people had to preserve enough food in as many ways as they could to last until the next butchering or harvest-time. Modern refrigeration has removed the necessity for the old-fashioned pantry, but the outmoded food-preserving techniques still linger on.

While you still will find recipes for some of these outdated pantry foods here, this book does not look at the pantry in that traditional way. It is, rather, a new-style pantry cookbook.

When Rodale approached me about writing a pantry foods cookbook that would feature foods made with healthful food preservation techniques, I was intrigued by the challenge. I spent the next year and a half developing recipes that would keep for some time, yet retain a fresh, just-cooked flavor. As I was working, I was struck by the way old-fashioned food preservation techniques continue to be recommended, even though they are known to be unhealthful. Rodale has been the leader in developing good-tasting recipes without using salt, refined grains, sugar, excessive amounts of fats, alcohol, caffeine (including chocolate), or cured or smoked fish or meats, and I have followed these guidelines throughout the book.

My aim in writing this book is to provide you with a variety of foods that stay in top condition anywhere from 1 week in the refrigerator to several months on the pantry shelf. But in working toward that goal, my prime concern was that the foods taste good: if something kept well but did not taste delicious, then I didn't include it.

When I started making some of my favorite foods without salt, I discovered an intriguing fact: most foods I kept in short-term storage had a much fresher flavor when salt was omitted, particularly if onions or garlic were included in the recipe. *Hummus* made with salt, for example, often develops a strong—almost unpleasant—flavor in storage, but when it's made without salt, the *hummus* tastes fresh for days. I suspect that the salt draws out any bitter juices, but whatever the reason, this fact is a real plus when cooking without salt.

If you have been cooking with salt and are just getting used to eliminating it, remember that it takes a while for your taste buds to adjust. It took me about 1 month to lose the taste for salt. I never used much to begin with, but I'd put a pinch here . . . or a pinch there . . . and it really added up. I think you have to be a much better cook when the salt shaker is packed away, for salt gives an intensity to flavors that has to be replaced in more creative ways.

The inspiration for much of my salt-free cooking is the extensive herb and vegetable garden in our back yard. Once you learn to cook with fresh herbs, I think you will find, as I did, that you don't miss salt at all. Sweet marjoram, basil, lovage, and sweet cicely are my favorite herb salt substitutes.

I've called this book *The Pantry Gourmet* because it was inspired by the interest we Americans have acquired in gourmet foods—wonderful regional American foods and ethnic foods from all over the world that bring new flavors to our tables. I'm speaking, for instance, about the pantry foods that you now find in the proliferating number of new gourmet shops and even special gourmet sections of supermarkets and department stores: raspberry vinegar that sells for $7 a bottle but that you can make at home for almost nothing if you have a berry patch or access to fresh raspberries; and unusual, flavorful mustards that are priced at $4.50 for ½ cup but that cost pennies to duplicate in your own kitchen.

My family enjoys traveling, and we have exchanged homes in Japan, Italy, England, and the Caribbean. I keep a travel diary and, everywhere we go, I fill pages with food ideas, sketches of beautifully prepared foods I've seen, and with recipes. I'm equally interested in American regional and ethnic foods: when the children were young, I'd pack them in the car and go looking for ethnic markets. Throughout the book you'll find a sampling of recipes from our travels, and adaptations of some of my favorite American ethnic foods.

The best part about cooking for me is that, no matter how good a cook you are, no matter how many different techniques and cuisines you've tried, there's always something new to learn.

I've been exchanging ideas and recipes with people since I began cooking, and I asked some of the good cooks I know to share their pantry food suggestions and recipes with me for this book. Some of these people are well-known cooks, others are not. What they all have in common is a love of good food, a curiosity about how it's prepared, and a wealth of knowledge that could come only from years of experience.

You'll discover how a restaurant chef prepares stocks and how a noted cooking teacher and food columnist adapts Chinese recipes to salt-free cooking. A Danish pastry chef shows how to bake light, delicate breads with whole grain flours, while a food historian talks about the old-fashioned methods of food preservation that seem so foreign to us today. You'll find these interviews, and others, scattered throughout the book.

A few final notes about storage: Foods keep much longer than you might expect—as long as you start with top-quality ingredients. In developing the recipes, I was constantly amazed at how well the foods kept. Often foods that I thought might spoil after a few days stayed in good condition for 1 week or longer. And these storage times were verified twice: once when I tested the recipes and a second time when the Rodale Test Kitchen retested the recipes, something it does with every recipe it publishes.

Food stored in glass in the refrigerator lasts longer than food stored in plastic. The Test Kitchen recently tested the same foods stored in both plastic and glass and found that in some cases the foods stored in glass kept 1 or 2 weeks longer without spoiling.

You don't need a great deal of space to store the foods in this book; a refrigerator and a few shelves should suffice. It's important, however, that foods stored on pantry shelves, such as bottled homemade vinegars, dried pastas, and home-canned goods, be kept in a cool, dark, dry spot—not near a radiator or in direct light or in a damp basement.

Where appropriate I've indicated whether or not a recipe freezes well, but this is not intended as a freezer cookbook. Rodale has just published *Rodale's Complete Book of Home Freezing*, and I suggest that you pick up a copy if you plan to do a lot of freezing.

Ingredients Used in This Book

When you're preparing pantry foods, it's essential to start with top-quality ingredients that will retain their fresh qualities in storage. The food you store is only as good as your raw ingredients. Super-ripe tomatoes from the garden are fine to use in a tomato sauce for dinner, but don't expect to store the sauce for any length of time, because it might spoil rapidly. This is particularly true when you're cooking relishes and preserves: if you want relishes that will keep in good condition, start with ripe, rot-free fruit and vegetables; don't try to be thrifty by cutting away bad spots and using what's left. Fresh ingredients also have more flavor, which is important when you're cooking without salt. When I say fresh I don't mean just the main ingredients, but also those that are there especially to add flavor, like lemon and lime juice, citrus zest, and hot peppers.

I've made a special attempt in developing the recipes for this book to use ingredients that are available at most supermarkets or natural food grocery stores. If an ingredient, such as almond oil, is hard to locate, I've given you a source. Most natural food or oriental grocery stores also stock the ethnic ingredients I've included.

Although soy sauce—and tamari—are favored ingredients of many natural food cooks, I use them sparingly. Aside from the fact that these ingredients contain sodium, I think they tend to overpower other flavors in a recipe and make everything taste the same. I prefer to use fresh herbs, spices, and other ingredients to develop a complex mix of flavors. In particular, I've found that a touch of something sour, such as lemon juice or a good-quality vinegar, compensates for the lack of salt.

You'll find several recipes for herb vinegars in this book, but I also use specialty vinegars for flavor. Two of my favorite vinegars are a pear vinegar (developed by the food mail-order company Harry and David, in Medford, Oregon), which is aged in wood before being sold, and sherry vinegars from Jerez de la Frontera, Spain. Jerez, the sherry-making capital of Spain, produces vinegars aged for different lengths of time. I use a vinegar imported by Dean and Deluca in New York City, available at many gourmet shops, and a stronger-tasting variety aged for 12 years, produced by the Morilla company in Jerez. These vinegars are worth tracking down because even a small amount gives an intense flavor to your cooking.

I found when I was testing recipes that the texture of whole wheat flour varied considerably depending upon the brand. Some companies milled a fine flour, while others left in large pieces of bran. To compensate for this variation, I've often given the amount of flour as a range—particularly in the cracker and bread recipes. Unless noted, the flour is whole wheat flour, not whole wheat pastry flour.

I prefer the varied texture of stone-ground cornmeal, and I usually buy it at natural food stores.

All the recipes in the book were tested with the lightest honey I could find, which is raspberry honey from Maine. I didn't pick this honey on a whim or because I liked the sound of the name. For years we had a country house near Belfast, Maine, midway up the coast. Our supermarket there sold locally produced raspberry and blueberry honeys. I became quite fond of these honeys and their excellent flavors. The honeys are packed by R. B. Swan and Son, 25 Prospect Street, Brewer, Maine 04412. The Swan company will mail these honeys as well as their mixed wildflower honey.

Whichever brand of honey you buy, the important point is to select a light honey. This is particularly important when you are preserving jams, because the honey flavor is pervasive and you want the fruit flavor to dominate. I cringe when I see recipes that call for buckwheat honey, which is so strong it will overpower every other flavor in the dish. Clover honey is a good compromise because it is a relatively light honey with a mild flavor.

Most recipes in this book call for fresh herbs. If you cannot locate the herbs (although I now see that many supermarkets and farm stands are stocking them all winter long), substitute 1 teaspoon of dried herbs for each tablespoon of fresh herbs called for.

Throughout this book you will find small symbols accompanying many of the recipes. I've placed them there to alert you to those foods that keep particularly well.

lets you know that this particular food cans well (see Basics chapter for canning instructions),

means that the food can be kept in the refrigerator for several weeks,

indicates that it's good for freezing (see Basics chapter again for some freezing tips), and

means that the food will keep well on the pantry shelf (a cool, dry, dark place) usually for months.

Maximum storage times can be found at the end of each recipe.

Watch for these symbols when you're looking for recipes that you know you'll want to keep more than the usual few days in the refrigerator: when, for instance, you want to turn just-right summer peaches into preserves that you can enjoy all winter long; when you want a bread recipe that you can double so that you have an extra loaf to freeze; or when you want to make up a sauce or spread and be sure that it will keep in the refrigerator for up to 1 month without losing its delicate flavor.

One of the best herbs to use in salt-free cooking is lovage. Although I use it a great deal, it is a fairly obscure herb, and for that reason I hesitated about including it in the book. I would never have started cooking with lovage had I not read Richard Olney's *Simple French Cooking*. Olney was so enthusiastic about lovage that I thought it was about time to have it in my own garden. That was at least 10 years ago, and lovage has been a fixture ever since.

Most herb farms stock lovage plants, and almost all the mail-order companies sell lovage seeds. (Be sure to get fresh seeds, for lovage seeds are like onion seeds—they lose their viability rapidly.)

What's so special about lovage? Lovage is an amalgamating herb. When you put it in a soup or stew and it cooks down, you can't pinpoint the flavor; you just know the food tastes good. In addition, it's one of the first herbs to emerge in the spring, so during April and May, when fresh herb choices are minimal, your lovage plants are in full production. Raw lovage has a slight celery flavor, and it is delicious in salads, particularly in the spring and fall, when its taste is milder. Of course, if you can't find lovage, you can always substitute parsley or a mixture of parsley and some other herb.

I've used unsalted butter and large eggs in all the recipes.

Finally, if you don't have an ingredient included in one of these recipes, think about what ingredient you could substitute, rather than decide not to make the recipe. Quite often it's possible to substitute other ingredients for the ones I have listed. As a matter of fact, some of my own favorite recipes—some found in this book—have evolved because I was out of an ingredient and decided to vary the recipe with ingredients I had on hand.

Condiments

Recently, while browsing in a New York gourmet shop, I happened upon the condiments section and was flabbergasted by the variety of home-style condiments for sale. I was tempted by the dozens of regional mustards, spiced oils, and vinegars flavored with fruits, herbs, and spices. But when cherry flavored vinegar costs $4.49 a pint, and a half cup of tarragon mustard goes for $5, it's easy to resist temptation and decide to make your own condiments at home.

For very little money and just a few hours in the kitchen, you can prepare mustards, vinegars, and oils that will fill a pantry shelf of condiments—to spice up meals on nights when you don't feel like cooking or to provide you with a supply of hostess gifts for the coming year.

Unusual condiments always elicit attention: At one elegant buffet dinner party I attended, the hostess had set out pickled shrimp, honey baked ham, a poached chicken loaf, and a smoked turkey and rice salad —all wonderful foods. But what the guests really fussed about was the bowl of sweet mustard the hostess had made just for the occasion. When

I cook for our annual Christmas Eve open house buffet, I now know to make a double supply of the Honey Mustard you'll find in this chapter. I have one guest who likes it so much he spreads it on bread, skipping the meat altogether because, he says, it interferes with the taste of the mustard.

The current boom in condiments ties in closely with a renewed interest in regional American cooking. You can find sweet, dark, German mustard far from the confines of Milwaukee, and Louisiana hot sauce even in small Maine supermarkets.

This interest in condiments is nothing new. Until refrigeration made fresh-tasting meats and vegetables an everyday occurrence, condiments were a necessity, giving variety to preserved meats that tasted much the same. During the 19th century people believed mustards accented the flavor of foods and aided digestion. A mustard pot was a standard fixture on the dining table, along with a silver plated cruet stand that held the assortment of vinegars and vinegar based sauces used to douse cutlets and roasts.

Every summer I bottle a number of herb vinegars to enjoy all winter long. I'll marinate lovage blossoms in white wine vinegar, or steep chive blossoms in white vinegar that turns an attractive pink after a few days. Come fall, I'll dig up fresh garlic cloves for Basil Garlic Vinegar, and I'll preserve tarragon in vinegar for sauces and salads. And I'll chop sweet cicely, sweet marjoram, or tarragon to flavor olive oil.

Condiments also play a major role in salt-free cooking, particularly in the winter, when fresh herbs are out of season. A spoonful of mustard contributes a complex flavor to most sauces, while a dash of vinegar in casseroles and soups helps compensate for the lack of salt.

In addition to the recipes you'll find here, there are others throughout the book that are flavorful enough to be used as condiments. Look especially at the recipes in Cold Sauces and Salad Dressings, such as Fresh Mint Sauce and Mint Garlic Sauce (see page 246). Check for more condiment ideas as you page through the other chapters, as well as the Index.

Tarragon Vinegar

    1¾   cups white vinegar
          tarragon sprigs

Heat the vinegar. Pack the tarragon loosely in a hot, sterilized pint jar. Fill the hot jar with the hot vinegar. Seal, and let the jar stand for 2 weeks, shaking the jar daily.

Strain the vinegar (if desired) through coffee filters or cheesecloth, and pour back into its jar. Seal, and store in a dark, cool spot, where it will keep for at least 6 months.

Makes 1 pint

Basil Garlic Vinegar

It's not necessary to strain and filter this vinegar if you don't mind a strong flavor. I just opened a jar of Basil Garlic Vinegar that had been stored in the fruit cellar for 6 months, and it was wonderful—the essence of basil on a cold winter day. However, if you skip the filtering step, use this along with another vinegar to tone down the taste.

    2   cups white vinegar
    ½   cup fresh basil
    3   cloves garlic, halved

Heat the vinegar in a stainless steel or enameled saucepan. Place the basil and garlic in a hot, sterilized pint jar. Pour in the hot vinegar, seal the jar, and let it stand for 2 weeks, shaking the jar occasionally.

Strain the vinegar through coffee filters or cheesecloth, and rebottle in the same jar. It will keep in a cool, dark spot for up to 6 months.

Makes 1 pint

Blueberry Vinegar

One day, while browsing through the gourmet section of a New York department store, Anne Adams was intrigued by a fancy bottle of blueberry vinegar priced at $5.60. She bought the vinegar, brought it back to her Vermont kitchen, and developed this recipe which—as she points out with pride—cost her only $0.29 a bottle. The vinegar has a lovely, deep purple color and a spicy flavor that sets off fruit salads or any of the chicken-in-fruit-flavored-vinegar recipes so popular with the proponents of nouvelle cuisine. The amount of blueberries depends upon whether you're using the more flavorful wild blueberries or the blander cultivated varieties.

¼ to ⅓	cup blueberries	1	tablespoon honey
2¼	cups white vinegar	1	cinnamon stick

Place all but 1 tablespoon of the blueberries in an enameled or stainless steel saucepan with the vinegar and honey. Bring the vinegar to a boil, lower the heat slightly, and boil slowly for about 8 minutes. Strain out the blueberries and pour the hot vinegar into a hot, sterilized pint jar. Add the remaining blueberries, the cinnamon, and additional vinegar if needed to fill the jar. Seal, and store in a cool, dark spot. The vinegar will keep for at least 6 months.

Makes 1 pint

Ginger Vinegar

Use this vinegar for making mayonnaise for chicken salad or in a vinaigrette sauce tossed in a julienne-vegetable-and-bean-sprout salad. You can also mix it with seltzer water and honey for a ginger ale. It's powerful, so a little goes a long way.

1	tablespoon chopped gingerroot
1	cup cider vinegar

Place the gingerroot in a sterilized jar and pour the vinegar over it. Cover the jar and let the vinegar steep for 3 to 5 days in a light, but not sunny, place. Taste after 3 days to see if it's the strength you wish.

Strain through coffee filters or cheesecloth, and rebottle in the same jar. Store in the refrigerator, where the vinegar will keep for several weeks.

Makes 1 cup

Chive Blossom Vinegar

Leonie Foy, who is a talented cook and editor, likes the fact that the blossoms turn this vinegar a delicate pink. It makes an attractive hostess gift or addition to the pantry shelf. You can make any amount of vinegar —the proportions suggested below work for a pint canning jar.

24   mature chive blossoms,
      at peak point of color
2   cups white vinegar

Loosely fill a sterilized pint jar with the chive blossoms. Add the vinegar, making sure all the blossoms are covered by the liquid. Cover the jar and set it in a sunny window.

After 3 to 4 days taste the vinegar, and if it is the flavor you like, strain off the blossoms and rebottle the vinegar in the same jar. The vinegar will keep for at least 1 year if stored in a cool, dark place.

Makes 1 pint

Lovage Vinegar

Lovage vinegar is one of the quickest vinegars to prepare. Lovage oils are so pervasive, the vinegar can be ready after 1 or 2 days of steeping. All summer long I clip off the lovage flowers before they are in full bloom and make up jars of vinegar for winter salads. The fresh lovage taste is particularly appreciated on a cold, snowy day.

½ to ¾   cup lovage flowers   1½ to 1¾   cups white vinegar
         and stems

Remove the lovage flowers from the stems and coarsely chop the stems. Place the stems and flowers in a sterilized pint jar. Pour in the vinegar, and seal. Let the vinegar steep for 1 or 2 days, then taste it.

Once the vinegar is the strength you wish, remove the lovage, if desired, and seal again. The vinegar will keep for up to 1 year in a cool, dark place.

Makes about 1½ cups

Lemon Mint Vinegar

This vinegar is fun to make in early spring, because mint is one of the first perennial herbs to appear in the garden. I use apple mint, which is milder than most varieties and my preferred choice for cooking. If you are substituting peppermint or spearmint, use only 5 mint leaves. Rice wine vinegar is sold in many supermarkets as well as in oriental and natural food stores, but if you cannot find it, substitute cider vinegar.

1	lemon	10	apple mint leaves or
1⅛	cups rice wine		5 spearmint or
	vinegar		peppermint leaves

Using a vegetable peeler, remove a thin strip of rind, about 1 inch wide and 3 inches long, from the lemon. Make sure none of the bitter white pith is attached.

Pour the vinegar into a hot, sterilized pint jar, and add the lemon rind and mint. Cover the jar and place it in a sunny spot for 1 or 2 days.

The lemon and mint flavor the vinegar rapidly, so it should be ready to use almost immediately. Taste the vinegar and remove the lemon and mint if you wish. Seal the vinegar and store it in a cool, dark place, where it will keep for several months.

Makes about 1 pint

Variations
• Lemon Lovage or Lemon Tarragon Vinegar: Substitute 1 tablespoon lovage or tarragon for the mint.

Sour Cherry Wine Vinegar

This vinegar is a specialty of Forcalquier, a town in the Provençal mountains of southern France. The cherries color the vinegar a lovely hue of reddish pink. At a gourmet shop you would pay more than $5 per bottle, but if you have a sour-cherry tree, such as a North Star variety, your only cost would be for white wine vinegar. (Canned cherries work well, too.) The vinegar is especially flavorful in chicken or turkey salads, in which the sharp taste is a counterpoint to the blandness of the poultry.

14 or 15	ripe sour	about 1¾	cups white wine
	cherries		vinegar

Place the cherries in a hot, sterilized pint jar. (A vinegar bottle with a cork top is even better.) Heat the vinegar almost to the boiling point, and pour it into the hot jar. Seal, and put the jar in a sunny window for a few days.

Then taste the vinegar. It should have a slightly sour-cherry flavor. Depending upon the degree of ripeness of the cherries, the vinegar should be ready in 1 to 2 weeks. Reseal the vinegar and store it in the refrigerator, where it will keep for several months.

Makes 1 pint

Raspberry Vinegar

The first time I made raspberry vinegar, I used only vinegar and raspberries. When I bottled the vinegar, it had a wonderful aroma that was the essence of raspberries and a lovely, deep, rich color. After I used the vinegar a few times, however, the color and much of the flavor remained, but the aroma had completely disappeared. Now when I bottle the vinegar, I add some honey syrup, which seems to fix both the aroma and the flavor, and—to be on the safe side—I store the vinegar in the refrigerator. The vinegar is delicious in chicken sautés, mayonnaise, and salad dressings.

1	quart raspberries	½	cup honey
1	quart white wine or white vinegar	½	cup water

Pick over the raspberries to make sure they're clean, and place them in a deep porcelain or stainless steel bowl. Add the vinegar and let the berries steep overnight.

The next day crush them slightly with a potato masher, and cover the bowl with plastic wrap. Let the berries sit for 2 days longer.

On the fourth day line a colander with coffee filters and strain the vinegar, pressing down on the berries to extract any extra juice.

Boil the honey and water together until a syrup is formed—the liquid will reduce at least a third. Stir 4 to 5 tablespoons of the honey syrup into the raspberry vinegar. (If there is any syrup left, use it for lemonade.) Pour the vinegar into sterilized jars, seal, and store in the refrigerator, where it will stay in good condition for several months. The honey syrup may settle to the bottom, so you may need to shake the vinegar before using.

Makes about 3¼ cups

Variation
• Raspberry Orange Vinegar: Add ¼ cup fresh raspberries and a 2 × ½-inch slice of orange zest to each pint of vinegar as you bottle it.

Profile

Daphne L. Derven

When Daphne Derven is not working as an archeologist for the Army Corps of Engineers in Texas, she can be found traveling around the country, talking about food. Daphne's extensive knowledge of food customs, recipes, and technology has made her a favored speaker and consultant at museums from Deerfield, Massachusetts, to New Orleans, Louisiana.

Daphne has culled manuscript cookbooks and other sources for early recipes to use in her demonstrations. Documenting food customs and recipes hasn't been easy, because written recipes were uncommon in early colonial times, when people relied upon an oral tradition of recalling recipes. Many old cookbooks (called memory cookbooks) just listed ingredients people were afraid they'd forget, along with unusual, special-occasion recipes. Familiar recipes usually were not written down.

I asked Daphne when white flour and refined sugar became standard parts of the American diet. Daphne said that although most early settlers used whole wheat flour, honey, and maple sugar in their everyday cooking, white flour and sugar were favored by the wealthy. Even in the 1600s there was a definite preference for white bread because it denoted high status. By the 18th and 19th centuries, white flour was more common, but whole wheat flour still was used for daily bread, which was called the household loaf. Cooks baked cakes with both whole wheat and white flours. The white flour, however, was nothing like the bleached, bromated white flour of today. When Daphne prepares period foods with white flour, she combines 5 pounds unbleached flour with ½ pound whole wheat flour and 3 ounces wheat germ to obtain a more authentic mixture.

"The sugar usage was similar to that of white flour," Daphne said. "The finest refined sugar, called loaf sugar, was the most expensive and was a status item to use. The less money you had, the less likely you were to cook with loaf sugar. Instead you would use other sweeteners such as maple sugar, honey, or molasses."

Although processed foods may seem to be a 20th century phenomenon, Daphne pointed out that there was concern in earlier centuries about adulterated foods. When Benjamin Franklin was a teenager, he became a vegetarian for a while after reading a book by Thomas Tryon recommending a vegetable diet. Tryon was concerned about the adulteration of foods: white flour, for example, contained chalk and alum to make it whiter. By 1765 Franklin was suggesting his countrymen make sugar from beets, honey, apples, and maple syrup, calling it a patriotic duty "to supply ourselves from our own produce at home."

I asked Daphne what she had discovered to be the most frequent ways of preserving foods in the past. She said most foods were preserved in sugar, fat, salt, or vinegar—or were smoked.

In the 1800s, when cookbooks became more common, extensive directions were given for preserving and curing meats in salt. *The Improved Housewife*, an 1845 book "by a married lady," explained how to make corned beef; Westphalian, western, and Virginia styles of cured hams; pickled hams and tongues; and how to "salt in snow." This last was an early form of cold storage that called for covering the bottom of a large, clean tub 4 inches deep with snow, adding meats and poultry, covering each layer with 2 to 3 inches of snow, and topping with a layer of tightly packed snow. "Cover your tub, and the colder its location, the better. The meat will remain as fresh and as juicy as when first killed. It will not freeze."

Cooks also used fat, brandy, or some other liquor to seal foods. An 1883 cookbook by S. Annie Frost calls for keeping sausage fresh all year long by cooking sausage cakes, packing them in stone jars, and covering them with the pan grease and melted lard to seal out the air.

Cookbooks published in the late 1800s also gave detailed instructions for building icehouses and root cellars. Root vegetables were stored in sand or leaves and layered in bins. Lemons were covered with water, which was changed weekly, and grapes were hung from the ceiling, with their stem ends coated with sealing wax.

A great deal of attention was devoted to preserving fruits, because fresh fruits were rare unless you were wealthy. People ate fruits in season, then preserved the remainder. Sometimes the fruits were put up in a sugar syrup with brandy and stored in crocks, other times they were made into fruit leathers by being cooked down, sweetened with sugar, and sun dried into paste. The easiest preserving method was to let the fruits dehydrate naturally in the sun.

In the 1877 *Buckeye Cookery* a "tomato figs" recipe was published that called for cooking tomatoes (or peaches) with brown sugar until translucent, then drying them in the sun. Dried and layered with powdered sugar, the author suggested, they tasted like figs.

I mentioned to Daphne that when I looked at a facsimile edition of an 1895 Harrod's department store catalog, there was an extensive listing of mustards, meat sauces, and various catsups for sale. "In the 19th century," Daphne said, "there was quite a popularity for all sorts of flavorings. Mustard was kept on the table and used at almost every meal." She added that there is a theory that before refrigeration became common, people actually preferred the taste of pickled meats to fresh meats but that the preserving techniques caused many of the meats to taste similar. A sprinkling of sauce in a soup or stew, or on pickled meats at the table, varied the flavors somewhat.

Vinegars were also used as seasonings and table condiments. Women made cider vinegar out of apples, but they also put up a number of flavored vinegars: herbs, raspberries, garlic, horseradish—even roses were utilized. (Daphne has made rose vinegar by steeping rose petals in vinegar, setting it in the sun for a few days, then bottling the mixture. The vinegar develops a perfumy aroma and taste.)

Cooks planned their meals around roasts and leftovers. "A lot of food was recycled," Daphne pointed out. "First you'd make a roast, then convert it into a hash, salad, or into croquettes." Stuffings were also a traditional way to use up roasted meats and poultry.

Colonial cooks paid a lot of attention to the way food was presented. In the 18th century, for example, symmetrical patterns were the fashion for serving food. There were corner dishes, and there were side dishes (which is how the phrase originated). Garnishes consisted of fried pieces of bread in various shapes, called sippets, pickled vegetables, herbs, hard boiled eggs, sweetmeats, and candied or preserved fruits. The preoccupation with how food looked led to bizarre practices: the dye cochineal was used to color food red—and Daphne has even found references to cooking in copper pots to give a green tinge to food (which we now know is a dangerous idea).

Many of the recipes Daphne has documented in her food research make ideal pantry foods. I picked out some unusual sauces and other seasonings I thought you might enjoy trying. Her recipes are found in this chapter and throughout the book.

Horseradish Vinegar

This is one of the condiment vinegars popular during the 19th century. Daphne Derven keeps a bottle on hand to add zip to salads and other foods. Remember that a little goes a long way. The vinegar also preserves the horseradish, if you want grated pickled horseradish for any recipes.

1	whole horseradish root	about 1	quart cider vinegar

Peel and grate the horseradish. Add it to the vinegar, and pour the vinegar into a sterilized quart jar. Periodically shake the jar. Depending upon the strength of the horseradish, the vinegar will be ready within a few days to 2 or 3 weeks.

Strain the vinegar before using, and rebottle in smaller sterilized jars if you wish. If the jars are capped, the vinegar will last for up to 1 year in a cool, dry place.

Makes 1 quart

Mushroom Catsup

In the 19th century, catsups were favored seasonings in England and America. These condiments, usually made from local ingredients, evolved from the original *ket'ciaps*, or pickled fish brines from the Indochina area. Daphne Derven says this mushroom catsup gave flavor to pan juices and was even carried by travelers as a condiment. She uses it in soups, sauces, stews, and vegetable dishes. Unlike tomato catsup, mushroom catsup is thin, like steak sauce.

1	pound mushrooms (whole, caps, or stems)	20	whole cloves
1	tablespoon ground nutmeg	¼	ounce whole mace or 1 tablespoon plus 1 teaspoon ground mace
3½	teaspoons ground allspice	1	quart red wine vinegar
2	tablespoons cracked black pepper		

Place the washed mushrooms and the nutmeg, allspice, pepper, cloves, mace, and vinegar in an enameled or stainless steel pan. Bring the mixture to a boil, reduce the heat, and simmer slowly until the mixture is reduced by half. Stir it occasionally. Strain the mixture and bottle the hot sauce in a hot, sterilized glass jar.

If the catsup is kept covered and stored in the refrigerator, it should keep in good condition for at least 2 months.

Makes 2 to 3 cups

Kitchen Pepper

This mixture of spices, documented by Daphne Derven in several cookbooks, was a favorite seasoning during the 1700s and 1800s. After Daphne had given out this recipe in one of her classes, a friend told her she knew kitchen pepper was something special because she had received it as hostess gifts from 4 different people. Daphne uses this seasoning on potatoes or white fleshed fish, rubs it onto roasts, and includes it in stuffing ingredients. Or try it as a seasoning for ground beef or sausage. Grinding whole spices in a coffee grinder and then combining them produces excellent results.

¼	pound cracked black pepper	1	ounce ground ginger
1	ounce grated nutmeg	1	ounce grated mace
1	ounce ground allspice	½	ounce cayenne pepper
		½	ounce ground cloves

Mix together the pepper, nutmeg, allspice, ginger, mace, cayenne, and cloves. Place in a tightly covered jar. The mixture will keep for several months if stored in a cool, dark spot.

Makes 1½ cups

Lemon Pickle Sauce

One of the most popular cookbooks during the 18th and 19th centuries was Hannah Glasse's *The Art of Cookery Made Plain and Easy*, first published in 1747. Glasse suggests using 1 spoonful of this sauce in white sauces and 2 spoonfuls in brown sauces—rather a concentrated amount for today's more subtle-tasting foods. Daphne Derven, who keeps this strongly flavored, almost bitter condiment on hand, suggests starting with 1 or 2 drops and increasing the amount to suit your taste. A touch will perk up a bland-tasting sauce or casserole.

4	lemons	4	cloves garlic, sliced
about 2	cups cider or wine vinegar	1	tablespoon bruised mace or 1 teaspoon ground mace
¼	cup mustard seeds		
1	nutmeg, cut into pieces (optional)	1	tablespoon bruised cloves

Remove the yellow zest from the lemons and grate it finely.

Make sure there is no white pith attached to the lemons, or the sauce will be bitter. Cut the white pith off the lemons and quarter them. Place the lemons in a stainless steel or enameled saucepan and cover with the vinegar. Add the grated lemon zest, mustard seeds, nutmeg (if used), garlic, mace, and cloves.

Bring the mixture to a boil, remove from the heat, and pour into a glass bowl. Cool the sauce and let the flavors meld for 1 to 2 hours before straining. For a stronger flavor cover the bowl with a plate and allow the sauce to stand at room temperature for a few days to meld the flavors.

Strain the sauce and pour it into a glass jar. Cap, and store the sauce in the refrigerator, where it should stay in good condition for several months.

Makes about 1½ cups

Piquant Sauce

This recipe, developed by Daphne Derven, originally came from Louisiana, but similar recipes can be found in Texas and Oklahoma.

8	scallions, finely chopped (about 1 bunch)	12	plum tomatoes or 6 garden tomatoes, finely chopped
4	cloves garlic, minced	3 to 4	jalapeño peppers, finely chopped
2	sweet green peppers, seeded and chopped		freshly ground black pepper
1	bunch coriander, chopped		hot pepper sauce
½	bunch parsley, chopped		lemon juice

Mix together the scallions, garlic, sweet green peppers, coriander, parsley, tomatoes, and jalapeño peppers. Add pepper, hot pepper sauce, and lemon juice to taste.

Store the sauce in a covered glass jar in the refrigerator, where it will keep for several weeks.

Makes 3 cups

Variation
• Omit the tomatoes.

Daphne L. Derven

Danish-Style Mustard

Don't expect this recipe to make a thick, American-style mustard. The day you make it, the mustard is thin, almost watery, but it thickens overnight in the refrigerator. This hot mustard goes well with cheese sandwiches or cold meats.

⅔	cup dry mustard	2	teaspoons Worcester-
¼	cup honey		shire sauce
⅓	cup boiling water	1	teaspoon cider or malt
1	tablespoon vegetable oil		vinegar

Combine the mustard and honey in a mixing bowl. Add the boiling water and beat until all the lumps are gone and the mustard forms a paste. Beat in the oil, Worcestershire sauce, and vinegar. Refrigerate in a covered jar. The mustard will keep for several months if tightly capped.

Makes ¾ cup

Spiced Mustard

This mustard, given to me by Debra Deis of the Rodale Test Kitchen, is made from whole seeds, which give it a pleasant, grainy texture. It will keep for up to 1 month in the refrigerator.

3	tablespoons mixed	½	cup white grape juice
	pickling spices	1	tablespoon honey
1	cup cider vinegar	2	tablespoons tamari or
¼	cup yellow mustard		soy sauce
	seeds		
¼	cup brown mustard		
	seeds		

Simmer the pickling spices in the vinegar in a covered saucepan for 5 minutes. Remove from the heat and let stand, covered, for 15 minutes.

Place all the mustard seeds in a blender. Pour the vinegar mixture through a strainer into the blender. Process until all the liquid is absorbed. Add the grape juice 2 tablespoons at a time, processing after each addition. (The mixture will thicken as the seeds become more finely ground.) Blend in the honey and tamari or soy sauce. Thin to the desired consistency by blending with more grape juice, vinegar, or water.

Transfer to jars and refrigerate. Check the mustard after 1 day, and thin further if necessary. It will keep in the refrigerator for up to 1 month.

Makes 2 cups

Honey Mustard

1	cup dry mustard	scant ½	cup honey
1	cup white or malt vinegar	2	tablespoons chopped dillweed
2	eggs		

Beat together the mustard and vinegar until smooth. Refrigerate, covered, for at least 24 hours.

Place the vinegar mixture in a bowl and beat in the eggs and honey. Cook in a double boiler over simmering water until thickened, 8 to 10 minutes. Cool before stirring in the dillweed. This mustard keeps for several months stored in a covered jar in the refrigerator.

Makes about 2 cups

Variation
• Add 2 tablespoons orange juice along with the eggs and honey.

Tarragon Mustard

This is a thin mustard when you make it, but it thickens a bit overnight in the refrigerator.

3	cloves garlic, minced	1	cup dry mustard
2	large onions, sliced	3	tablespoons honey
1¾	cups Tarragon Vinegar (see page 2)	1	tablespoon olive oil

Combine the garlic, onions, and tarragon vinegar in a glass mixing bowl, and let sit for 24 hours.

Strain the vinegar. Beat ½ cup vinegar into the mustard. Continue beating until all lumps are removed. Bring the remaining vinegar to a boil and, stirring constantly, slowly add the mustard mixture.

Simmer, stirring frequently to remove any lumps, for 5 minutes. Add the honey and simmer for 3 minutes more. Cool slightly. While the mustard is still warm, add the oil. Pour into a jar, and seal. Stored in the refrigerator, it will keep for several months.

Makes about 1¾ cups

Orange Hot and Sweet Mustard

Serve this pungent mustard, also created by Debra Deis, with broiled meats, or add it to sauces or stews just before serving. To make a zesty dip for vegetables or fruits, stir 3 to 4 tablespoons of mustard into 1 cup yogurt.

1⅛ cups dry mustard (3¼-ounce can)	½ cup honey
1 cup orange juice	½ teaspoon ground cinnamon
¼ cup lemon juice	2 tablespoons vegetable oil
2 teaspoons grated orange zest	
1 teaspoon grated lemon zest	

Place the mustard in a double boiler but not over the heat. Add the orange and lemon juices a little at a time, stirring after each addition to keep the mustard from lumping. Add the orange and lemon zest.

Heat, covered, over simmering water for 15 minutes, scraping the sides of the pan occasionally with a spatula. Stir in the honey, cinnamon, and oil.

Transfer to jars and refrigerate. Check the consistency after 1 day, and thin with a little water if necessary. It will keep well for up to 1 month.

Makes 2 cups

Soy Mustard

Use this very hot mustard to accompany Chinese food.

½ cup dry mustard	1 tablespoon soy sauce
¼ cup water	

Combine the mustard, water, and soy sauce. Dry mustard tends to lump, so make sure no lumps remain. Cover, and let stand for at least 4 hours to blend the flavors.

Pour into a jar. The soy sauce tends to bead, so stir before using. If the mustard is tightly covered, it will last for up to 2 months in the refrigerator.

Makes about ⅓ cup

Green Peppercorn Mustard

Bottled or freeze-dried green peppercorns, imported from Madagascar, are available in many gourmet shops. They add a gentle bite and flecks of color to this flavorful mustard. Like many mustards, this one will thicken as it cools.

2	onions, chopped	1	tablespoon plus 1
3	cloves garlic, chopped		teaspoon bottled or
2	cups white vinegar		freeze-dried green
1	cup dry mustard		peppercorns,
¼	teaspoon Worcester-		drained if bottled
	shire sauce		hot pepper sauce
2	tablespoons honey		

Coarsely purée the onions and garlic in a food processor. Add the vinegar, and pulse on and off for just a moment. Pour the mixture into a glass bowl, cover, and let it steep for at least 4 hours.

Strain the vinegar, reserving the puréed onions and garlic. Beat the mustard to remove any lumps, then add ½ cup of the vinegar, the Worcestershire sauce, and the honey. Mix until smooth.

Heat the remaining vinegar and gradually add it to the mustard mixture. Put the mixture in the food processor bowl, and process until the mixture is smooth and free from lumps.

Place the mustard in a stainless steel or enameled pan, bring it to a boil, add the peppercorns, and cook at a gentle boil for 5 minutes, stirring constantly with a whisk. The mixture will thicken. Season with 1 to 2 dashes hot pepper sauce.

Process the mustard in the food processor until the peppercorns are broken down and distributed throughout the mustard. If you like a mustard with texture, add a tablespoon of the reserved puréed onions and garlic, and process it until combined.

Cool the mustard, then pack it in jars. Seal the jars and store them in the refrigerator, where the mustard will keep for several months.

Makes 1½ cups

Variation
• Omit the peppercorns and add 1½ tablespoons finely chopped tangerine zest (be sure to remove the bitter white pith) that has been simmered in water for 10 minutes and drained. Add to the mustard mixture before boiling it.

Mustard Butter

Spread this butter on thinly sliced dark rye bread as a flavorful base for tongue or roast beef sandwiches. Or use it for basting chicken: just loosen the skin on a roast chicken, and dot the butter under the skin. Or try it over vegetables such as cauliflower or baked potatoes.

½	cup butter, softened	1	teaspoon Worcester-
1½	tablespoons Dijon		shire sauce
	mustard	⅛	teaspoon cumin
1	tablespoon lemon		powder (optional)
	juice		cayenne pepper

Beat the butter with a mixer or in a food processor until it is whipped. Add the mustard, lemon juice, Worcestershire sauce, cumin (if used), and cayenne to taste, and beat until thoroughly combined.

Store in a covered glass container in the refrigerator. The butter should stay in good condition for up to 3 weeks. For longer refrigerator storage omit the lemon juice; or freeze it for up to 3 months.

Makes about ⅔ cup

Variation
• Add 1 tablespoon grated horseradish and 1 teaspoon caraway seeds.

Honey Butter

This is a nice hostess gift on days when you're rushed or have nothing in the pantry. Spread the butter on bran muffins or cream scones—it melts right in.

½	cup butter, softened	1	teaspoon grated
½	cup honey		orange or lemon
			zest (optional)

Cream together the butter, honey, and orange or lemon zest (if used) until fluffy. Cover and store in the refrigerator, where it will keep for at least 1 month.

Makes 1 cup

Kimchi or Korean
Pickled Vegetables

This crisp and spicy-hot condiment, developed by the Rodale Test Kitchen, can be eaten before meals or can be chopped and added to other foods in need of some zip.

1	pound Chinese cabbage stalks (leaves removed)	3	tablespoons cider vinegar
1	large carrot	1	teaspoon minced gingerroot
¼	pound white radishes	2	cloves garlic, minced
2	scallions, thinly sliced	2 to 4	2-inch-long dried red chili peppers, split and seeded
¼	cup soy sauce		
½	cup water		
2	tablespoons honey		

Julienne the Chinese cabbage, carrot, radishes, and scallions. Toss with the soy sauce and water. Cover loosely and let stand overnight at room temperature.

Drain the liquid from the vegetables into a bowl. Add the honey and vinegar to the liquid, and stir well to dissolve the honey. Add the gingerroot, garlic, and chili peppers to the vegetables, and pack them in a sterilized quart jar. Pour the liquid into the jar to cover the vegetables completely. If more liquid is needed, add water.

Cover loosely with a sterilized lid, and let sit at room temperature for 3 to 5 days to ferment, making sure the vegetables are kept beneath the liquid. The liquid will bubble and the flavor will become sour.

The kimchi should then be refrigerated. In 3 or 4 days the cabbage will become translucent and will be ready to serve. Kimchi can be stored in the refrigerator for up to 2 months.

Makes 1 quart

Spicy Catsup

10	pounds plum tomatoes, peeled, quartered, and seeded
3	onions, chopped
1	sweet green pepper, chopped
2	stalks celery, chopped
¾	cup cider vinegar
1 to 2	teaspoons whole allspice or 1 tablespoon ground allspice
2	teaspoons dry mustard
1	teaspoon ground cloves
½	teaspoon black pepper
½	tablespoon ground sweet Hungarian paprika
1	teaspoon ground cinnamon
½	cup honey

Mix together the tomatoes, onions, sweet green peppers, celery, vinegar, allspice, mustard, cloves, pepper, paprika, cinnamon, and honey in a large enameled or stainless steel pot.

Cover and bring the mixture to a boil. Uncover, reduce the heat, and simmer for 2 hours. Remove from the stove, purée the vegetables, and sieve them. Return the sieved purée to the liquid in the pot and cook for another 2 hours, or until thickened.

Spoon the boiling hot catsup into hot, clean pint jars, leaving a ½-inch headspace. Process for 10 minutes in a boiling water bath.

The catsup will keep for up to 1 year if stored in a cool, dark place. You can also freeze this catsup for up to 1 year, but freeze in small quantities so that you can use it up quickly once it is defrosted.

Makes about 4 pints

Dried Hot Pepper Sauce

Use this sauce with tacos, enchiladas, or huevos rancheros—or add a touch to zip up hamburgers or a barbecued-chicken sauce.

18	large dried hot red peppers (such as Anaheim*)	1	tablespoon chopped oregano (or 1 teaspoon dried)
3	cups hot water	½	teaspoon cumin powder
3	cloves garlic		freshly ground black pepper
¼	cup vegetable oil		

Preheat the oven to 400°F.

Spread the hot red peppers out on a baking sheet. Place in the oven for 1 to 2 minutes. Turn the peppers over and put back in the oven for another 1 to 2 minutes. The peppers should give off a lightly roasted aroma. Watch carefully: if the peppers scorch, they will become bitter. Cool the peppers.

Stem and seed the peppers. Rinse them, drain, then cover with the water. Soak the peppers for 1 hour.

Remove the peppers, reserving the soaking water. Place a few of the peppers in a blender or food processor, add some of the soaking water and some of the garlic, and blend until a purée is formed. Continue this process until all the peppers are blended.

Combine the puréed peppers with any remaining soaking liquid, then pour through a medium sieve, and discard any solids left in the sieve.

Place the purée back in the blender, and combine with the oil, oregano, cumin, and pepper to taste. Put the purée in a saucepan, and simmer for 15 minutes, stirring occasionally. Cool.

Store the sauce in a jar in the refrigerator, where it will keep in good condition for several weeks. Or freeze for up to 1 year.

*Do not substitute small, dried chili peppers, or the sauce will be too hot.

Makes 3 cups

Chili Oil

This recipe is from Nina Simonds's *Classic Chinese Cuisine*. In the Chinese provinces of Sichuan and Hunan, where chili peppers are used to give a fiery flavoring to cooking, chili oil is added to dipping sauces and dressing. A little goes a long way.

1	cup sesame oil	6	slices of gingerroot, smashed
1	tablespoon Sichuan peppercorns	½	cup ½-inch pieces dried chili peppers
6	stalks scallions, smashed		

Heat the oil in a pan until smoking. Add the peppercorns, scallions, gingerroot, and chili peppers. Turn off the heat, cover the mixture, and let it sit for 30 minutes. Strain out the seasonings and transfer the oil to a sterilized jar. The chili oil will keep indefinitely in a cool, dark spot.

Makes ¾ cup

Garlic Oil

This mildly flavored oil, which is a staple at Alice Senturia's home, keeps for several months. She uses it in salad dressings and as a cooking oil. Alice keeps 2 versions on hand: one made with safflower oil (which is refrigerated) and another with olive oil (kept on the pantry shelf).

1   quart olive or
    safflower oil
6   large cloves garlic

Place the oil in a sterilized jar (or remove a little oil from its original bottle so you have room for the garlic), and drop in the garlic. Leave the oil at room temperature for 5 to 7 days.

Remove the garlic and rebottle the oil. Store the olive oil in a cool, dark place and the safflower oil in the refrigerator. Both will last for several months.

Makes 1 quart

Herb Oil

Use this oil in vinaigrette salad dressings, to baste grilled lamb or poultry, or to sauté vegetables. The flavor of lovage becomes stronger as the season progresses, so use it only in the spring.

lovage   olive oil
tarragon   vegetable oil
thyme

Fill a sterilized jar ⅓ full with the herbs. They should be picked before they flower, because that is when the oils are concentrated. Fill the jar with equal amounts of olive and vegetable oils to completely cover the herbs. Seal, and store in a dark place for at least 2 weeks.

Strain the oil and rebottle it. The oil keeps for several months in a cool, dark place.

Makes 1 jar

Escaveke Sauce

Daphne Derven found this recipe in *The Cook's Own Book*, by a Boston Housewife (Mrs. N. K. M. Lee), published in 1832. This highly spiced, sharp condiment would have been kept in a cruet on the table, to add a dash of flavor to bland foods. Daphne says *escaveke* (es ka vesh´) sauce is particularly good with mild-tasting fish such as flounder or turbot, as a dipping sauce with fried foods, or to add a bite to stews or soups. Be sure to remove the white pith from the lemon zest, for otherwise the sauce will be bitter.

2   cups wine vinegar   ½   teaspoon cayenne
    zest of 1 lemon   pepper
1   tablespoon coriander   6   cloves garlic, crushed
    seeds   6   shallots, crushed, or 3
2   tablespoons grated   small onions,
    gingerroot   quartered

Bring the vinegar to a boil. Immediately add the lemon zest, coriander seeds, gingerroot, cayenne, garlic, and shallots or onions. Lower the heat and let the mixture simmer for 5 to 10 minutes.

Cool the mixture, strain, and bottle it. If stored in a cool spot, this sauce will keep for several weeks.

Makes about 1⅓ cups

Appetizers, Salads, and Soups

I could make a whole meal out of vegetable appetizers. Hand me a dish of *Hummus* from the Middle East or a helping of Caponata from Italy and a serving of pita bread to use as an edible scoop and I'm content. Every country has equally interesting appetizers, many of which are ideal pantry foods.

I've had some of my most appealing hors d'oeuvres in France. There a meal might begin with diced leftover vegetables in a mustard mayonnaise, grilled peppers in an herb anchovy vinaigrette, or a plate of julienne Celeriac *Remoulade*. Even in the well-known restaurants, simple vegetable preparations are featured: at a Michelin-starred restaurant in southwestern France, diners study the menu while they nibble on Piquant Onions surrounded by chicory marinated in an orange vinaigrette sauce.

Middle Eastern cooks are particularly adept in preparing long-lasting vegetable appetizers. Stuffed Syrian Eggplants, *Hummus*, and *Baba Ghanoush* all stay in good condition for several days—sometimes weeks—on the refrigerator shelf.

Several recipes in this chapter make excellent vegetarian main dishes, such as the Italian Marinated Zucchini and Peppers and the Hearty Italian Vegetarian Torta. One year, when I was evaluating school programs for the National Endowment for the Arts, I ended up in upper Michigan, where I discovered the local snack was Cornish pasties. These turnovers usually include potatoes, chopped beef, and turnips, but my vegetarian version uses broccoli *raab*, and cumin for flavor. The pasties keep for almost 1 week in the refrigerator and also freeze well.

Salads are not usually considered to be good keepers, but if they're made with top-quality fresh ingredients, they will hold for up to 1 week in the refrigerator. I've given you a few recipes for my favorites and my mother's potato salad.

I've highlighted the soups that freeze well with the freezer symbol, and they all will keep for several days in the refrigerator.

Cold Broiled Tomatoes

Prepare these tomatoes to ring a cold vegetable salad, or use them as part of a vegetable antipasto. Serve them at room temperature.

4	large tomatoes	1	teaspoon chopped sweet marjoram
1	tablespoon finely chopped garlic		freshly ground black pepper
3	tablespoons finest quality olive oil	1	tablespoon lemon juice
½	teaspoon chopped rosemary		

Halve the tomatoes crosswise. Place them in a broiling pan small enough to hold them closely together. Sprinkle with the garlic, oil, rosemary, sweet marjoram, and pepper to taste.

Broil the tomatoes for at least 10 minutes, or until they barely begin to brown. Do not let them burn, or the herbs and garlic will be bitter.

Cool, sprinkle with the lemon juice, then refrigerate the tomatoes in a loosely covered container. They should keep in good condition for at least 5 days.

Serves 4

Alsacian Appetizer Sticks

While my husband, Gordon, and I were waiting for the menu in a lovely restaurant in Strasbourg, France, a waiter arrived with a plateful of these flaky nibbles. The caraway seeds are an unusual, yet delicious touch.

¼	recipe Easy Puff Pastry (see page 187)	1	egg white
about 1	teaspoon caraway seeds	1 to 2	tablespoons grated Parmesan cheese

Roll out the pastry dough to ¼ inch thick on a floured surface to form a rectangle of about 9 × 11 inches. The size doesn't really matter, as long as the pastry is ¼ inch thick.

When the pastry is just about thin enough, sprinkle with the caraway seeds, and continue rolling for 1 or 2 seconds, until the seeds are slightly pressed into the dough. Brush the dough with the egg white, then sprinkle with the Parmesan cheese.

Preheat the oven to 400°F.

Cut the dough into ¾-inch-wide strips. I like to make them about 3 inches long, but it doesn't really matter. Place the pastry strips on a lightly greased baking sheet, and bake for 8 to 10 minutes, or until lightly browned.

Cool on a rack. If the pastry strips are stored in a covered tin, they should keep in good condition for at least 1 week. Reheat the strips in the oven if you wish.

Makes about 30 sticks

Celeriac Remoulade

The celeriac (which also goes by the name of celery root) in this French vegetable appetizer is tenderized by the *remoulade* dressing and actually improves in storage. Count on a lot of waste with celeriac—you'll end up discarding almost ½ the weight because of its thick skin and convoluted surface area. This same dressing and technique are excellent for Chinese turnips or kohlrabies.

4	cups celeriac (1 large), cut into matchstick pieces acidulated water (1 to 2 tablespoons lemon juice in 1 cup water)	3	tablespoons lemon juice
		⅞	cup combined vegetable and olive oils
3	tablespoons Dijon mustard	1	tablespoon chopped parsley
2	egg yolks	2	teaspoons chopped tarragon
¼	cup boiling water		freshly ground black pepper

Celeriac discolors upon exposure to air, so keep it in the acidulated water until you toss it in the dressing.

Place the mustard and egg yolks in a food processor or blender, and process for 1 second to combine them. Keep the machine on and add the water and lemon juice. Then add the oils in a slow, steady stream. The mixture will thicken. Stir in the parsley and tarragon, and season with the pepper.

Drain the celeriac, pat dry, and toss it in the dressing. (After the celeriac is completely coated, you may have a little extra dressing. Serve any extra dressing with hard boiled eggs, asparagus, broccoli, or green beans.)

Put the celeriac in a covered bowl, and store in the refrigerator for at least 1 day before serving. If the celeriac is kept refrigerated and is covered by the *remoulade* dressing, it should last for at least 1 week in storage.

Makes about 4 cups

Marinated Curried Broccoli and Peppers

Spoon the marinade over the broccoli daily so the oil doesn't sepa-rate from the vinegar. The curry powder and the vinegar give the vege-tables a slightly yellowish cast.

1 to 1½	pounds broccoli, trimmed into florets	1	teaspoon curry powder
2	onions, halved then thinly sliced	2	tablespoons honey
1 to 1¼	cups cider vinegar	3	sweet peppers (pre-ferably a mixture of red, yellow, and green), peeled
½	cup vegetable oil		
¼	cup plus 1 tablespoon Dijon mustard	4	cloves garlic, sliced

Blanch the broccoli and onions in a large pot of boiling water for 2 to 3 minutes. Immediately remove to the sink, and let cold water run into the pot until they are cool. Remove the broccoli and onions, drain, and set aside.

Beat together the vinegar, oil, mustard, curry, and honey.

Layer the broccoli, onions, and sweet peppers in a deep glass bowl, tucking in a piece of garlic from time to time. Pour the marinade over them. Don't worry if the marinade doesn't quite cover the vegetables, for after a few hours the vinegar will draw the vegetable water out of the broccoli. At that point press down firmly on the broccoli, and spoon the marinade over it. Let sit for at least 1 day before serving.

If kept in the refrigerator, loosely covered with foil, the vegetables should stay in good condition for up to 2 weeks. The crisper it is, the better the broccoli keeps.

Makes about 10 cups

Caponata

Caponata is a sweet-sour eggplant appetizer that originated in Sicily, Italy. During the winter, when fresh plum tomatoes are nonexistent, substitute a 1-pound can of Italian plum tomatoes. A true caponata would also have chopped black Italian olives and sometimes capers. It is good served with Italian or French bread or rolls.

1	firm large eggplant (about 1½ pounds) juice of ½ lemon	1¼	cups diced celery
		1¼	pounds Italian plum tomatoes (about 12), peeled
¾ to 1	cup good-quality olive oil	¼ to ½	teaspoon aniseed (optional)
3	onions, thinly sliced	3	tablespoons honey
1	sweet green pepper, seeded and thinly sliced	⅔	cup red wine vinegar freshly ground black pepper
1	sweet red pepper, seeded and thinly sliced		

Peel the eggplant, dice it into ¾- to 1-inch cubes, and toss with the lemon juice. Let it sit for 15 minutes while you peel, seed, or cut up the remaining vegetables as needed.

Dry the eggplant and fry in ¾ cup oil until softened and lightly browned on all sides. The eggplant will still be slightly firm. Remove the eggplant with a slotted spoon, and let it drain on paper bags.

Add the onions and all the sweet peppers to the oil in the frying pan. (You may need to add the remaining oil.) Cook, stirring frequently, for about 5 minutes, then remove from the pan and set aside.

Drain all but a thin film of oil from the pan, and add the celery, tomatoes, and aniseed (if used). Mash the tomatoes with a potato masher, then simmer for 20 minutes, or until thick. Stir frequently to keep the mixture from burning.

In another pan, over medium heat, stir the honey and vinegar together just long enough to dissolve the honey, and pour into the tomato mixture. Add the eggplant, onions, and peppers to the tomato mixture, and stir to coat all the vegetables with the sauce. Cover the pan and simmer over low heat for 30 minutes to blend the flavors. Stir frequently to prevent the caponata from burning.

Taste for seasoning and add the pepper and lemon juice or additional vinegar if necessary. Chill before serving.

If the caponata is stored in a covered glass bowl in the refrigerator, it will keep for at least 2 weeks.

Makes 6 to 7 cups

Tourshee or Armenian Pickled Vegetables

In Armenia these mild pickled vegetables are served with flat cracker bread and cheese. The 2-quart glass jars that commercial mayonnaise comes in are a good size for these pickles. Or check your local deli for pickle or pepper jars. Sometimes local takeout stores will be glad to let you have their discarded jars—it's certainly worth a try. If you can't locate these jars, use quart canning jars.

6	cloves garlic	3	sweet red peppers
3	dried hot peppers	3	large Spanish onions
1	pound carrots	1½	tablespoons mixed
8	stalks celery		pickling spices
1½	pounds cauliflower	1	quart cider vinegar
2	pounds cabbage	2½	quarts water

Peel and thinly slice the garlic and divide it between 3 hot, clean 2-quart jars. Remove the seeds from the hot peppers, and place 1 pepper in each jar.

Peel, seed, or core the vegetables as needed. Cut the carrots and celery into 1-inch pieces. Divide the cauliflower into florets, and cut the cabbage into at least 12 wedges. Slice the sweet red peppers into 1½-inch pieces. Cut the onions into small wedges. Pack the vegetables into the jars. Add ½ tablespoon pickling spices to each jar.

Combine the vinegar and water and heat them to the boiling point, then pour them over the vegetables. Seal, and store in the refrigerator for at least 1 week before serving. These vegetables keep for up to 2 months in the refrigerator.

Makes 6 quarts

Stuffed Syrian Eggplants

In Syria and other parts of the Middle East, baby eggplants are stuffed with a salty walnut mixture and preserved in oil. Omitting the salt gives the preserved eggplants a firmer texture—and slightly different flavor—but they are still delicious.

3	pounds baby egg-plants (2 to 3 inches long*)	3	tablespoons minced garlic
			vegetable oil
1	cup finely ground walnuts		red wine vinegar

30

Wash the eggplants and remove their leaves and stems. Boil a large pot of water, add the eggplants, cover, and cook for 7 to 10 minutes, until they are cooked all the way through but not soft. Drain and cool them.

Slit each eggplant lengthwise, cutting to within ½ inch of the opposite end so that you form a pocket. Place the eggplants slit side down, and let them drain for 3 hours or overnight.

Mix together the walnuts, garlic, and 1 teaspoon oil. Fill each eggplant with about 1 tablespoon of this mixture, pressing together the sides of each eggplant as you finish, to close the slit. Place the eggplants in quart jars. Cover each jar with a dish, invert the jars, and let the eggplants drain for several hours.

Fill the jars with a mixture of 2 parts vinegar and 1 part water, making sure all the eggplants are covered. Tightly close the jars. Store in the refrigerator for 1 week.

Drain the vinegar mixture, and replace with oil. Refrigerate the eggplants for 1 more week before using. Cut into rounds before serving.

The eggplants will last for several months in the refrigerator, as long as they are covered with oil and capped.

*Baby eggplants can be harvested throughout the season, but they may be most plentiful at the end of the year, when they must be harvested to avoid frost damage.

Makes about 2 quarts

Italian Marinated Zucchini and Peppers

2	pounds zucchini (about 5 medium-size)	3	cloves garlic
½	cup olive oil	½	cup water
2	sweet peppers (red peppers are most attractive)	1½	cups white vinegar
2	onions	1	tablespoon chopped basil
			black pepper

Cut the zucchini into ½-inch-thick strips lengthwise. Heat the oil in a heavy frying pan, and sauté the zucchini until lightly browned and cooked through. Remove to paper bags or paper toweling to drain.

Slice the sweet peppers and onions and mince the garlic. Sauté these vegetables lightly in the same oil. Cool briefly, then add the water and vinegar, and simmer for 10 minutes.

With a slotted spoon place the peppers and onions in a deep earthenware or glass bowl, reserving the liquid. Toss the peppers and onions with the zucchini and basil. Season with the pepper. Pour the hot liquid over the vegetables and cool.

Cover and refrigerate the vegetables for at least 2 days before serving. Serve cold. They will keep for at least 1½ weeks in the refrigerator.

Makes 8 to 11 cups

Swedish Pickled Cucumbers

Swedish and Danish cooks serve these cucumbers both as a salad and as a side garnish for open-faced sandwiches. I think they stay crisper when cut into ¼-inch slices, but the traditional way of preparing the cucumbers is to slice them into paper-thin pieces.

3½	pounds firm large cucumbers (about 5)	3	cups white or cider vinegar
1	cup honey		chopped parsley (optional)

Score the cucumbers by running the tines of a fork down their sides. Thinly slice, and place them in a deep mixing bowl.

Mix together the honey and vinegar, stirring until the honey is suspended in the mixture. Pour the marinade over the cucumbers, and press down with your hands or the back of a wooden spoon. Let the cucumbers sit for about 30 minutes, toss, and press down once again. The liquid should cover the cucumbers. Chill. Sprinkle the cucumbers with parsley before serving if you like.

The cucumbers will keep for up to 3 weeks if stored in a covered container in the refrigerator.

Makes 11 to 12 cups

Sweet Peppers in Oil

In Italy and Provence cooked sweet peppers are a favored appetizer. Tossed in garlic and oil, garnished with anchovies and capers, or served in a vinaigrette sauce, their rich, smoky flavor whets the appetite. These peppers are easy to prepare, and I think once you try them, you'll want to have a jar on hand at all times.

5   large sweet red
        peppers
     olive oil

Preheat the broiler.

Place the sweet red peppers in a single layer in a broiling pan, and set on the rack closest to the broiler. Once the skins have charred on 1 side, in 2 to 3 minutes, turn the peppers. Continue turning until all the surface skins have blistered.

Immediately place the peppers in a closed paper bag, and let them sit for 15 minutes to loosen the skins.

Under running water, peel the peppers and remove the stems and seeds. Dry and then cut them into 1-inch-wide strips.

Layer the pepper strips in a jar with the oil, leaving at least ½ inch of oil above the peppers. Store in the refrigerator, where the peppers will keep for up to 4 weeks. Serve at room temperature.

Makes 1 pint

Peperonata

This Italian vegetable appetizer is delicious served at room temperature, accompanied by crusty peasant bread.

⅓ cup olive oil
8 cups thinly sliced red and yellow frying peppers
2 large onions, slivered
3 cloves garlic, minced

2½ cups Tomato Sauce (see page 268)
¼ cup minced basil (optional)
black pepper

In a large frying pan heat the oil and sauté the frying peppers and onions for 2 minutes, stirring constantly. Add the garlic and tomato sauce, cover, and cook until the peppers are tender, about 10 minutes. Uncover the pan, add the basil (if used), and cook for another 1 to 2 minutes, until the basil is slightly wilted. Season with pepper to taste.

Cool to room temperature before serving. Store in a covered dish in the refrigerator, where the *peperonata* will keep in good condition for up to 2 weeks. The mixture may also be frozen for up to 6 months.

Makes about 3 cups

Armenian Walnut Eggplant Dip

Sherry vinegar is difficult to find but is worth looking for because its nutty flavor accentuates the walnuts. As this purée has a rather gray color, serve it in a bowl lined with Boston lettuce, surrounded by red cherry tomatoes.

1 2-pound eggplant
2 teaspoons soy sauce
½ cup chopped walnuts
2 cloves garlic, mashed
2 tablespoons sherry or wine vinegar

3 tablespoons cold water
chopped lovage (optional)

Preheat the oven to 425°F.

Place the eggplant in a shallow baking pan, and insert a stainless steel fork in the eggplant up to the point where the tines end. The fork conducts heat into the center of the vegetable so that it cooks faster. Bake the eggplant until cooked through and soft, 40 to 50 minutes.

While the eggplant is still hot, remove the skin. Cool the pulp slightly and drain off the juices. Beat the pulp until it is puréed. Add the soy sauce and set aside.

Make the walnuts and garlic into a paste. This takes but a moment in the food processor, but you can also use a mortar and pestle. (If you are using the food processor, first whirl the nuts and garlic until they are finely ground, then add the liquids and continue processing until the nuts form a purée.) Add the vinegar and water. Stir this mixture into the eggplant pulp. Just before serving, sprinkle with the lovage if you wish.

This mixture keeps for at least 1 week stored in a covered container in the refrigerator but starts to lose some flavor after 5 days.

Makes 3 cups

Hummus

This Middle Eastern snack is a wonderful party dish served with a bowl of pita bread torn into pieces. Just double or triple the quantity. The water gives a lighter consistency to the dip—omit it if you prefer.

2	cups cooked chick-peas	⅓	cup water
⅓ to ½	cup lemon juice		olive oil (optional)
3 to 4	cloves garlic, minced	2	tablespoons chopped
⅓	cup tahini (sesame		Bermuda onions
	seed paste)		(optional)
	cayenne pepper		
⅛ to ¼	teaspoon cumin		
	powder		

Purée the chick-peas and lemon juice in a food processor or blender. (If using a blender, add the water before you purée.) Add the garlic and tahini and process until the garlic is incorporated. Season to taste with cayenne and cumin. If the *hummus* is too thick, thin with the water.

For serving, spoon into a bowl, make a depression in the center, pour in the oil, and surround the *hummus* with the onions. Or omit the oil and onions and sprinkle with paprika.

If the *hummus* is stored in a covered bowl in the refrigerator, it will last for at least 10 days.

Makes 2⅓ cups

Variations
• Add ¼ cup chopped mint along with the tahini and blend lightly.
• Substitute cooked (fresh) shell beans for the chick-peas.

Baba Ghanoush
or Eggplant Caviar

1	1½-pound eggplant	olive oil
1	clove garlic	chopped onions
⅛ to ⅓	cup lemon juice	chopped mint
¼ to ½	cup tahini (sesame seed paste)	Boston lettuce or pita bread

Preheat the oven to 425°F.

Place the eggplant in a shallow baking pan. Insert a stainless steel fork in the eggplant up to the point where the tines end. The fork conducts the heat into the center of the eggplant so that it cooks faster. Bake the eggplant until cooked through and soft, 35 to 50 minutes. It's not important if the eggplant chars, for in some versions of this dish, the eggplant is cooked over coals, which gives it a pleasant, smoky flavor.

While the eggplant is still hot, remove the skin. Cool slightly, and drain off the juices, which tend to be bitter. Mash the garlic and place in a mixing bowl. Add the eggplant pulp and the lemon juice and tahini to taste. Vary the proportions of each depending upon whether you want the lemon or the sesame flavor to dominate. Beat with a mixer or in a food processor, pulling out only stringy parts, until mixed well.

Place the mixture in a serving bowl, make a depression in the center, and fill with about 1 tablespoon oil. Garnish with the onions and mint. Serve with the lettuce or with pita bread to use as a scoop. This *baba ghanoush* (băbă gănŏosh) will keep, refrigerated, for up to 2 weeks.

Makes about 2 cups

Variations
- Russian-Style: Omit the tahini and add ¼ cup each cooked chopped sweet green peppers and tomatoes and 1 teaspoon chopped fresh coriander.

- Omit the tahini and add ½ cup cooked chopped onions and ⅓ cup cooked chopped tomatoes. Just before serving, stir in 1 cup cooked whole chick-peas.

Guacamole

Guacamole can be as simple or as fancy as you wish. A traditional recipe has only avocados, lemon juice, garlic, and salt. The peppers, onions, and chili powder in this version add so much flavor that even the bland avocados don't need salt. A food processor makes this a snap to prepare.

2	tablespoons vegetable oil	3	ripe avocados (about 2¾ pounds)
⅓	cup chopped sweet green peppers	2	teaspoons minced garlic
⅓	cup chopped onions	⅜ to ⅓	cup lemon juice
2	tablespoons chopped hot red pepper (about 1)		chili powder cumin powder (optional)

Heat the oil in a frying pan, and sauté the sweet green peppers, onions, and hot red pepper for about 4 minutes, or until cooked through and limp. Set the vegetables aside.

Peel and slice the avocados.

Turn on the food processor and add the garlic while the blade is turning. Immediately add ⅜ cup lemon juice and the avocados, and process until the mixture is combined. Add the reserved vegetables and pulse the machine on and off until the guacamole is the texture you prefer. Stop before the guacamole is completely smooth. Taste the mixture and add the remaining lemon juice, 1 or 2 dashes of chili powder, and a dash of cumin if you wish. The guacamole is now ready to serve.

Store it in a deep glass container such as a peanut butter jar. Seal the guacamole with a thin layer of oil so it doesn't discolor. If the guacamole is covered with oil and refrigerated, it will last for at least 1 week.

Makes 3 to 4 cups

Variations
• Guacamole Salad Dressing: Thin the guacamole with mayonnaise and sour cream or yogurt to taste.
• Add chopped coriander and chives and a chopped raw tomatillo or green tomato.
• Substitute roasted sweet red peppers for the sweet green peppers. There's no need to sauté the red peppers if you do this.

Hearty Italian
Vegetarian Torta

Many chic food specialty shops sell a version of the Italian *Torta Rustica*—at $3 to $4 per slice. This version, which features homegrown vegetables and herbs, costs very little—and improves in flavor after it sits for 1 day. Any leftover filling is wonderful in omelets or scrambled eggs.

1½	pounds zucchini	5	sweet red peppers, roasted, peeled, and chopped
⅜	cup vegetable oil		
2	cups chopped onions		
3½	cups sliced mushrooms	¼	pound provolone cheese, sliced
3	tablespoons chopped lovage or basil	1½	cups ricotta cheese
1	recipe Whole Wheat Pie Crust (see page 191)	4	eggs
		¼	cup grated Parmesan cheese
½	cup grated Cheddar cheese		

Shred the zucchini, squeeze it, and place in a colander for 30 minutes to allow the juices to drain. Squeeze dry again, and set aside.

Heat ¼ cup oil in a heavy frying pan, and sauté the onions until limp, about 5 minutes. Remove 2 tablespoons of the onions and set aside. Add the mushrooms to the pan containing the onions, and sauté over high heat, stirring constantly, for 5 minutes. You want the mushrooms to release their moisture, then dry out. Set the mushroom mixture aside.

Squeeze the zucchini dry once again, and sauté in the remaining oil. Cook over high heat, stirring constantly, until the zucchini has cooked slightly and is dried out. Add the lovage or basil and the reserved 2 tablespoons onions. Cook for 2 minutes longer. Set aside on a paper bag to drain.

Reserve ⅓ of the pastry. Roll out the rest to between ⅛ and ¼ inch thick. Line an 11 × 7-inch baking dish with the dough, extending it up the sides of the pan.

Preheat the oven to 400°F.

Sprinkle the Cheddar cheese over the pastry. Evenly distribute ½ the sweet red peppers, then ½ the mushrooms, over the Cheddar, and top with the provolone cheese. Sprinkle the remaining peppers and mushrooms on top.

Mix the zucchini with the ricotta cheese, eggs, and Parmesan cheese, and spoon over the top. Cover with the rolled-out reserved pastry, prick with a fork to allow steam to escape, and crimp the edges.

Bake for 35 to 40 minutes, or until the mixture is set and a knife inserted in the center comes out clean. Allow to cool before serving, to give the flavors a chance to meld.

The torta will keep for up to 1 week in the refrigerator if wrapped in foil. Serve at room temperature or slightly warm.

Serves 8 to 10

Pepper and Eggplant Dip

The peppers add colorful flecks to this low-calorie appetizer that's delicious spread on pita bread or used as a dip for raw vegetables. Although I've given directions for preparing the dip in a food processor, you can also use a mixer or make it by hand. I like to serve the dip in a glass bowl garnished with mint leaves, placed on a large platter filled with cherry tomatoes to pick up the color of the red peppers. Separated wedges of red Bermuda onions make an attractive scoop for eating the purée.

2	large eggplants (3 to 4 pounds)	¼	cup lemon juice
2	large sweet red peppers	2	tablespoons olive oil
2	hot red peppers (such as Anaheim)		hot pepper sauce (optional)
3	cloves garlic	2	tablespoons chopped basil
⅓	cup yogurt	1	tablespoon chopped mint
1	scant tablespoon cumin powder		

Preheat the oven to 400°F.

Place the eggplants in a baking dish, and insert stainless steel forks into them up to the point where the tines end, for better heat penetration. Bake the eggplants until cooked through and soft, 45 to 60 minutes. If the eggplants char a little, it doesn't matter, because it just adds a smoky flavor.

Peel away a little of the skin to allow the steam to escape, and let the eggplants sit for a moment. While they are still hot, peel the eggplants and press down on them to remove the bitter juices. Place the peeled eggplants in a food processor, and process until they are puréed.

Broil all the peppers on all sides until blackened. Immediately put the peppers in a paper bag, and let them sit for 5 to 10 minutes, then place them in the sink. Peel the peppers and remove their seeds and stems.

Put the peppers in the food processor along with the garlic, yogurt, cumin, lemon juice, oil, and a dash of hot pepper sauce, if desired. Process in short bursts until the ingredients are combined but still chunky. Add the basil and mint, and process for just a moment.

If the dip is stored in a glass jar in the refrigerator, it will keep for at least 1 week.

Makes 5 to 6 cups

Vegetarian Cornish Pasties

These pasties were inspired by the beef-and-potato turnovers that miners in Cornwall, England, packed for meals. In parts of upper Michigan and other sections of the Midwest with Cornish settlements, pasties are a local snack. Spinach or kale may be substituted for broccoli *raab*, but this green is well worth planting or searching for in Italian markets, where it is often called rappini. Its full, rich flavor is accentuated by the cumin and provolone cheese. A pastry richer than the one suggested here might pull apart and be difficult to work with.

1½	pounds broccoli *raab*	2	recipes Whole Wheat
¼	cup butter		Pie Crust (see
½	cup minced onions		page 191)
2	cloves garlic, minced	13 to 16	slices of provolone
¼ to ½	teaspoon cumin		cheese
	powder		milk
	freshly ground black		
	pepper		
2 to 3	cups diced, peeled		
	boiled potatoes		
	(⅜-inch cubes)		

Trim the broccoli *raab* and blanch it in a large pot of boiling water for 2 to 3 minutes. Drain, then squeeze to remove excess moisture. Coarsely chop.

In a large frying pan melt the butter and stir in the onions and garlic. Cook for 3 to 5 minutes, until slightly wilted. Stir in the cumin and the broccoli *raab*. Cook over medium heat, stirring constantly, until the broccoli *raab* has dried out somewhat. Cool slightly, then season with pepper to taste. Toss with the potatoes. Cover, and set aside.

Roll out the pastry. I find this easiest when it is divided into quarters. On a lightly floured surface, roll out the dough to ½ inch thick. Cut circles, using a 6-inch-diameter plate as a guide. Save the pastry scraps and roll them out later.

Preheat the oven to 400°F.

Line up the pastry circles on a counter, and center a slice of provolone cheese in each circle. Place ¼ cup of the filling on 1 side of each round, moisten the edges with water, then fold in half to enclose the filling. Press the turnover edges together firmly, then crimp with the tines of a fork or make a pie crust edge with your fingers.

Place the turnovers on ungreased baking sheets, and cut 2 1-inch-long slits in the top of each turnover. Brush lightly with the milk, and bake in the middle of the oven for 15 minutes. Reduce the heat to 350°F, and bake for 20 to 30 minutes longer, or until the turnovers are golden brown. Do not overcook or the cheese will become slightly tough near the slits. Serve hot or at room temperature.

Both the filling and the pastry dough separately will keep for several days in the refrigerator if covered tightly. Or you can store the cooked pasties in the refrigerator for up to 5 days.

Makes 13 to 16 pasties

Middle Eastern Bean Dip

This dip is more subtly flavored than a chick-pea *hummus*. As it has a delicate pink color, an attractive way to serve it is in a bowl surrounded by wedges of red Bermuda onions. Break off onion slices to use as scoops, or use pieces of pita bread.

2	cloves garlic	½	cup lemon juice
1	cup cooked red kidney beans	⅜	cup tahini (sesame seed paste)
1	cup cooked fava beans (if using fresh, skin first)	½	teaspoon cumin powder

Mash the garlic with a mortar and pestle, or chop it and mash with a knife blade. Purée all the beans in a food processor or mixer. Add the garlic and purée for 1 minute. Add the remaining ingredients and purée until combined. This appetizer keeps for up to 1 week in the refrigerator.

Makes about 2½ cups

Profile

Alice W Senturia

Energetic Alice Senturia is the least harried hostess I know. She plans a dinner party like a campaign, preparing all of the food in advance so that, when the guests come, she is free to circulate and make sure the party is going smoothly.

Alice calls upon her years of experience as a faculty resident in a women's dormitory at the Massachusetts Institute of Technology, where her husband, Steve, is a professor of electrical engineering. During the years the Senturias served as dorm parents—and hosted dinner parties for 50 to 75 students at a time—Alice honed her skills for do-ahead cooking.

Appetizers may include Texas-style Hot Pickled Onion Slices—which have marinated for several days—or a long-lasting Leek Mayonnaise, prepared as a dip for raw vegetables. She always serves a main course that tastes best at room temperature, so there's no last-minute fussing in the kitchen. Dessert is fresh fruit, or a cake from the freezer.

When Alice cooks, she cooks in quantity. "I always make a double recipe," Alice told me. "If I'm broiling chicken, I'll fix 2 or 3, rather than one, and freeze the extras. I use my freezer the way other people use their refrigerators or pantries."

The freezer and refrigerator in the Senturias' Boston condominium are filled with delicious homemade food, including some of the Southwestern specialties Alice enjoyed growing up in Texas. Alice has a tiny kitchen, so every inch has to count.

Her pantry shelves include a special, homemade garlic flavored oil Alice uses for sautéeing foods and for dressing salads, as well as several kinds of exotic vinegars, while the refrigerator is stocked with a selection of vegetable appetizers the family enjoys.

When sweet peppers are in season, Alice buys a batch and broils, peels, and slices them, then layers the peppers in a glass jar. Covered with her garlic flavored oil and a little vinegar, they'll keep for 1 or 2 weeks in the refrigerator.

Or she'll poach a variety of vegetables in chicken stock and marinate them in a sauce *à la greque* made with loads of lemon juice and spices. Treated this way, the vegetables stay in good condition for 1 week in the refrigerator. Alice uses the same technique for Florence fennel.

For lunch or dinner there are usually at least 4 homemade salad dressings on hand, chosen because they'll last for at least 1 week. Croutons fixed the Senturia way are a snap: Alice toasts bread, rubs it with raw garlic, then cuts it into cubes. The croutons end up with a crunchy texture and subtle garlic flavor minus the greasy aftertaste (and calories) of croutons sautéed in butter.

Alice's busy schedule as a real estate executive gives her little time to shop, so even salad greens receive a do-ahead treatment. She washes the lettuce leaves under running cold water, then drains them in a colander for about 30 minutes. Then she arranges the lettuce, 1 layer deep, on tea towels or on strong paper toweling, rolls up the towels, and places them in large, unsealed plastic bags. (Leaving the bags unsealed allows the moisture to evaporate.) Alice stores the bags in the central section of the refrigerator (not the vegetable crisper), where the lettuce stays crisp for at least 1 week. She'll also dice raw vegetables in advance, place them in dampened towels, wrap them in foil, and store them in the refrigerator, where they'll keep in good condition for 1 or 2 days, ready to be used in salads or casseroles.

Even though the Senturias live in the middle of the city, whenever possible Alice shops at a nearby farmer's market for the fresh herbs she uses to add flavor to her salt-free cooking. Ever since 1965—long before it became fashionable—Alice has been cooking without salt.

Similar to other good cooks experimenting with salt-free cooking, Alice relies upon spices, herbs, and sours to accentuate the flavors of food. She uses cayenne pepper (or imported sweet Hungarian paprika, one of her favorites) to give a bite to foods, and she adds lemon or lime juice to give just a touch of tartness. "I find a little tart edge makes me think that nothing is missing," she told me. "When I'm converting a recipe to salt-free cooking, I'll also use far more pepper and herbs than originally required."

Alice shared several of her do-ahead recipes with me, which you'll find throughout this book. Included are her method for making a mildly flavored Garlic Oil (see page 22) and her recipes for salad dressings and such Texas specialties as Spicy Barbecue Sauce (see page 245) and, in this chapter, Coleslaw Texas-Style and Hot Pickled Onion Slices.

Leek Mayonnaise

Alice Senturia serves this mayonnaise with poached vegetables as an appetizer or uses it as the base for a salad dressing. She says it is particularly good with bitter greens such as arugula, spinach, or dandelions. You'll need a food processor or blender for this recipe.

2	leeks, white parts only, sliced	¼ to ⅜	cup lemon juice
2	eggs, at room temperature	¼	teaspoon white pepper
2	teaspoons Dijon mustard	1½	cups olive oil

Place the leeks, eggs, mustard, lemon juice, pepper, and ¼ cup oil in a food processor or blender, and blend for a moment. With the motor running, add the remaining oil slowly, drop by drop, until the mixture thickens. Then add oil by the teaspoon until you get the desired texture.

Spoon into a glass jar, and store, covered, in the refrigerator. The mayonnaise will keep for at least 2 weeks.

Makes about 1¾ cups

Coleslaw Texas-Style

Alice Senturia says this slaw gets better the longer it sits. Hold it for at least 2 days before serving.

1½	pounds cabbage, shredded	¼	cup vegetable oil
1	large sweet green or red pepper, chopped	¼	cup cider vinegar
		½	teaspoon dry mustard
½	cup chopped red onions	2	teaspoons honey
		½	teaspoon black pepper

In a large mixing bowl combine the cabbage, sweet peppers, and onions. Stir together the oil, vinegar, mustard, honey, and pepper. Pour the marinade over the vegetables and mix thoroughly.

Cover the salad and refrigerate it. Stir the mixture about once a day. It should keep for up to 1 week if kept tightly covered.

Makes 8 cups

Hot Pickled Onion Slices

These Texas-style onion slices are often an appetizer at Alice Senturia's home. They remind her of the kinds of condiments out-of-the-way Texas restaurants serve with barbecued or grilled meats. Alice prefers the taste of sweet, white Bermuda onions but varies the type of vinegar depending upon the flavor she wants. She says a mild wine vinegar tastes fine undiluted, but white vinegar should be diluted ½ and ½ with water.

3	onions, sliced into rings	1	tablespoon chopped oregano
3	fresh jalapeño peppers, seeded and sliced		wine or white vinegar
¾	teaspoon cracked black pepper		

Place the onions in a colander in the sink, and pour boiling water over them. Drain the onions well.

Layer the onion rings with the jalapeño peppers, pepper, and oregano in a 1½-quart jar. Fill the jar with wine vinegar, or white vinegar diluted with an equal amount of water. Cover, and store in the refrigerator, where the onions will keep for at least 3 weeks.

Makes 3 to 4 cups

Alice W Senturia

Potato Salad

My mother, Marie O'Day, makes potato salad that is so filling that it's practically a meal in itself. Roast pork, spread with mustard before cooking and served at room temperature, is a delicious accompaniment.

8 to 10	waxy potatoes		freshly ground black
¾	cup diced onions		pepper
4	stalks celery, diced	1	cup mayonnaise
8	hard boiled eggs	¼	cup chopped lovage
2	tablespoons vinegar		

Boil the potatoes in their skins until cooked through, then cool.

Peel and cut the potatoes into ¼-inch cubes. Mix with the onions, celery, and 7 eggs, coarsely chopped. Toss until combined. Sprinkle on the vinegar and the pepper to taste and toss again. Mix in the mayonnaise and lovage. Let blend for at least 4 hours or overnight in the refrigerator.

Adjust the seasoning to taste. Slice the remaining egg and garnish the salad with it before serving.

If stored in a tightly covered container, the salad will keep in good condition for at least 5 days in the refrigerator.

Serves 10 to 15

Tabbouleh

If you're going to hold the *tabbouleh* (tă bŏo'lēe) for more than 1 day, add the tomatoes and cucumbers just before serving. Yellow tomatoes add an attractive accent.

1	cup bulgur	1	tablespoon lovage
1	onion		(optional)
5	tomatoes	¼	cup lemon juice
1	cucumber	½	cup olive oil
½	cup finely chopped mint		freshly ground black pepper
¼	cup finely chopped parsley		mint leaves

Cover the bulgur with water, and let stand for at least 1 hour until it has softened.

Meanwhile, chop the onion, tomatoes, and cucumber. See aside.

Taste the bulgur and, if the grains are soft yet chewy, drain, and place in a clean towel. Squeeze the bulgur dry and place in a bowl. Add the onions, tomatoes, cucumbers, mint, parsley, and lovage (if used). Stir in the lemon juice, oil, and pepper to taste. Garnish with mint leaves before serving. *Tabbouleh* will keep for at least 1 week in the refrigerator.

Makes 3 to 4 cups

Brown Rice–Sweet Pepper Appetizer Salad

If you plan to serve this salad for several days, divide up the pine nuts and add them just before serving, as they soften in storage. Pear vinegar is delicious in this salad.

2	cups brown rice	½ to 1	teaspoon sesame oil
2½	quarts water	1	tablespoon soy sauce
5	large sweet red peppers	2	tablespoons lemon
¼	cup plus 1 tablespoon		juice
	minced scallions,	½	cup pine nuts
	white parts only		black pepper
¼	cup vegetable oil	3	tablespoons chopped
¼	cup cider or pear		parsley
	vinegar		

Boil the brown rice in the water, uncovered, until cooked through yet still slightly chewy. Add additional boiling water as needed. The rice will take about 40 minutes to cook. Rinse and drain the rice; set aside.

Meanwhile, broil the sweet red peppers for about 4 minutes on each side. The skins should be blistered and completely charred. Place them in a paper bag, close it, and let the peppers sit for 20 minutes to loosen the skins.

Peel and seed the peppers, and dice them into ¼-inch pieces. Combine the rice and peppers in a deep serving bowl. Add the scallions, vegetable oil, vinegar, sesame oil, soy sauce, lemon juice, and pine nuts. Add pepper to taste. Stir in the parsley.

The salad keeps for at least 4 days in the refrigerator, but the lemon flavor diminishes slightly in storage. Add additional lemon juice and soy sauce if you wish.

Makes about 8 cups

Barley, Carrot, and Cabbage Soup

When you have turkey leftover from Thanksgiving dinner and have run out of inspiration, try this meal-in-one soup developed by my mother. The vegetables must be finely diced, which is an easy task with a food processor.

1	quart boiling water	4	cups finely diced cabbage
1¼	cups barley		
2	quarts turkey or chicken stock	2	cups cubed turkey (1-inch cubes)
4	cups finely diced carrots		black pepper

Pour the water over the barley, and let sit for at least 1 hour.

Drain the barley, place it in a deep soup kettle, and add the stock. Bring the stock to a boil, reduce the heat, and simmer for 30 minutes, until the barley is cooked through but still slightly chewy.

Add the carrots and cabbage and enough water to cover the vegetables with 2 inches to spare. I find the final stock usually reduces by about 2 cups, which should leave you with plenty. Simmer the vegetables and stock for 15 minutes. Add the turkey and simmer for 5 minutes longer, or until the turkey is heated through. Add pepper to taste.

Remove from the heat, and let the soup sit for at least 30 minutes before serving, to let the flavors blend. Reheat before serving.

The soup keeps in good condition for up to 5 days in the refrigerator and for 6 months in the freezer.

Serves 12 to 14

Variations
- My mother always makes this soup from scratch, using a whole chicken. She simmers the chicken in water along with an onion and a celery stalk until cooked through. Then she removes the chicken meat from the bones and serves it in large chunks in the soup.
- For a spicier soup add 2 cloves garlic, minced, and 1 teaspoon thyme when you add the vegetables to the pot.

Lamb Lentil Soup—
Three Ways

By adding a few ingredients, you can make leftover soup seem different each time you serve it. Start with a flavorful stock.

Day 1

2	tablespoons vegetable oil	4	onions, chopped
2	pounds lamb shanks	3	cloves garlic, minced (about 1 table-spoon)
1	cup lentils		
3	quarts beef, lamb, or vegetable stock		

Heat the oil and brown the lamb.

Meanwhile, wash the lentils and boil them for 10 minutes in 3 cups stock. Add the remaining stock and the lamb, onions, and garlic. Simmer for 1 to 1½ hours, or until the lamb is tender. Remove the meat from the shank bones, and return it to the soup. Reduce the stock by cooking briskly if not flavorful enough. Leftover soup can be "renewed" for . . .

Day 2 (based on 8 cups soup)

⅔	cup chopped tomatoes	2	scallions, white parts only, chopped
1	cup cooked chick-peas		
2	tablespoons lemon juice		

Reheat the soup and add the tomatoes and chick-peas. Simmer for 20 minutes. Just before serving, stir in the lemon juice and scallions. Any leftover soup can move on to . . .

Day 3 (chopped cabbage)

Measure the soup and chop ¼ to ½ cup cabbage for each 1¼ cups soup. Reheat the soup to a simmer, add the cabbage, and continue simmering for 3 to 4 minutes, or until the cabbage is cooked through but not limp.

This soup will keep for at least 4 days in the refrigerator. You can also freeze it for up to 9 months.

Serves 10 to 12

Onion Soup

Do cook the onions the length of time indicated, because they reduce to almost a purée and develop a mellow flavor.

¼	cup butter	2	quarts chicken or
7 to 8	cups thinly sliced onions		beef stock black pepper
2	tablespoons whole wheat flour or ½ cup mashed potatoes		

Melt the butter in a large saucepan. Add the onions, stirring to coat with butter. Cover the pan and slowly simmer the onions for 20 minutes. Uncover and cook for 30 minutes longer.

Remove the onions from the heat, stir in the flour (if using potatoes, see below), place the pan back on the stove and cook, stirring, for 3 minutes. Heat the stock and whisk it into the soup. (If you prefer to thicken with potatoes, whisk them in at this point.)

Cover the pan and simmer slowly for 20 minutes longer. Taste and season with pepper.

The soup will keep for up to 5 days in the refrigerator if, after the third day, you boil it to keep the stock from spoiling.

Makes 8 cups

Carrot Soup

The turnip and parsnip are essential for the complex flavor of this soup.

2	tablespoons butter	1	turnip, chopped
1	cup chopped onions	1½	quarts chicken or
4	cups chopped carrots		vegetable stock
1	stalk celery, chopped		pinch of nutmeg
1	potato, chopped		black pepper
1	parsnip, chopped	1	cup light cream

Melt the butter in a large, heavy pot. Stir in the onions and cook over low heat for 2 to 3 minutes, or until barely wilted. Stir in the carrots, celery, potatoes, parsnips, and turnips, and continue stirring until the vegetables are coated with butter.

Pour in the stock, bring it to a boil, and reduce the heat. Cover the pan and simmer for 30 minutes, or until the vegetables are cooked through. Do not overcook; the vegetables should retain some texture.

Cool the soup slightly and, with a slotted spoon, remove and reserve about 2 cups of the vegetables. Finely purée the remaining vegetables and stock. Add the nutmeg and pepper to taste. Stir in the cream and the reserved vegetables. Reheat, but do not let the cream boil.

If you're holding the soup in the refrigerator, it will keep for up to 5 days, as long as you boil it after the second day to keep the chicken stock from spoiling. (Boiling is not necessary if you've used vegetable stock.) If you are storing the chicken-stock-based soup, the cream should be added only to the amount of soup you plan to eat in 1 day. This soup can also be served as a chilled cream of carrot soup; try garnishing it with a spoonful of yogurt.

Serves 6 to 8

Melon Soup

This soup, made with whatever melons are sweet and fresh at the time, is a summertime favorite at Chillingsworth restaurant on Cape Cod. Nitzi Rabin would add 1½ cups champagne just before serving.

2	cups tightly packed cantaloupe pieces	3	tablespoons honey
2	cups tightly packed honeydew melon pieces	1½	cups minced cantaloupe
		1½	cups minced honeydew melon
2	cups orange juice	½	cup whipped cream
¼	cup lime juice		mint leaves

Blend together, in a blender or food processor, the cantaloupe and honeydew pieces along with the orange juice, lime juice, and honey until puréed. You may need to do this in 2 batches.

Pour the blended mixture into a bowl, and stir in the minced cantaloupe and honeydew. Taste, and adjust the flavor and consistency by adding more blended melon, or orange or lime juice.

Chill the soup and let it sit for at least 2 hours before serving. Garnish each serving with a spoonful of whipped cream and the mint leaves.

The soup base (without champagne) will keep for up to 1 week in the refrigerator if stored in a covered container. Nitzi says it's important to start with top-quality ingredients, otherwise the soup won't last as long.

Makes 9 cups

Variations
• Use different varieties of melons, or substitute papaya for 1 of the melon varieties.

Relishes and Pickled Vegetables

Americans have rediscovered their heritage of homemade relishes and pickled vegetables. It's become chic to serve grandmother's chowchow or a bowl of homemade Pickled Jalapeño Peppers as part of an all-American-foods dinner. As a friend said to me, "When *Vogue* magazine has a recipe for corn relish, you know something has changed."

Chic or not, there's something very satisfying about putting up jars of homemade relishes. I had a crash course in tasting relishes, if not making them, when I worked for the food department of *Farm Journal* magazine the year the kitchen was testing recipes for *The Freezing and Canning Cookbook.*

Until then I hadn't realized how much variety relishes could contribute to a meal and how different homemade relishes tasted from the store-bought versions. I've been making some of those *Farm Journal* recipes, such as Victory Relish, ever since, and even when I'm busy at harvesttime, I manage to squeeze in some time to put up at least a few jars.

I suspect that part of the current enthusiasm for making relishes is tied in with the resurgence of home gardening. A bushel of tomatoes waiting to be picked, or 14 pepper plants drooping with peppers, is an incentive to get out the family recipes and go to work.

I had a difficult time selecting the recipes for this chapter from the dozens we've enjoyed through the years. I chose some of our family favorites as well as unusual recipes you won't find in any general preserving book. The relishes call for ingredients that should be available at farm stands or are commonly planted in most gardens.

Pickled vegetables make satisfying snacks and are also a great pantry food to bring out for unexpected company. Some of these pantry foods came to my rescue when one of the best cooks I know dropped by; there was literally no fresh food in the house. (I was dieting and had removed every last morsel of temptation.) However, on the pantry shelf I found a jar of *Giardiniera* (Italian Pickled Vegetables), and in the refrigerator there were some Pickled Hot Pepper Rings and Pickled Jalapeño Peppers that went nicely with some crackers and Tillamook cheese, which came from Oregon.

Even once they're opened, the vegetables in this chapter are good keepers, and many of the foods, such as the Hungarian Peppers Stuffed with Cabbage, will keep crisp for weeks.

Use these recipes as inspiration for converting your own family favorites to recipes that use natural ingredients. Remember to use about ½ as much honey as sugar and to stir the relishes frequently while you're cooking, because honey can stick and burn as the relishes thicken. Honey does tend to darken the color of relishes, but the flavor remains much the same.

Beet and Horseradish Relish

This is the traditional accompaniment to gefüllte fish.

1	cup freshly grated horseradish	1	teaspoon honey
½ to ¾	cup finely grated (raw) beets	¾	cup vinegar

Combine the horseradish and beets. Mix the honey and vinegar together until the honey is thoroughly incorporated, then pour them over the horseradish and beets. Spoon into a sterilized jar, and press down so the horseradish and beets are submerged under the vinegar. Let sit refrigerated for at least 24 hours before serving.

This relish will keep for several weeks in the refrigerator, as long as the beets and horseradish are covered with the vinegar.

Makes about 1¾ cups

Red Cabbage Relish

This cabbage recipe falls halfway between a salad and relish. Try it with roast pork or lamb, as a sandwich ingredient, or in Hungarian Peppers Stuffed with Cabbage (see page 64). This recipe provides a good way to use up any partially finished small bottles of vinegar. A particularly flavorful combination is malt, white, and red wine vinegars—but you can use just cider, red wine, or white if you prefer. Adding the beet helps retain a bright color, as does substituting beet juice for some of the water.

¼	cup honey	8	cups thinly sliced red
3	cups water		cabbage
1½	cups vinegar	4	cups sliced onions
	pinch of ground	1	small beet, cooked
	allspice		and sliced
1	teaspoon celery seed		

Boil the honey, water, and vinegar for 5 minutes in a large enameled or stainless steel pan. Stir in the allspice, celery seed, cabbage, onions, and beets. Cook for 2 minutes, stirring constantly, until the cabbage and onions are slightly wilted and the marinade covers the vegetables.

Cool, and refrigerate in a tightly covered container. Wait at least 1 day before serving. The relish will keep for up to 3 weeks in the refrigerator.

Makes about 2 quarts

Variation
• Replace 1 cup cabbage with 1 cup sliced green peppers.

Dilly Beans

Adjust the honey, depending upon how sweet you'd like the beans to be.

2	pounds string beans	2	large onions, thinly
2½	cups water		sliced
2½	cups white vinegar	about ½	teaspoon hot pepper
¼ to ⅓	cup honey		flakes
½	teaspoon coriander	5	cloves garlic
	seeds	10	dill sprigs
6	peppercorns		

Blanch the beans in boiling water for 3 minutes. They should still be crisp. Drain, rinse in cold water, and set aside.

Combine the water, vinegar, honey, coriander seeds, peppercorns, and onions in an enameled or stainless steel saucepan. Bring to a boil, lower the heat, and simmer for 10 minutes.

Pack the beans upright in hot, sterilized pint jars, alternating with onion slices. Top with about ⅛ teaspoon hot pepper flakes, 1 clove garlic, and 2 dill sprigs per jar. Cover with the hot vinegar mixture. Seal the jars immediately.

Let sit for at least 1 week in the refrigerator before using. The beans will keep for up to 2 months under refrigeration, as long as they are sealed.

Makes 4 to 5 pints

Pickled Carrot Strips

This is a good way to rejuvenate older carrots. You can also experiment with other herbs such as tarragon and chervil.

3½ to 4	pounds carrots, cut into 4-inch-long strips	1	tablespoon mustard seeds
	dill sprigs	4	cloves garlic, sliced
	lovage leaves	3½	cups vinegar
18	peppercorns	2½	cups water
		⅓	cup honey

Stand the carrots upright in 6 hot, sterilized pint canning jars, occasionally adding a dill sprig or lovage leaves. Divide up the peppercorns, mustard seeds, and garlic, and sprinkle an equal amount in each jar.

Boil the vinegar, water, and honey together until the honey dissolves. Pour hot over the carrots, covering them completely.

Seal, and refrigerate for at least 1 week before using. These carrots keep for up to 2 months, but I prefer to use them up within 1 month.

If you wish to can them for longer keeping, cover the carrots with the boiling liquid, but be sure to leave a ½-inch headspace. Process in a boiling water bath for 10 minutes. Store in a cool, dark place for up to 1 year.

Makes 6 pints

Giardiniera or Italian Pickled Vegetables

These vegetables look best in gallon containers. I buy mine from a restaurant that has leftover commercial pickle jars. If you can't find a source, then use quart containers—anything smaller is too much trouble to pack.

2	pounds carrots (about 8 medium-size)	2	quarts white vinegar
3	sweet peppers	4	quarts water
2	hot peppers	1½	cups honey
1	3-pound cauliflower	⅓	cup mustard seeds
1	bunch celery (about 1¾ pounds), trimmed	1	tablespoon fennel seeds (optional)
1¾	pounds white boiling onions	1	tablespoon celery seed
		1	teaspoon peppercorns
		4	cloves garlic

Peel and halve the carrots lengthwise, and cut them into 2-inch-long pieces. Seed all the peppers and cut them into 1½-inch pieces. Divide the cauliflower into 1½-inch florets. String the celery, then slice it lengthwise and cut it into 2-inch-long pieces. Peel the onions and cut crosshatches in their bases.

Place the vinegar, water, honey, mustard seeds, fennel seeds (if used), celery seed, and peppercorns in a 10-quart enameled or stainless steel pot. Bring the mixture to a boil, and boil until the honey dissolves, about 5 minutes. Stir, then skim off any foam on the surface.

Add the onions and cook for 3 minutes. Stir in the carrots, celery, and cauliflower. When the mixture returns to a boil, cook for 5 minutes. Add the peppers and cook for 3 minutes longer.

Spoon the vegetables into 2 hot, sterilized gallon containers. Pour the hot vinegar mixture over them, and make sure the spices are distributed evenly. Add 2 garlic cloves to each container. Seal the jars and store them in the refrigerator. Let the vegetables marinate for at least 1 week before serving. Treated this way, the vegetables should keep for several weeks.

Makes about 2 gallons

Variation
• Substitute sliced Florence fennel for the celery, and reduce the fennel seeds to 1 teaspoon.

Pickled Mushrooms

In colonial days pickling was an important technique for preserving perishables. Daphne Derven has found pickled mushroom recipes (receipts) in several books from the 1700s. This version appeared in *The Receipt Book of Elizabeth Raper, 1756–1770*.

1	pound small to medium-size mushroom caps (about 1½ pounds whole mushrooms)	1	nutmeg, grated
		10	whole cloves
		1	tablespoon cracked black pepper
1	quart cider vinegar		whole mace (optional)
1	slice of gingerroot		

Put the mushrooms, vinegar, gingerroot, nutmeg, cloves, pepper, and mace (if used) in an enameled or stainless steel pan. Slowly bring the mixture to a boil. Turn off the heat and allow the mushrooms to cool.

Place the mushrooms in a quart jar, making sure they are covered with the liquid, and store in the refrigerator for several days before using. The mushrooms will keep for at least 2 weeks in the refrigerator.

Makes 1 quart

Profile

Nina Simonds never planned to be one of the country's leading experts on Chinese cooking. Her goal, from the time she was in high school in Andover, Massachusetts, was to combine a study of language, culture, and food—preferably in France.

When she was in college, however, Nina was given the name of a woman in Taiwan who ran a cooking school and wanted her books translated into English. Fortunately, Nina had studied Chinese in high school, so she headed for Taiwan and a fruitful 3½-year collaboration with Huang Su-Huei—as well as a translation of 3 Chinese cookbooks and apprenticeships in 2 restaurant kitchens.

From Taiwan Nina went to Paris, where she received a *grand diplôme* in classic French cuisine from LaVarenne cooking school while teaching Chinese cooking at night.

An editor from *Gourmet Magazine* attended her cooking class and asked Nina to write a series of columns on Chinese cooking. The *Gourmet* series formed the basis for her book, *Classic Chinese Cuisine*, and led to her food demonstrations around the country.

Chinese cooking relies heavily upon salt and preserved foods, such as bean paste and soy sauce, for flavor. Although Nina normally uses salt in her cooking, while she was in France, she worked as a chef for several months for a French actor who was on a salt-free diet but craved Chinese food. Nina devised several ways to add flavor to Chinese food without salt. When the food had a sauce, she would make a concentrated sauce from unsalted bouillon cubes, which she used to replace water in Chinese recipes.

"The way for people to cook Chinese food without salt is to step up the seasonings," Nina explained. "Increase the quantities of garlic, scallions, and gingerroot. Very often I would add rice vinegar to give the food a type of sharpness that salt would give. Or I would use interesting flavorings such as sesame oil, which is a prime seasoning in Chinese vegetarian cooking.

"Because salt heightens the taste sensation, you have to replace it with ingredients that will continue to excite the palate. Textures can serve this important function."

Certain cooking techniques, Nina thinks, lend themselves to salt-free Chinese cooking.

"Stir-frying intensifies and accentuates food's natural flavors and textures. Deep frying is also a good cooking method for no-salt cooking; you end up with a wonderful, crisp texture and good flavor. And use tart and sour dipping sauces to heighten the taste sensation.

"Steaming is great because it also accentuates the natural flavorings of the foods, and you can add pungent flavorings such as gingerroot, or fresh herbs such as cilantro. In addition, you could make a fragrant oil such as a red-pepper oil—or a ginger oil—and use it to season the food. Using these flavor intensifiers, there's no need for salt or soy sauce.

"Like other cultures," Nina added, "the Chinese have developed a number of pantry foods which will keep at room temperature and increase in flavor as they steep. A good example is pickled vegetables, where seasonings such as vinegar, sugar, and Sichuan peppercorns are used to flavor and preserve foods. In many of these pickled dishes, the liquid is retained and reused over and over again. The Chinese believe that each additional use adds to the flavor of the finished pickle."

Nina reminded me that sauerkraut is said to be a Chinese invention, made up by Chinese workers building the Great Wall during the Han dynasty. The workers, who existed on a diet of cabbage and rice, used rice wine to preserve the cabbage from summer to winter. When the Tartars controlled China, they adapted the pickled cabbage to suit their own tastes, substituting salt for rice wine. Sauerkraut was introduced to Europe in this form.

In ancient China condiments were developed as preservatives for foods when refrigeration and transportation were limited. Although they are ideal pantry foods, no one makes condiments such as bean sauce or soy sauce at home, because they need fermenting. Also, she added, for centuries the Chinese have had an extensive market network, which means that items such as dumpling skins or pickled vegetables are bought at the market rather than prepared at home.

Chinese cooks, however, do make short-term pickled salads at home. The vegetables marinate for hours at room temperature, and then they're seasoned and stored in a cool spot. These refrigerator salads make ideal pantry foods because they last for several days.

I asked Nina how she would make pickled salads without salt. "Basically, when you make any kind of pickled salad, you salt the vegetables to draw out the natural liquids so that the marinade can go into the vegetables and flavor them accordingly. I would suggest air drying the vegetables before you make a salad. The Chinese customarily do this, and it would help remove the liquids. Cut the vegetables up, spread them out on a tray covered with a linen dish towel for at least a few hours, and then make the pickled salads."

Nina suggests several techniques for storing Chinese ingredients. She keeps fresh unpeeled gingerroot in a pot of sand or places it, peeled, in a jar of rice wine or dry sherry in the refrigerator.

Leftover canned bamboo shoots or water chestnuts can be stored in the refrigerator. Because they both have strong flavors, they should be plunged into boiling water before being used at all, then refreshed in cold water. Cover bamboo shoots or water chestnuts with cold water, and refrigerate them in a covered jar. If you change the water weekly, they will keep for several weeks.

Nina has given me several pantry food recipes which appear in her book, *Classic Chinese Cuisine*, in slightly different form. You'll find them scattered throughout the book.

Cantonese Pickled Vegetables

This sweet and sour salad of Nina Simonds can be eaten alone or used as a garnish for sweet and sour pork or shrimp.

1	*daikon* radish (Chinese turnip, about ½ pound)	¼ to ⅜	cup honey
		½	cup clear rice vinegar
4	carrots, peeled	12	thin slices of gingerroot, smashed
6	pickling cucumbers		

Peal the *daikon* radish, remove the root and stem ends, and halve lengthwise. Then cut each half lengthwise into thirds, and roll-cut each section into 1-inch pieces. (To roll-cut, make a diagonal cut at the end of the section, roll the section ¼ turn, and make another diagonal cut. Continue rolling and cutting until you've cut the entire section into several 1-inch pieces that are all cut on the diagonal at each of their ends.)

Roll-cut the carrots into 1-inch pieces as well. Halve the cucumbers lengthwise. Seed them and cut each half lengthwise into thirds. Roll-cut the cucumbers into 1-inch pieces. Place the vegetables in a single layer on trays, cover with a dish towel, and let sit for several hours.

Combine the honey and vinegar, stirring well. Add this mixture and the gingerroot to the vegetables, and toss lightly to coat. Refrigerate for at least 3 hours, or overnight, before serving.

The vegetables will last for up to 1 week in the refrigerator if stored in a covered container.

Makes about 6 cups

Sichuan Pickled Salad

Nina Simonds says the air drying technique compensates to some extent for the lack of salt. The longer the salad sits, the spicer the flavor will be. If you prefer more dressing, double the oil and spices.

1	pound *napa* (Chinese cabbage)	6	dried hot red peppers, seeded and cut into ¼-inch pieces
1	*daikon* radish (Chinese turnip, about ½ pound)	2	scallions, white parts only, smashed
4	carrots, peeled	2	tablespoons finely shredded gingerroot
2	tablespoons corn oil	2	teaspoons Chinese black vinegar
1	tablespoon sesame oil	1	teaspoon honey
1	tablespoon Sichuan peppercorns		

Core the *napa* and cut the leaves into 2-inch squares. Lightly bruise the *napa* pieces by smashing them with the flat side of a cleaver.

Peel the *daikon* radish and cut off the root and stem ends. Halve it lengthwise. Then cut each half lengthwise into thirds, and roll-cut it into 1-inch pieces. (See Cantonese Pickled Vegetables, page 60, for roll-cutting directions.) Roll-cut the carrots into 1-inch pieces.

Spread the vegetables out on trays exposed to the air, and let them sit for at least 1 hour, but preferably all day. Turn the cabbage at least once. The air drying will evaporate some of the liquid from the vegetables.

Combine the corn and sesame oils in a saucepan, and heat until they are smoking. Add the peppercorns, hot red peppers, and scallions. Cover the pan and remove it from the heat. Let it sit, covered, for 30 minutes.

Using a fine-mesh strainer, remove the seasonings and retain the oil.

Mix the oil with the vegetables along with the gingerroot, vinegar, and honey. Toss until the vegetables are coated with the mixture. Refrigerate the salad for at least 4 hours before serving.

If the salad is stored in the refrigerator in a covered container, it should last for at least 1½ weeks.

Makes about 6 cups

Piquant Onions

Make these onions 1 day before serving, to allow time for the flavors to mellow. They go nicely with roast pork or duck.

2	pounds small white onions (about 26, 1-inch diameter)	4 to 5	tablespoons tomato paste
2½	cups water	⅓	cup olive oil
1⅓	cups red wine vinegar	1	teaspoon freshly ground black pepper
⅓	cup honey	¼	teaspoon cumin powder
½	cup raisins		

Bring a large saucepan of water to a boil. Drop the onions into the water, and boil for 1 minute to loosen the skins. Drain them, peel, and pierce a cross in each root end, to help the onions keep their shape while cooking.

Place the 2½ cups water and the vinegar, honey, raisins, tomato paste, oil, pepper, and cumin in a 4-quart enameled or stainless steel pot. Bring the liquids to a boil, then simmer until the honey dissolves, about 2 minutes. Add the onions.

Simmer the onions slowly for 1 hour, or until they are tender but still hold their shape. It may be necessary to add water while cooking, because the liquid should cover the onions. Stir occasionally.

Store the onions in a dish, loosely covered with foil, in the refrigerator. They will keep for at least 5 days. If you have refrigerated the onions, remove them from the refrigerator 1 hour before serving, to allow time for the olive oil to come to room temperature.

For longer storage, can them. Pour boiling hot into hot, clean pint canning jars, and leave a ½-inch headspace. Process in a boiling water bath for 10 minutes. Store for up to 6 months in a cool, dark place.

Makes 5 to 6 cups

Pickled Jalapeño Peppers

As you might expect, these are hot and can burn the roof of your mouth if you aren't careful. (My teenage son, however, munches on them with sandwiches.) A smidgen of the peppers perks up tartar sauce and Russian dressing and is good in coleslaw. Or try draining the peppers and adding them to tomato sauce.

2	cups white vinegar	1	red Anaheim pepper, cut into thin rings (optional)
⅔	cup water		
1	tablespoon mixed pickling spices	1	onion, thinly sliced
⅓ to ½	pound fresh green jalapeño peppers	2	cloves garlic, slivered

In an enameled or stainless steel saucepan, heat the vinegar, water, and 2 teaspoons pickling spices. Bring the mixture to a boil, remove it from the heat, and let the spices steep in the vinegar while you prepare the jalapeño peppers.

Wash and dry the jalapeño peppers, and trim the stems to within ¼ inch of the tops.

Place ½ teaspoon pickling spices in the bottom of each of 2 hot, sterilized pint canning jars. Pack ½ of the jalapeño peppers, Anaheim pepper rings (if used), and onion slices in each jar, placing garlic slivers throughout.

Reheat the vinegar and water mixture, and pour it over the peppers. Seal. Place the peppers in a sunny spot for at least 1 week before serving.

Store in the refrigerator, where they will keep in good condition for 1 month. For longer storage, don't place the jars in the sun first. Rather, fill the jars with the hot vinegar and water mixture, leaving a ½-inch headspace. Seal, and process in a boiling water bath for 10 minutes. Store for up to 1 year in a cool, dry place.

Makes 2 pints

Hungarian Peppers Stuffed with Cabbage

I recently sampled a jar of peppers imported from Budapest. The Hungarians had stuffed red cabbage into large sweet cherry peppers shaped like tomatoes. Unfortunately, large cherry peppers, which are easy to stuff, are uncommon in the United States—although small hot cherry peppers are available from specialized seed companies. I've substituted Italian frying peppers in this recipe. If the chunky, slightly hot Romanian pepper is available, it's also excellent in this recipe. Note that the color of the peppers fades, but the red cabbage stuffing remains brightly colored, as does the marinade.

8 to 10	Italian frying peppers (4 to 6 inches long)		red wine vinegar
1	recipe Red Cabbage Relish (see page 54; add to it 1 teaspoon ground sweet Hungarian paprika [optional], and omit 2 cups onions)	4	cloves garlic

The peppers should be at room temperature, otherwise they will be difficult to seed. Lay the peppers flat, and make a slit along the length of each pepper almost to the stem. Then, at a right angle to the slit near the stem, make another connecting cut, just long enough to allow you to seed and stuff the pepper. The opening in each pepper will look like an upside down *L*. Remove the stem of each pepper, cutting it as close to the flesh as possible. Seed the peppers.

Blanch the peppers in a large pot of boiling water for 2 minutes, which will be long enough to soften their texture and make the peppers more pliable. Immediately run them under cold water to stop the cooking process, then drain. Set the peppers aside.

Prepare the Red Cabbage Relish with the adjustments noted in this recipe's ingredients list.

Lay the peppers out in a row on the counter. Stuff the peppers with the relish. You will probably have about 1½ cups relish leftover for another meal.

Pack the peppers in 2 hot, sterilized quart jars, placing the stem ends at the top of the jar. You should be able to pack 4 or 5 peppers in each jar. Reheat the pickling juice from the relish, and pour it over the peppers. The juice should be sufficient to fill each jar almost all the way to the top. If you need more pickling liquid, boil together equal parts red wine vinegar and water, and use to fill each jar to the top. Add 2 cloves of garlic to each jar, cover, and refrigerate for at least 1 week before serving.

The pickled peppers will last for at least 2 months in the refrigerator, as long as they are covered with the pickling liquid. You can also can them, using the boiling water bath method. If you plan to do so, leave a ½-inch headspace and process for 15 minutes. They will keep for up to 1 year in a cool, dry place.

Makes 2 quarts

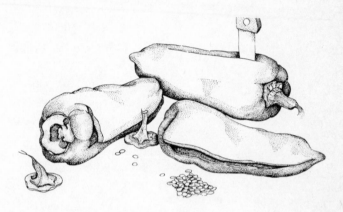

Daikon Radish (Chinese Turnip) Pickles

2½	cups water	2 pounds (8 cups) *daikon*
½	cup honey	radishes (Chinese
⅔	cup rice wine	turnips), thinly
	vinegar	sliced

Combine the water, honey, and vinegar in a stainless steel or enameled pan. Bring the liquid to a boil, and boil just until the honey dissolves. Cool, then pour over the *daikon* radishes. Cover tightly and let stand in the refrigerator for at least 3 days before serving.

The pickles will keep for at least 1 month if kept tightly covered in the refrigerator.

Makes 8 to 9 cups

Pickled Hot Pepper Rings

Anaheim, or California, peppers are the mildest hot peppers you can grow. (They are also among the largest.) Substitute a hotter variety if you wish, but the "heat" will war with the garlic and coriander flavors. The pepper rings are ready after about 1 week, although they improve in storage. As the seeds contain volatile pepper oils, don't touch your eyes while you are seeding the peppers. The vinegar marinade makes an excellent dipping sauce for broiled fish or chicken.

½	pound red Anaheim peppers (about 12)	1	teaspoon coriander seeds
3	cloves garlic, sliced	1	cup water
4	basil sprigs		
2	cups white vinegar		

Cut the tops off the peppers, scoop out the seeds with a paring knife, and then slice them into thin rings about ⅛ inch thick. This takes a bit of time, but don't try to rush the job by washing out the seeds, because you might breathe in the fumes.

Divide the peppers, garlic, basil, and coriander seeds between 2 hot, sterilized pint containers. Mix the vinegar and water together in a pot and bring to a boil. Pour over the peppers to within ½ inch of the top. Add more boiling water if necessary.

Seal the jars and let them sit in a sunny spot for about 1 week, then store in the refrigerator, where they will keep for at least 2 months. Or process in a boiling water bath for 10 minutes, and store in a cool, dark place, where they will keep for up to 1 year.

Makes 2 pints

Green Tomato Refrigerator Pickles

These pickles are a wonderful accompaniment to a pot roast in winter or as a snack to curb a dieter's appetite. The firm texture of the tomatoes makes them an ideal pickling choice.

6	large cloves garlic	3	onions
3	small hot peppers, seeded	2	sweet red peppers
3	small dill heads	4	large carrots
3	teaspoons mixed pickling spices	5	green tomatoes
		5	cups water
		2	cups white vinegar

Peel and quarter the cloves of garlic, and divide them among 3 sterilized quart jars. Halve the hot peppers and put 1 pepper in each jar. Place 1 dill head and 1 teaspoon pickling spices in each jar.

Cut the onions into thin wedges. Then slice the sweet red peppers and carrots into strips, and cut into 1½-inch lengths. Core the tomatoes and cut each tomato into 6 wedges. Distribute the vegetables in the jars.

Heat the water and vinegar to the boiling point. Put a spoon in each jar to disperse the heat and prevent the jars from cracking, then pour the hot water and vinegar mixture into the jars. Cover the jars and refrigerate. Let sit for at least 2 weeks before eating. The pickles keep for at least 1 month if refrigerated.

Makes about 3 quarts

Variation
• Add 1 teaspoon hot pepper flakes to each jar.

Tomato Relish

14	large tomatoes	1½	cups honey
2	large onions	2	cups cider vinegar
2	large sweet green peppers		

Peel the tomatoes and onions. Seed the sweet green peppers. Coarsely chop the vegetables and place in a stainless steel or enameled pan along with the remaining ingredients. Simmer for 2 hours, or until thickened. Spoon into hot, sterilized pint jars and seal. Store in the refrigerator for up to 2 months.

To can, spoon hot into hot, clean pint canning jars, leaving a ½-inch headspace. Process in a boiling water bath for 10 minutes. Store in a cool, dark place for up to 1 year.

Makes 4 pints

Victory Relish

This relish, adapted from a *Farm Journal* recipe, is my family's favorite topping for barbecued Italian sausages or hamburgers. It's also a good spread on slices of Cheddar cheese for a quick snack.

22	large ripe tomatoes (8 to 10 pounds)	2	sweet green peppers
7	large onions	1	cup whole pickling spices
5	pears	3	cups cider vinegar
10	peaches	2¼ to 2¾	cups honey

Peel and coarsely chop the tomatoes and onions. Set them aside. Peel and core the pears, and peel and pit the peaches. Seed the sweet green peppers. Coarsely chop the pears, peaches, and peppers in a food processor or meat grinder. Tie the pickling spices loosely in a piece of cheesecloth.

Place all the ingredients in a stainless steel or enameled pan, and bring them to a boil. Lower the heat and simmer, stirring occasionally, for 2 hours, or until the mixture is thick.

Place the hot relish in hot, sterilized jars and seal. Cool, then store in the refrigerator for up to 2 months.

To can, pour hot into hot, clean pint canning jars, leaving a ½-inch headspace. Process for 15 minutes in a boiling water bath. Store in a cool, dark place for up to 1 year.

You can also freeze the relish for up to 1 year.

Makes 10 to 13 pints, depending upon the size of the tomatoes

Fruit Preserves

Homemade fruit preserves turn any breakfast into an occasion. My standard company breakfast is buttered scones served with a selection of preserves or jams—and sometimes eggs. The preserves are a treat for me as well as the company.

I like European-style preserves, which often contain chunks of the whole fruit and are less sweet than American versions. They also have a less solid texture than those you may be accustomed to eating.

Aside from personal taste, there is a practical reason for not making preserves too sweet if they're made with honey. When you are preparing natural preserves, particularly single-fruit recipes, the honey flavor tends to dominate. If you make an ultrasweet preserve, all you will taste is the honey: the fruit flavor will recede into the background.

I've 2 solutions to this problem. First, multiple-fruit preserves often have a complexity of flavors that overcomes the honey taste. Also, after much experimentation I've discovered that lime juice cuts any of the cloying qualities of honey more effectively than lemon or orange juice.

In addition to the flavor consideration, honey sometimes will darken the preserves, so you may end up with a less-vibrant fruit color than you expect.

Even with these reservations about fruit preserves made with honey, I must add that the recipes in this chapter are among my favorites in the book. English Lemon Curd has been a family favorite ever since we bought a jar in Ripon, England. Tomato Peach Marmalade has an unexpected meld of flavors that's a good choice for afternoons when a friend drops by and you bring out the biscuits and tea. Spiced Fresh Prunes or Spiced Seckel Pears can turn a mundane dinner into an occasion, while Spiced Blueberries are an attractive addition to a game or pork dinner.

I hardly need to say that fruit preserves are traditional canned foods. Canning jars filled with colorful preserves and spiced fruits look beautiful lining a pantry shelf, bringing back memories of spring and summer.

Spiced Cherries

The cherry juice stains terribly, so wear old clothes and be prepared for purple hands. Any leftover juice is good stirred into Peach Blueberry Jam (see page 76) or basted over a roast pork or lamb. The cherries should be served as a side dish with roast meats or poultry. They're particularly good in a French-style roast duck with cherries; just susbstitute them for the cooked cherries called for in the recipe.

2	cups honey	¼	teaspoon ground ginger
1½	cups white vinegar	⅛	teaspoon ground nutmeg
6	cups pitted sweet cherries	1	tablespoon chopped orange zest
1	teaspoon ground cinnamon	⅓	cup lime juice
¼	teaspoon ground allspice		juice of 1 orange (about ⅓ cup)
½	teaspoon ground cloves		

Boil together the honey and vinegar in an enameled or stainless steel pan for 3 to 4 minutes, or until they form a syrup. Add the cherries, cinnamon, allspice, cloves, ginger, nutmeg, orange zest, lime juice, and orange juice. Cook, stirring frequently, until the cherries are cooked and the juices have reduced. The cooking time, which should be about 15 to 20 minutes, depends upon the amount of juice the cherries contain.

With a slotted spoon, ladle the hot cherries into 2 hot, sterilized pint jars. Cover the cherries with the syrup, and seal. Allow them to cool, then store in the refrigerator for up to 2 months.

To can them, ladle the hot cherries into 2 hot, clean pint canning jars and cover with syrup, leaving a ½-inch headspace. Process for 15 minutes in a boiling water bath. Store for up to 1 year in a cool, dry place.

Makes 2 pints

Cherries in Syrup

This 18th century recipe calls for roseflower water, which was a common flavoring in that era. Daphne Derven, who makes this recipe in her food demonstrations, says vanilla wasn't used until the 19th century; until then people flavored with roseflower and orangeflower waters. The best place to find roseflower water is at a Middle Eastern shop. If you are buying it elsewhere, make sure it is made for consumption and not for cosmetics. The bottle should be marked "distilled from rose petals and water."

¼ pound honey
1 cup water
2 tablespoons rose-
   flower water

1 pound cherries with
   stems

Boil together the honey and water until the honey is dissolved, lower the heat to simmer, and add the roseflower water and cherries. If the syrup doesn't cover the cherries, add more water. Bring the syrup to a gentle boil, remove the pan from the heat, and allow the cherries to cool in the syrup. Serve the cherries stem up.

If the cherries are covered with syrup, sealed, and stored in the refrigerator, they will last for at least 2 weeks.

Makes about 3½ cups

Apricot Honey

My friend Michael Padnos dreamed up this recipe one year when his bees produced a bumper crop of honey. He varies the proportion of apricots to honey, sometimes stirring in 2 parts apricot purée to 1 part honey for a thick jam while other times using a smaller amount of apricot, just to flavor the honey. This is delicious drizzled on scones or pancakes.

⅓	pound dried apricots (1¼ cups)
2	cups honey

Place the apricots in a 1-quart pan, barely cover with water, and bring the mixture to a boil. Lower the heat and simmer until the apricots are cooked but not mushy. This will take about 15 minutes.

Purée the apricots in a food processor or blender. Stir the purée into the honey. Pour into a sterilized jar, seal, and store it, covered, in a cool, dark spot.

As long as the purée is distributed throughout the honey, the honey will keep for several weeks at room temperature and for several months if refrigerated. As you use the apricot honey, pour in plain honey to seal the bottle.

Makes about 3 cups

Blackberry Jam

Many of the towns of southern France and northern Spain have a tradition of cooking with honey, which carries over into preserving. Last fall, when we visited Barcelona, I bought several jars of fruit-and-honey preserves made in the Spanish town of Calahorra, in the Rioja wine region. In general, European preserves are less sweet than those made in America—as is this jam, which is almost identical to its Spanish prototype. If you have an ultra-sweet tooth, you may wish to increase the amount of honey—but taste it first before you do. The seeds are not strained out, giving this jam an interesting texture.

5	cups blackberries (mixture of ripe and underripe)	1½	cups honey
		2	tablespoons lime juice

Put the blackberries and honey in a large enameled or stainless steel pot, crush them slightly with a potato masher, and let sit for 20 minutes to bring out the juices.

Bring the mixture to a boil. Add the lime juice. Boil over medium heat until thick, 10 to 15 minutes, until the spoon leaves a path on the bottom of the pot. The cooking time depends upon how juicy the berries are.

Spoon the hot jam into hot, clean pint canning jars, leaving a ½-inch headspace. Process for 15 minutes in a boiling water bath. It will keep for up to 1 year in a cool, dry place. Or if you prefer, store the unprocessed jam in a jar in the refrigerator, where it will keep for several weeks.

Makes about 3½ cups

Variation
• Blackberry Sauce: Boil the berries until the juices are released and the sauce thickens slightly. Sieve to remove the seeds. Five cups berries will produce 4 to 4½ cups sauce. Store as for jam.

Spiced Blueberries

Serve these berries with cold roast meats. If you end up with more syrup than berries, don't toss it out. Save the syrup and mix it with seltzer water for a blueberry shrub.

3	quarts blueberries	1	teaspoon whole cloves
1	teaspoon whole allspice	3¾	cups honey
2	cardamom seeds	1½	cups cider or white vinegar
2	cinnamon sticks		grated zest of 1 lemon

Wash and drain the blueberries. Tie the allspice, cardamom, cinnamon, and cloves in a small cheesecloth bag. In a large, heavy saucepan mix together the honey, vinegar, and lemon zest. Add the cheesecloth spice bag and ½ the berries, and simmer slowly until they are tender, about 12 minutes.

Using a slotted spoon, remove the berries and put in 3 hot, clean pint jars. Repeat with the remaining berries, and spoon into 3 more hot, clean pint jars.

Pour the syrup over the berries until the jars are filled. Seal, and store for 1 month in the refrigerator before serving. These will keep for up to 3 months in the refrigerator.

You can also can them. To do so, pour hot into hot, clean canning jars, leaving a ½-inch headspace. Process for 15 minutes in a boiling water bath. Store for up to 1 year in a cool, dry place.

You can freeze the extra syrup for up to 1 year.

Makes 6 pints

Fresh Blueberry Syrup

I prefer native low-bush blueberries for this recipe. When using the blander high-bush varieties, increase the amount of lemon juice to taste. If the berries are particularly juicy, you will have a higher syrup yield and will need to simmer the syrup longer. This syrup is wonderful on waffles, hot cereal, vanilla ice cream, and yogurt.

3	cups blueberries	⅔	cup water
⅓	cup honey	¼	cup lemon juice

Simmer together the blueberries, honey, water, and lemon juice for 10 to 15 minutes, or until the berries are incorporated into a syrup.

Place in a covered jar in the refrigerator, and use within 2 weeks. Or freeze for up to 1 year.

Makes 1⅔ cups

Italian Fruit Relish

This *mostarda di Cremona* is based on a recipe in Giuliano Bugialli's *Classic Techniques of Italian Cooking*. Bugialli says this fruit relish originated in the Lombardy town of Cremona. Be sure to use slightly under-ripe fruits and varieties that will retain their shape when cooked. The first time I made this, I used Granny Smith apples, which turned to mush in an instant. Serve this relish with roasted or boiled meats or poultry.

1½	pounds apples (such as Cortland, Yellow Delicious, or Baldwin), cored	9½	cups cold water
		2	cups honey
		6	tablespoons lemon juice
1½	pounds pears, cored	3	tablespoons mustard seeds
1½	pounds peaches, pitted	10	whole cloves
¼	pound pitted cherries		hot pepper sauce

Peel the fruits, then cut them into 1-inch pieces. Keep the varieties of fruit separate.

Place 3 saucepans on the stove. In each pan put 3 cups cold water, ½ cup honey, and 2 tablespoons lemon juice. Simmer this mixture for about 20 minutes, then add the fruits.

Place the apples in the first pan, the pears in the second pan, and the peaches and cherries in the third. Simmer until the fruits are cooked but still firm. Remove the pans from the heat, but let the fruits cool in the syrup. This will take about 45 minutes. When the fruits have cooled, remove them to a baking dish, and pour all the cooking juices into 1 pan.

Preheat the oven to 375°F.

Bake the fruit for 15 minutes. Then remove the fruit from the oven, stir, and let stand.

To the juices in the saucepan add ½ cup honey, the mustard seeds, ½ cup water, and the cloves. Simmer together until a thick syrup forms (the cooking time depends upon the amount of cooking juices). Reduce to 3 cups. Then add the hot pepper sauce to taste.

Add the fruit to the syrup, and simmer for about 10 minutes, stirring frequently. Cool and cover and store in the refrigerator, where the *mostarda* will keep for at least 2 weeks.

To can, ladle the hot fruit into hot, clean canning jars, and cover with the syrup, leaving a ½-inch headspace. Process for 10 minutes in a boiling water bath. Store in a cool, dry place for up to 1 year.

Makes about 8 cups

Tropical Jam

This golden colored jam has a softer texture than you might expect from a jam. It's delicious spooned over scones or bran muffins. Add a little extra orange juice, and you end up with a topping for pound cake or ice cream. Use only ripe mangoes.

1	pound mangoes (about 3), peeled and chopped	¾ cup orange juice
		⅓ cup honey
		2 limes, thinly sliced

Combine the mangoes, orange juice, honey, and limes in a heavy stainless steel or enameled pan. Cook, stirring frequently, for 10 to 15 minutes, or until the mangoes have turned into a purée and the orange juice has evaporated. The shorter the cooking time, the sweeter the jam, because the lime flavor dominates if the jam is cooked too long. The jam will set a bit more as it cools.

Cool, then spoon into a jar and store in the refrigerator, where the jam will keep for at least 1½ weeks. You can freeze it for up to 1 year.

Makes about 2 cups

Peach Blueberry Jam

Use at least ¼ underripe fruit to ensure sufficient pectin for the jam to jell. This jam is wonderful on muffins.

7	cups sliced or chopped peaches (about 12)	1	cup sliced strawberries (optional)
1	cup blueberries	¾	cup honey

Place the peaches, blueberries, and strawberries (if used) in an enameled or stainless steel pot with a large surface area. Crush them slightly with a potato masher. Add the honey, stir the fruits, and place the pot on the stove.

Bring the fruits to a boil, stirring constantly, and boil for 2 to 3 minutes. Then skim off the foam, lower the heat, and cook the preserves at a gentle boil for 15 to 20 minutes. By this point the mixture should have a jamlike consistency. If the jam has too much liquid, remove the fruit pieces with a slotted spoon, and rapidly boil down the liquid to the consistency you desire. Then add the fruit pieces.

Place the jam in a jar, seal, and store in the refrigerator, where it will keep for at least 1 month.

For longer keeping, can the jam. After adding the fruit pieces, reheat the jam and pour it hot into clean, hot pint or ½-pint canning jars, leaving a ½-inch headspace. Process for 15 minutes in a boiling water bath. If stored in a cool, dark place, the jam should keep for at least 6 months.

Makes 2 pints

Peach and Plum Chutney

4 to 5	small plums	⅓	cup mustard seeds
2½	pounds yellow peaches	1	cinnamon stick
1 to 1¼	cups honey	1	teaspoon cloves
¾	cup raisins	2	cups cider vinegar
2	tablespoons finely chopped gingerroot		

Peel and halve the plums. Peel and quarter the peaches. Mix together in a large enameled or stainless steel pot. Stir in the honey, raisins, gingerroot, mustard seeds, cinnamon, cloves, and vinegar.

Bring the mixture to a boil, and boil for 15 minutes, stirring frequently. Skim off any foam. Remove from the heat, and let stand for at least 6 hours or overnight to plump the fruit. Stir from time to time.

Reheat the mixture and cook for 15 minutes, stirring frequently. Watch carefully because the honey will stick and burn.

Pour into sterilized jars, and cap. If you wish a stronger cinnamon taste, break the cinnamon stick into 3 pieces and put a piece in each jar; otherwise discard. Store in the refrigerator for up to 2 months.

For longer storage, can it. Spoon hot into hot, clean pint or ½-pint canning jars, leaving a ½-inch headspace. Process for 10 minutes in a boiling water bath. It will keep for up to 1 year if stored in a cool, dark place.

Makes about 3½ pints

English Lemon Curd

One year we exchanged houses with a family in Yorkshire, England. At the village food shop I found a lemon curd bottled by a local farmwife; it was delicious served with scones and buns. After stocking up on several jars to bring home, I discovered this spread keeps for months. Although the traditional English lemon curd, or "cheese," is made with sugar, I understand the Scottish version uses honey.

¼	cup butter	2	egg yolks
½	cup honey		grated zest of 1 lemon
½	cup lemon juice		(optional)
1	egg		

Melt the butter in the top of a double boiler set over simmering water. Stir in the honey and cook for a moment, until it is incorporated. Add the lemon juice.

Beat together the egg and egg yolks. Stir them into the lemon mixture, continuing to stir until the mixture thickens, which can take as long as 10 minutes. (It will thicken further as it cools.) Add the lemon zest if you like.

Pour into sterilized jars and cool. It will keep for several months in the refrigerator.

Makes 1¼ cups

Variation
• Fruit Tart Filling: English cooks often fill tarts with lemon curd. Use only a small amount, for the mixture is rich. Spread a thin layer of the curd on the bottom of a cooked pie crust or individual tart shells, and top with fresh fruit such as blueberries, blackberries, peaches, raspberries, or strawberries.

Peach Conserve

This is a tart conserve that mellows in storage. Be aware that the honey flavor will overpower the peaches if you increase the amount of honey in an effort to make the conserve sweeter. I like to coordinate the preparation of this jam with that of either Spiced Blueberries or Spiced Cherries. Any syrup leftover from the preparation of these other recipes makes a delicious addition to this peach conserve and gives it a softer consistency.

5	pounds peaches	⅓	cup orange juice
1	cup honey	½	cup lime juice

Dip the peaches into boiling water for 2 minutes, and then run them under cold water to loosen the skins. Remove the skins and mash the peaches with a potato masher until some of their juices have been released. Remove the pits, place the peaches in a 6- or 8-quart enameled or stainless steel kettle, and stir in the honey. Bring the mixture to a boil quickly over medium-high heat, and cook for 5 minutes, skimming off any foam as it accumulates.

Add the orange and lime juices and cook for 20 to 30 minutes, stirring frequently. As the liquid reduces, you will need to stir constantly—otherwise the honey may burn.

The conserve can be spooned into jars and stored in the refrigerator, where it will keep for up to 2 months.

You can also can it, should you want to keep it longer. Spoon the hot conserve into clean pint or ½-pint canning jars, leaving a ½-inch headspace. Process for 15 minutes in a boiling water bath. Stored in a cool, dark place, the conserve will keep for up to 1 year.

Makes about 3½ cups

Variations
• Add ½ cup syrup from either Spiced Blueberries or Spiced Cherries (see page 73 or 70) to ½ this recipe.

Pear and Pineapple Medley

1	quart water	½	pound fresh pine-
1	cup honey		apple (1½ cups)
1	lemon, thinly sliced	6 to 8	fresh prunes, peeled
1	pound pears (about 3),		and halved
	peeled, seeded, and	4	ounces cranberries
	sliced		(1½ cups)

In a large enameled or stainless steel pan, boil together the water, honey, and lemon for approximately 10 minutes. Add the remaining fruits and cook until the pears are tender but not mushy.

For refrigerator storage, spoon into hot, sterilized jars, seal, and let meld for a few weeks before using. Discard the lemon slices before serving as a fruit compote. It will keep for several weeks.

For longer keeping, can it. Spoon hot into hot, clean pint or ½-pint canning jars, leaving a ½-inch headspace. Process for 15 minutes in a boiling water bath. It will keep for up to 1 year if stored in a cool, dry place.

Makes 3 pints

Spiced Seckel Pears

24	1½-inch seckel pears	1½	cups honey
	(3 pounds)	1	teaspoon whole cloves
2½	cups white vinegar	2	1-inch cinnamon
	plus 1 tablespoon		sticks
	cider vinegar		

Peel the pears, retaining the stems; do not core. As you work, drop the pears into water to which you've added 1 tablespoon cider vinegar so they don't discolor.

Bring the white vinegar, honey, cloves, and cinnamon to a boil and skim off the foam. Drain the pears and add them to the liquid. Simmer for 10 to 15 minutes, until cooked through. The time will vary depending upon the size of the pears.

Pack the hot pears into hot, sterilized pint jars. Cover with the preserving liquid, and seal. If you wish a less spicy taste, strain out the cloves and cinnamon before adding the liquid to the jars. Allow to cool, then store in the refrigerator for up to 3 months.

To can them, pack the pears in hot, clear pint canning jars, and cover with the liquid, leaving a ½-inch headspace. Process for 15 minutes in a boiling water bath. Store in a cool, dry place for up to 1 year.

Makes 2 pints

Two-in-One Pear, Peach, and Raspberry Jam

This recipe makes either a delicious fresh sauce or a jam. If you stop the fruits from cooking after 5 minutes, the mixture is an excellent topping for ice cream or custard. To end up with jam, continue cooking for another 10 to 15 minutes.

3 cups peeled, quartered, and seeded pears (about 12 ounces)	½ cup raspberries
	1 cup honey
3 cups peeled and quartered peaches (about 12 ounces)	

Coarsely chop the pears and peaches—a food processor works well; pulse the machine on and off. Place in a stainless steel or enameled pan, and stir in the raspberries and honey. Bring the fruits to a boil, stirring constantly until they release their juices. Lower the heat, skim off the foam, and simmer for 15 minutes, or until thickened, stirring as needed to keep the honey from burning.

Spoon into hot, sterilized jars and seal. Cool, then store in the refrigerator for up to 3 months.

You may also freeze or can the jam for up to 1 year. To can, spoon hot into 3 hot, clean ½-pint canning jars, leaving a ½-inch headspace. Process in a boiling water bath for 15 minutes. Store in a cool, dark place.

Makes 3 cups

Spiced Fresh Prunes

2 cups honey	3 pounds fresh prunes
2 cups cider vinegar	
8 cloves	
1 slice of gingerroot (size of a quarter)	

In a large enameled or stainless steel pot, simmer together the honey, vinegar, cloves, and gingerroot until a syrup forms. Skim off the foam as it accumulates. This will take about 5 minutes.

Prick the prunes with a sewing needle, and cook them in the syrup until tender. (If you prefer skinned prunes, just cook without pricking, and slip off the skins before bottling.) The skins add a rich color to the syrup.

Let the prunes cool, then pack them in hot, sterilized jars, cover with syrup, and seal. Allow to cool, then store in the refrigerator for up to 3 months.

To can, pack the hot prunes into hot, clean pint canning jars, and cover them with syrup, leaving a ½-inch headspace. Process for 15 minutes in a boiling water bath. Store in a dark, cool place for up to 1 year.

Makes 3 to 4 pints

Tomato Peach Marmalade

This mellow orange preserve's sweetness is delightfully balanced by the bitterness of the lime. It is excellent for English muffins or bagels with cream cheese or as a complement to lamb.

3	pounds tomatoes, peeled, seeded, and coarsely chopped	2	lemons, seeded and very thinly sliced
2	limes, seeded and very thinly sliced	4	peaches, peeled and chopped
		1½ to 2	cups honey

Place the tomatoes, limes, lemons, peaches, and honey in a stainless steel or enameled pan and stir together. Cook slowly, stirring frequently, for 2 to 3 hours, or until thick.

Place in hot, sterilized jars and seal. Refrigerate for up to 3 months.

To can, pour hot into hot, clean pint canning jars, leaving a ½-inch headspace. Process in a boiling water bath for 20 minutes. Store in a cool, dark place for up to 1 year.

Makes 2 pints

Yellow Plum
Tomato Preserves

When our children were young, they snacked on yellow plum tomatoes fresh from the garden as if they were candy. Every once in a while, I managed to hoard some of the tomatoes to make this preserve.

4	pounds yellow plum or pear tomatoes	3	cups honey
2	lemons	1	cup water

Wash and dry the tomatoes. Cut the lemons into paper-thin slices. Place the tomatoes, lemons, honey, and water in an enameled or stainless steel saucepan. Bring the mixture to a boil, lower the heat, and simmer until thickened. Cool, and then spoon into sterilized jars, seal, and store in the refrigerator for up to 3 months.

You can also freeze or can it for up to 1 year. To can, spoon hot into hot, clean pint canning jars, leaving a ½-inch headspace. Then process for 15 minutes in a boiling water bath. Store in a cool, dark place.

Makes about 8 pints

Greek Quince Compote

8	large quinces (11 cups sliced quinces)	1	cinnamon stick
3	cups water	4	whole cloves
¾	cup honey	2	tablespoons lemon juice

Peel, quarter, and seed the quinces, then thinly slice them. Place the quinces in a large pot, and add the water, honey, cinnamon, and cloves.

Simmer for 1 hour, or until the fruit is tender. Cool slightly and stir in the lemon juice. Cool completely before serving.

As long as the quinces are covered with the syrup, they keep well in the refrigerator for at least 2 weeks.

Makes about 8 cups

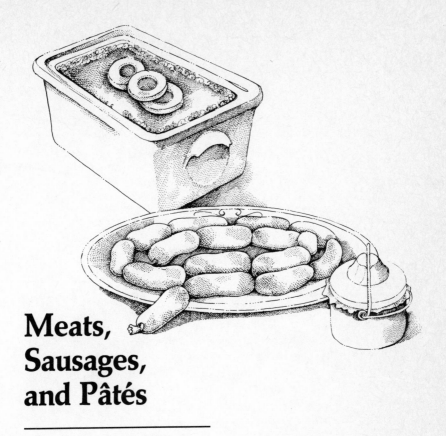

Meats,
Sausages,
and Pâtés

A few years ago my husband and I had a farmer raise a pig for us. I made loaves of headcheese from the head, pots of French rillettes (shredded pork packed in pork fat) out of the scraps and fat, and even tried grilling the ears and serving them with a mustard sauce—certainly not one of my better dishes. I had dreams of feasting on country-style hams once the long, slow curing period was over, but when we took the hams to the butcher, he surprised me by announcing that they would be ready in only 2 weeks.

When I asked how that could be possible (because I knew that curing usually took much longer), he responded that the packing house used a modern curing method; it injected the pork with a curing solution that worked immediately, rather than let the hams sit in a cure that would be slowly absorbed by the meat. The hams looked fine, but they had an unpleasant aftertaste and a soft texture that never seemed right to me.

This experience started me wondering about how the cured meat we ate was processed, and it got me interested in curing meat at home. I had another reason to get interested: we have a beef animal raised every year on our farm in central Massachusetts, and it was pleasant to vary the 500 pounds of meat, usually stored in the freezer, by curing some of it. I started making corned beef, spiced beef, salt cured beef, air dried salted sausages, and other meat products.

The first thing I discovered was that most recipes called for too much salt and too long a curing period. Corning beef in a strong salt solution for 2 weeks or longer, as many recipes suggest, makes it unbelievably salty. I cut back on the amount of salt and the curing time and produced delicious corned beef in less than 1 week. The beef had a cured taste but with more of the flavor of the pickling spices and much less of a salty aftertaste.

Then, when I started cooking without salt or sugar, I carried my curing experiments a step further by eliminating those ingredients. I tried vinegar, water, and spice marinade with varying success: if I marinated the meat for more than 4 days, it usually became too sour, and I had to add honey (or gingersnaps, as you would with sauerbraten) to the cooking liquid, to compensate for the lip-pursing taste. Honey and vinegar marinade worked all right for a short-term cure, but the meat had a heavy honey overtone, and the texture became somewhat pulpy, which made me wary. I finally decided it wasn't possible to end up with the traditional cured flavors without using the traditional curing methods: To get the taste of corned beef, you're going to have to use salt. For a sugar cured ham, you'll have to use sugar.

At the same time, however, I was also developing some very successful recipes for salt-free meats that have some of the storage capabilities of cured meats. I think these new-style pantry meats have a wonderful fresh flavor that I find far more palatable than that of the old-style cured meats. My taste has changed; now that my body has become sensitized to salt, salty meats almost taste unpleasant to me.

In this chapter you'll discover no-salt sausages that hold in the refrigerator or freezer, meat turnovers and pies made flavorful with herbs and spices, and ground meat specialties that stay fresh much longer than you'd expect.

You'll also find some pâtés because pâtés are good keepers, particularly when sealed with a coating of butter. I've changed some of my favorite pâté recipes, removing the salt and alcohol and cutting down considerably on the fat from the originals. Although I enjoy the traditional pâtés occasionally, I now prefer the lighter taste and texture that vegetables add to a ground meat mixture. I've developed several pâté recipes that are held together with a vegetable binder, which not only keeps the pâtés moist but also means that they contain much less fat than traditional versions.

I particularly like poultry stuffed with ground meats and vegetables that create beautiful mosaics of colors when you slice them. These are attractive party dishes, and they stretch a small amount of poultry and meat a long way.

I think you'll discover that the meat recipes in this chapter have a fresh, pleasant taste, that the reduced fat content makes them easier to digest, and that you may end up substituting them for cured meat products, as I have.

Persian Lamb Balls

Leftover lamb balls are delicious served sliced in a pita bread sandwich with pepper rounds, Garlic Yogurt Sauce (see page 248), lettuce, tomatoes, and chick-peas.

1	pound ground lean lamb	¼	teaspoon cumin powder
2	mealy potatoes, boiled and riced	¼	teaspoon ground cinnamon
1	egg, lightly beaten		olive oil
¼	cup pine nuts freshly ground black pepper	1	recipe Tomato Sauce (see page 268)
2	tablespoons minced parsley or mint		

Combine the ground lamb, potatoes, egg, pine nuts, pepper, parsley or mint, cumin, and cinnamon. Film a frying pan with olive oil, fry 1 teaspoon of the lamb, and taste for seasonings. The mixture should be flavorful. If it seems bland, increase the amount of spices and parsley or mint.

Form the lamb into ping-pong-size balls. Sauté in the oil until brown, adding additional oil as needed. Heat the tomato sauce, add the lamb balls, and simmer together for 10 to 15 minutes.

Serve over kasha or brown rice. The lamb balls keep for at least 1 week in the refrigerator.

Serves 6 to 8

Italian Meatballs in
Tomato Sauce

Pork, fresh parsley, and Parmesan cheese are the key ingredients for authentic Italian meatballs.

1	cup fine, dry whole wheat bread crumbs		freshly ground black pepper
¼	cup water or Beef Stock (see page 260)	2 to 3	tablespoons finely chopped Italian parsley
1	pound ground beef		
¼	pound ground pork	2	tablespoons olive oil
1	clove garlic, minced	1	recipe Fresh Tomato Sauce (see page 267)
¼	cup freshly grated Parmesan cheese		
2	eggs, lightly beaten		

Mix together the bread crumbs and water or stock, and let sit for 5 minutes. Combine with the ground beef, ground pork, garlic, cheese, eggs, pepper to taste, and parsley. Moisten your hands and form 1½-inch meatballs. The easiest way to do this is to toss the meat mixture from hand to hand to form each ball.

Heat the oil in a large frying pan, and brown the meatballs, turning them gently because they are soft until browned and fall apart easily. As the meatballs cook, they release fat, so it will be unnecessary to add additional oil. Remove them from the fat with a slotted spoon.

Simmer the meatballs in the tomato sauce until just cooked through, 25 to 30 minutes. Serve over spaghetti that is cooked through yet still slightly chewy (al dente).

The meatballs and sauce will keep for at least 1 week if covered and stored in the refrigerator. Freeze for longer storage, up to 6 months.

Makes about 22 meatballs

Variation
• Italian Stuffed Eggplant: Prepare the meatball mixture, but do not brown it. Peel an eggplant. Cut a thin lengthwise slice from one side to steady the eggplant. Place sliced side down, then thinly slice the eggplant diagonally. Dip each slice first into flour, then into a mixture of 2 beaten eggs, chopped parsley, and pepper. In the center of each eggplant slice, place about 1 tablespoon meatball mixture. Roll up the eggplant and hold each slice together with a toothpick. Cook each eggplant slice in olive oil until golden brown.
Preheat the oven to 350°F.

Remove the toothpicks and arrange the stuffed eggplant slices in a casserole. Pour tomato sauce over the eggplant, sprinkle it with Parmesan cheese to taste, and bake for 30 minutes.

The eggplant will keep for about 1 week in the refrigerator. Freeze for longer storage, up to 6 months.

Beef Sandwich Spread

This is an excellent way to use beef that you've simmered for stock. The beef should be practically falling apart and should be measured after all fat and gristle have been removed. The spread takes but 1 minute to prepare in the food processor, but you can grind the beef and beat in the seasonings by hand as well.

1	onion, minced	¼	teaspoon ground allspice
¼	cup Beef Stock (see page 260)	½	teaspoon dry mustard
½	cup butter, softened	¼	teaspoon cumin powder
1	tablespoon Dijon mustard	1	pound simmered beef (2 pounds uncooked stewing beef)
¼	cup lemon juice		black pepper
1	tablespoon tomato paste		
1	tablespoon malt or red wine vinegar		

Process the onion with the stock until puréed. Beat in the butter until thoroughly combined. Then add the Dijon mustard, lemon juice, tomato paste, vinegar, allspice, dry mustard, and cumin. Add the beef and process until the texture is fine. Season with pepper to taste.

Chill before serving. The spread will keep in good condition for up to 1 week in the refrigerator.

Makes about 4 cups

Rich Chicken Liver Pâté

This delicious but super-rich pâté is based on one of Jacques Pepin's recipes. I've added spices, cut down on the butter, and omitted the Cognac, but his idea of simmering the chicken livers in stock and folding in whipped cream creates a texture and flavor similar to that of a goose liver pâté. Don't agonize about the fat content—you can't eat much of this pâté at a time. I once catered a party for 75 where people nibbled on the pâté all evening, and there was still some left over. I bother with the aspic only for a fancy party, but it is a pretty conceit to make flowers out of carved carrots with leek, tarragon, or scallion stems. Use your imagination for the vegetable cutouts. If you omit the aspic, sprinkle the pâté with minced parsley or tarragon before serving it.

Pâté

1	pound chicken livers, trimmed of membranes		freshly ground black pepper
2	onions, thinly sliced	½	teaspoon dry mustard
2	cloves garlic, thinly sliced	½ to ¾	teaspoon ground mace or nutmeg
1	cup Chicken Stock (see page 262)	1	tablespoon minced tarragon (or 1½ teaspoon dried)
1	cup butter, softened	½	cup heavy cream

Aspic

1	envelope unflavored gelatin	1	egg white

Make the Pâté

Place the chicken livers, onions, garlic, and stock in an enameled or stainless steel saucepan. Bring the stock to a boil, lower the heat, and simmer for 10 minutes. Do not let the stock boil, or the texture of the livers will become grainy. Remove the pan from the heat, and let the livers sit in the stock for 10 minutes, then drain off the stock, reserving it for the aspic.

Put the chicken liver mixture in a food processor. Add the butter and pulse on and off until the texture is smooth. Add a generous amount of pepper, the mustard, ½ teaspoon mace or nutmeg, and the tarragon. Process again. Taste the pâté, and add more mace or nutmeg only if you think the flavor of the pâté is too bland. (The spices should accentuate the flavor of the pâté, not overpower it.) Spoon the mixture into a clean bowl and refrigerate for 15 minutes.

Meanwhile, whip the cream until stiff. Fold the whipped cream into the pâté, place in a serving dish, cover with plastic wrap, and refrigerate once again. The pâté is soft and fluffy at this point but will firm up as it chills.

At this point you can either chill the pâté for a few hours before serving plain, or you can make an aspic for a fancier presentation.

Make the Aspic (optional)

Strain the stock reserved from simmering the livers. I find the easiest method is to strain it through coffee filters, but cheesecloth also works well.

Mix the gelatin with the stock, and place it in a saucepan. Beat the egg white with a fork for a few seconds, and add it to the liquid. Place the pan on medium heat, and cook until it comes to a boil, stirring constantly with a wooden spoon to prevent scorching. A heavy crust will start to form on top of the liquid. The moment the liquid boils, strain it through a double layer of cheesecloth. You should end up with about ¾ cup clear stock. Let the stock cool.

While the stock is cooling, make vegetable flowers and decorate the pâté. I find a colorful and easy presentation to be carrot rounds, cut about ⅛ inch thick, shaped with a paring knife into flower forms. I add a center of tarragon and form stems and leaves with green scallion or leek pieces.

Once the aspic has cooled to the consistency of a heavy syrup, pour a layer over the pâté. This seals it and keeps the chicken livers from darkening.

Refrigerate the pâté for at least 5 hours before serving. Serve with thin toast or rounds of French bread. This pâté will keep for at least 6 days in the refrigerator.

Makes about 6 cups

Easy Chicken Liver Pâté

This pâté is most flavorful made 1 day ahead of time to give the flavors a chance to meld.

½ cup butter
2 onions, minced
¼ teaspoon dried thyme
¼ teaspoon dried tarragon
1 slice of gingerroot (size of a quarter)
1 pound chicken livers, trimmed of membranes
2 tablespoons Chicken Stock (see page 262)

2 teaspoons red wine vinegar
½ teaspoon Worcestershire sauce
⅛ teaspoon cayenne pepper
1 teaspoon Dijon mustard
½ teaspoon black pepper
⅛ teaspoon cumin powder

Melt the butter in a large frying pan, and cook the onions for 5 minutes, until wilted but not browned. Add the thyme, tarragon, gingerroot and chicken livers, and cook rapidly until the livers are cooked through but still pink in the center. This will take 4 to 5 minutes. Remove the gingerroot.

Place the mixture, including all the butter, in a food processor or blender. Add the stock, vinegar, and Worcestershire sauce. Process until smooth. Then add the cayenne, mustard, pepper, and cumin. Continue processing until all the flavorings are absorbed. The pâté will be thin, but it will thicken as it cools.

If you plan to use the pâté within 4 days, cover tightly with foil and refrigerate. If you plan to hold it for 1 week, it will be necessary to seal the top with melted butter. Smooth out the surface, and top with melted butter at least ½ inch thick.

Makes 2½ cups

Making Pâtés

A traditional pâté is nothing more complicated than a ground meat mixture combined with fat, eggs, and seasonings that is baked in a water bath and weighted down before serving. Technically, a pâté is baked in a crust, and a terrine is not—but usage has led to calling all such mixtures pâtés.

You can use practically any combination of meats or poultry to make a pâté, but veal and pork are the traditional choices. The *pâté maison* found in French bistros is ground meat combined with chopped onions, garlic, and other ingredients. A fancier version is made with strips of meat marinated in wine or Cognac and alternated with the ground meat mixture in rows along the length of the baking dish. When the pâté is cut, each slice ends up with a mosaic pattern. I think the textural contrast and the visual variety make these pâtés worth the single extra step in preparation. You could buy the meats ready ground, but a meat grinder or food processor is still a big help in preparation.

The key ingredient in any classic pâté is plenty of fresh pork fat. The fat continuously moistens the ground meat during cooking and keeps the loaf from drying out. If you skimp on the fat, you will end up with a pâté that has an unpleasant, tough texture.

When I first started making pâtés more than 20 years ago, it was difficult to find fresh pork fat, so I would cut it off pork roasts and chops and hoard it in little packets in the freezer. Now that meat is so expensive, most supermarkets sell pieces of fresh pork fat for seasoning.

Fat makes these pâtés tasty, but it also makes them heavy and somewhat hard to digest, so I have developed some alternative recipes using a vegetable binder that retains moisture while basting the meat. Zucchini turns out to be an excellent binder: its bland taste doesn't detract from the basic flavor of the pâté, and it adds a lighter texture that's particularly nice during the summer.

Pâtés with vegetable binders have a slightly different texture from those with a higher fat content, but I find the lighter taste and texture a pleasant change of pace from standard pâtés. And they've got a bonus: fewer calories.

Cognac is another traditional pâté ingredient. When you omit it, you must add extra amounts of herbs and a more complex mixture of spices to make up for the loss of flavor.

Once you've mixed the ground meats and seasonings, it's important to make a small patty and sauté it, to taste test it for proper seasoning. Never taste the raw meat. Remember that you will be serving the pâté chilled and the seasonings will flatten out, so you want the ground meat mixture to be well seasoned.

Baked pâtés should cook in a water bath, which serves the purpose of maintaining a constant temperature and of keeping the sides of the pâté from drying and forming a crust. As a rule of thumb, count on about 30 minutes cooking time per pound of meat. When the pâté is cooked, the fat will have lost its cloudy characteristics and will run clear.

Once the pâté is cooked, weight it down with soup cans or something equally heavy, and let it rest overnight before you remove the weight. (Weighting the pâté removes any air pockets that would make the pâté difficult to slice.) The pâté's flavor improves in the refrigerator as it ages, and if the surface is sealed with melted fat or butter, the pâté should keep for 7 to 10 days in the refrigerator.

Layered Pork-Vegetable Pâté

This light pâté is a beautiful addition to a summer buffet. I've suggested an order for layering the ingredients. Change it if you wish, but start and end with a layer of the pork forcemeat. You may end up with a little of the escarole left over—just chop it up and add it to an omelet.

1¼	pounds escarole	3	tablespoons chopped tarragon
5	tablespoons butter		
½	pound mushrooms, diced (1½ cups)	3	eggs
		½	cup grated Parmesan cheese
2	cloves garlic, minced		
2	tablespoons minced lovage or parsley	¾	cup ricotta cheese
		2	pounds ground pork
	freshly ground black pepper	½	tablespoon *Quatre Épices* (see page 266)
2	onions, minced		
1	pound (unpeeled) zucchini, shredded (2 cups)	¼	pound provolone cheese, sliced
1	teaspoon chopped sweet marjoram or oregano		

Trim the escarole, removing any thick ribs, and blanch in a large pot of boiling water for 3 minutes. Immediately place the pot in the sink, and run cold water into it to stop the cooking process. Squeeze the escarole dry and set it aside.

Melt 2 tablespoons butter in a large frying pan, and sauté the mushrooms and garlic, stirring frequently, until the mushrooms are cooked through and the juices have dried up. Stir in the lovage or parsley, season generously with pepper, and remove from the pan.

In the same frying pan melt 2 tablespoons butter, and sauté the onions for 3 to 4 minutes, or until limp. Squeeze the zucchini and add to the pan. Cook, stirring frequently, until the zucchini is lightly cooked and the vegetable juices have dried up. Stir in the sweet marjoram or oregano and tarragon and season with pepper. Set the zucchini aside to cool.

Beat together the eggs, then mix with the Parmesan and ricotta cheeses. Place the ground pork in a food processor, add ½ the zucchini mixture, ¾ cup of the egg mixture, and the *Quatre Épices*. Process until combined.

Add about 3 tablespoons of the egg mixture to the remaining zucchini. You will have a little of the egg mixture left to add as a binder as you assemble the pâté.

Preheat the oven to 325°F. Butter a 9 × 5-inch loaf pan.

Smooth out ⅓ of the pork forcemeat in the bottom of the pan. Add a thin layer of the egg mixture, then top with some of the escarole, smoothing each leaf out as you work. Then add a layer of provolone cheese, and top with ½ the mushrooms.

Add another thin layer of the egg mixture, top with some more of the escarole, then smooth on a layer of the pork forcemeat.

Top with the zucchini mixture, add more escarole, then add a layer of provolone cheese. Sprinkle with the remaining mushrooms, and add any remaining egg mixture. Top with the remaining pork forcemeat. Dot the top with the remaining butter.

Cover the pan with foil. Crimp the edges so the foil does not extend down the pan, or water could seep into the pâté. Place the loaf pan in a deep pan. Pour boiling water into the deep pan, halfway up the sides of the bread pan.

Bake the pâté for 1½ hours, or until the pâté is cooked through. When the pâté is done, a knife inserted in the center will come out clean. Cool in the pan, then pour off the accumulated cooking juices and wrap in foil. (You can also weight down the pâté with cans if you prefer a denser texture.)

If wrapped in foil, the pâté will stay in good condition for at least 1 week in the refrigerator.

Makes 1 loaf

Variations
• Substitute other vegetables for the escarole and mushrooms. Diced roasted sweet red peppers or chopped broccoli are also good choices. You can also substitute a mixture of grated Cheddar and Muenster for the provolone cheese.

Country Pâté

This pâté is similar in texture to versions you'd find in French country inns but with a milder flavor. I like to crush fresh peppercorns with my meat pounder, but you can also use coarsely ground fresh pepper. Caul fat, a lacy membrane available from some specialty butchers, is preferable for lining the bread pan, but fresh pork fat works well and is much easier to find.

¼	cup butter	½	teaspoon ground allspice
2	onions, finely chopped		
3	cloves garlic, finely chopped	½	teaspoon cayenne pepper
1¼	pounds pork liver	1	teaspoon dried thyme
1	pound ground fresh pork fat	½	teaspoon ground mace or nutmeg
2	pounds coarsely ground pork	1	tablespoon cornstarch
3	eggs	¼	pound caul fat or pork fat, thinly sliced
2	teaspoons cracked black pepper	3	bay leaves

Heat the butter in a frying pan, add the onions and garlic, and cook, stirring frequently, for 5 minutes. Do not let the onions and garlic brown — you want to cook them only slightly. Set them aside to cool.

Remove any sinew from the pork liver, and cut it into 2-inch pieces. Using a food processor (or a meat grinder), purée the liver and the ground pork fat together in small batches. Put the mixture in a large bowl. Add the ground pork and lightly mix together.

Scrape the onions and garlic into a food processor bowl, and purée until combined. Add the eggs and pulse on and off a few times. Place the egg mixture in the large mixing bowl containing the meat mixture, and add the pepper, allspice, cayenne, thyme, and mace or nutmeg. Thoroughly combine the eggs and spices with the ground meats but do not overmix. Mix in the cornstarch.

Lightly film a frying pan with butter, make a patty, and panfry it until cooked through. Let the patty cool slightly, taste to check the seasonings, and correct them if necessary.

Preheat the oven to 325°F.

Line the sides and bottom of a 9 × 5-inch loaf pan with the sliced caul or pork fat. Spoon in the pâté mixture. Wet your hands and smooth out the top. Place the bay leaves in a row along the top of the pâté, and cover with fat. It may be necessary to round the top of the pâté, or you can bake any extra mixture in a small Pyrex dish.

Cover the pan with foil. Crimp the edges up near the top, or water could seep into the pâté. Place the pan in a large roasting pan, and pour warm water into the pan until it comes ¾ of the way up the sides of the pâté pan.

Bake the pâté for 2¼ to 2¾ hours, or until the pâté has an internal temperature of 155 to 160°F when checked with a meat thermometer.

Cool the pâté to room temperature, then refrigerate it for at least 1 day before serving. If you wish, weight down the pâté with cans before refrigerating.

To unmold, run a knife around the edges of the pâté, then invert it. Slice it into ½-inch pieces, and serve them on a bed of lettuce garnished with cornichons (small pickled cucumbers available at gourmet shops) and/or pickled onions, along with some crusty French bread.

If the pâté is sealed with fat and is left unsliced, it should stay in good condition in the refrigerator for up to 1½ weeks.

Makes 1 loaf

Variations
• Before baking, layer with strips of raw duck, pork, or turkey that have been marinated in orange or apple juice and dusted with black pepper.
• Mix in 1 pound blanched and squeezed fresh spinach or Swiss chard leaves that have been chopped or sliced into short, thin strips.
• Center raw Italian sausages (that have been removed from their casings) in the pâté as you assemble it.
• Vary the herbs. Use 1 tablespoon fresh tarragon or a mixture of tarragon and sweet cicely.
• Substitute 2 teaspoons *Quatre Épices* (see page 266) for the allspice, cayenne, and nutmeg.

Chicken Vegetable
Party Loaf

This gallantine is easier than it sounds, because the steps can be done at spare intervals throughout the day. Try this loaf for a buffet party dish on a summer's night. It's festive, pretty, and has a light texture that's easy to digest when the temperature is high.

1	3¾ pound chicken	½	cup coarsely chopped sweet red peppers
3	tablespoons lemon juice	3 to 4	tablespoons chopped fresh lovage or 2 tablespoons chopped fresh basil
	freshly ground black pepper		
½	pound (unpeeled) zucchini	¼ to ½	teaspoon ground nutmeg
¾	pound asparagus, peeled and trimmed	1	tablespoon chopped tarragon
2 to 3	ounces spinach, trimmed and stemmed	1	egg
4	tablespoons butter	1	tablespoon minced parsley
8	scallions, white parts only, chopped		ground allspice
			ground ginger

Bone the chicken. If you follow the directions that come next, you'll end up with almost the entire chicken skin intact as 1 piece, with the breast meat—but not the thigh or leg meat—attached. The skin will be larger than the meat attached to it, so it can be wrapped around the filling.

Begin by splitting the chicken down the back. Use a small, sharp paring knife to separate the back bones, ribs, and breast bone from the breast meat. Leave the breast meat attached to the skin. Don't worry if the meat separates slightly, because it will adhere to itself as it cooks.

Next cut off the wings. Then remove the meat and bones from the legs and thighs, being careful to leave the skin intact. The easiest technique is to place your fingers between the skin and meat and completely loosen the skin before peeling it from the meat. Small tears at the tips won't be any problem.

Now spread out the chicken skin, meat side up. As you look down on the chicken skin, you will see the breast in the center and the leg and thigh skin to each side. With a sharp knife make 2 cuts from the center of the breast so that you can butterfly the top part of the meat on each side of the breast and fold it down to cover as much skin as possible. Try to keep the layer of meat uniform.

Remove the meat from the wings, legs, and thighs and set aside.

Place the chicken skin, meat side up, on a buttered sheet of foil. Sprinkle evenly with 1 tablespoon lemon juice, and then sprinkle with the pepper.

Grate the zucchini, squeeze slightly to release some of the juices, and set aside.

Blanch the asparagus in a large pot of boiling water for 2 minutes. Immediately run cold water into the pot to stop the cooking process. Lift the asparagus onto a folded kitchen towel to drain.

Blanch the spinach in a pot of boiling water for 30 seconds. All you want to do is to make the spinach limp. Run cold water into the pot to stop the cooking process, and drain the spinach in a colander. Squeeze the leaves into a ball to remove moisture. Lay on the counter and cut the spinach into ¼-inch strips. The strips will be irregular.

Melt 3 tablespoons butter in a large frying pan, and sauté the scallions for 4 to 5 minutes, or until softened but not browned. Add the sweet red peppers and cook for 2 minutes, stirring constantly. Squeeze the zucchini again and add it to the pan. Cook for another 2 minutes, stirring constantly until the moisture is removed. Stir in the lovage or basil and nutmeg and set aside to cool.

Cut about ½ cup of the reserved wing, thigh, and leg meat into ½-inch-wide strips, and roll in the tarragon. Set aside.

Place the remaining reserved meat in a food processor or meat grinder, and process until smooth. (If you are using a meat grinder, select the finest setting.) Add the egg, remaining lemon juice, and parsley, and process for just 1 second, until the mixture is combined. Stir it into the zucchini mixture. Add a generous pinch of allspice and a pinch of ginger, and season to taste with the pepper. Toss the spinach to separate, and gently stir it into the zucchini mixture.

Heat the remaining butter in a frying pan, and panfry a small patty of the ground meat mixture until cooked through. Cool the patty slightly, then taste to check for seasonings. Correct the seasonings if necessary.

Preheat the oven to 350°F.

Place the chicken skin in front of you. Cover it with ½ the zucchini mixture. Top with the asparagus spears, which should run lengthwise. Arrange the spears as if they were in a sardine can, alternating bottoms and tops. Fill in with the sliced chicken, and top with the remaining zucchini mixture.

Bring the long sides of the stuffed chicken together, barely overlapping the skin. The asparagus will bunch in the center, which is what you want. Fold over the ends of the skin.

Roll the chicken in the foil, enclosing the chicken as if you were rolling up a piece of paper. Bring the sides of the foil over the folded bird and fold tightly. Then fold in the ends of the foil. If you wish, tie with a length of kitchen string.

Place the chicken in a shallow baking pan, and bake for 50 to 60 minutes. Fold back the foil to allow the chicken skin to brown, and bake for another 15 to 20 minutes, basting the skin frequently with the pan juices.

This chicken loaf is delicious served either hot or at room temperature, but let it rest for at least 20 minutes before serving. If you are planning to refrigerate it, drain the foil of all the pan juices before you wrap it up. Bring the loaf to room temperature before serving in thin slices.

If the loaf is tightly wrapped in foil and stored in the refrigerator, it will keep for at least 4 days.

Makes 1 loaf

Low-Calorie Chicken Loaf

1	4-pound chicken	1	envelope unflavored
5	carrots, peeled		gelatin
2 to 4	tablespoons chopped lovage	2 to 4	tablespoons lemon juice

Cover the chicken with water, bring to a boil, lower the heat, and poach the chicken for 1¼ hours, or until cooked through. Cool the chicken, skin it, and remove the meat. Cut the meat into thin strips and set aside.

Boil down the chicken stock to concentrate the flavor. Cool the stock and skim off the fat. Measure out 3 cups stock.

Grate the carrots on the coarsest side of a grater, and place in a bowl. Mix in the chicken and lovage. In a small saucepan dissolve the gelatin in 1 cup cooled stock. Heat while stirring until completely dissolved. Remove from the heat and stir in the remaining 2 cups stock and the lemon juice. Mix the chicken and vegetable mixture with the stock.

Spoon the mixture into a deep 9 × 5-inch loaf pan that has been rinsed in cold water to cool it, and chill until set. Serve on a bed of ruby lettuce or raw spinach. The loaf will keep for up to 5 days in the refrigerator.

Makes 1 loaf

Variations
• Add whole hard-cooked eggs, sautéed strips of red pepper, or sliced Florence fennel.

Stuffed Chicken Loaf

This is impressive party fare which is easier to prepare than similar loaves cooked inside chicken skins.

1	cup brown rice	¼	pound chicken livers, trimmed of membranes and thinly sliced (½ cup)
2½	cups water		
1	7-pound roasting chicken		
4	carrots (about ¾-inch diameter), peeled	1	tablespoon soy sauce
2	onions	1	egg, lightly beaten
2	cloves garlic	3	tablespoons minced tarragon
4	tablespoons butter		

Cook the rice in the water until chewy, about 25 minutes. Drain, and set aside to cool.

Bone the chicken (see page 96 for directions, except do not remove the wings). Set the dark meat aside for another meal.

Simmer the carrots, in enough water to cover, until slightly cooked through yet still crunchy. Drain them and set aside. Chop the onions and mince the garlic.

In 3 tablespoons butter sauté the onions and garlic. Add the chicken livers and cook briefly, until they have stiffened and begun to cook through. Place the mixture in a bowl, and stir in the cooked rice, soy sauce, egg, and tarragon.

Preheat the oven to 400°F.

Place the chicken skin, meat side up, on a large piece of foil. Spread the rice mixture over the meat. Push the carrots lengthwise into the center of the stuffing. Fold over the skin to cover the stuffing, shaping a long loaf. Place the chicken loaf and foil on a jelly-roll pan. Turn the chicken loaf breast-side up on the center of the foil. Dot with the remaining butter, and encase in the foil.

Bake for 1 hour. Then fold back the foil and cook for another 20 to 30 minutes, or until the chicken is cooked through and the meat is slightly browned. Baste from time to time with the pan juices.

Let cool slightly before serving, so the stuffing doesn't fall apart. Serve thinly sliced, warm or cold. The chicken loaf will keep in good condition in the refrigerator for up to 4 days.

Serves 8 to 10

Savory Corn Cake

Add a sliced tomato-onion-and-basil salad and a cooling lemon ice, and you have a complete meal. This corn cake is also a delicious picnic choice.

2 tablespoons olive oil
1 pound hot Italian
  sausages, with
  casings removed and
  finely chopped
1¾ cups chopped onion
  (about 1 large)
2 hot peppers, minced
2 sweet red peppers,
  chopped
1 large clove garlic,
  minced
3 tablespoons minced
  basil
¼ cup butter

3 eggs
1 cup sour cream
1⅔ cups corn kernels
  (about 2 ears)
1⅓ cups cornmeal
½ cup whole wheat flour
1 teaspoon baking soda
1 teaspoon baking
  powder
½ cup milk
6 ounces Cheddar
  cheese, grated
  (1¾ cup)
  hot pepper sauce

Heat the oil in a large frying pan, and sauté the sausage until just barely cooked through. Remove the meat with a slotted spoon, and drain it on a paper bag.

In the same oil sauté the onions, all the peppers, and the garlic until lightly wilted, about 5 minutes. Stir in the basil and cook for 1 minute longer. Remove the mixture with a slotted spoon, and place in a colander to drain.

In a large mixing bowl beat together the butter and eggs. Add the sour cream, corn, and ¾ of the sautéed pepper mixture (about 2 cups).

Mix together the cornmeal, flour, baking soda, and baking powder. Add to the butter mixture alternately with the milk. Stir in the cheese and a dash of hot pepper sauce.

Mix together the remaining pepper mixture and the sausage.

Butter a 10-inch tube pan. Preheat the oven to 350°F.

Spoon ⅓ of the cornmeal batter into the tube pan. Sprinkle with ½ the meat mixture, then add another layer of batter, then the meat mixture, and top with the remaining batter.

Bake the corn cake for 45 to 50 minutes, or until completely cooked through. Cool in the pan. Serve either at room temperature or cold.

Wrap the corn cake in foil or plastic wrap, and store in the refrigerator, where it will keep in good condition for up to 1 week. Or freeze for up to 1 month.

Makes 1 cake

Cima or Genoa-Style Stuffed Meat Roll

An authentic *cima* (chē mǎ) from the Genoa region of Italy would be made from a boned veal breast. Veal breasts in my area are hard to come by, and when I finally locate a butcher who stocks them, the price is exorbitant. I think a boned chicken works just as well, although purists might disagree. The contrasting colors of the stuffing ingredients make this a beautiful presentation—worthy of a special occasion. The raw peas are essential for texture and color.

1	pound spinach	1 to 2	tablespoons chopped basil
¾	pound sweet Italian sausages (4)	2	tablespoons chopped sweet marjoram
3	tablespoons butter	3	tablespoons lemon juice
2	cloves garlic, chopped		
1¼	cups chopped onions (about 2)	¼	teaspoon ground allspice
2	small zucchini, peeled and quartered	½	teaspoon ground mace or nutmeg
½	cup chopped sweet red or frying peppers	1	egg
		½	cup grated Parmesan cheese
3	slices light rye bread, crusts removed	2	tablespoons grated Romano cheese
⅔	cup milk	1¼	cups raw shelled peas
1	4-pound chicken		
½	pound finely ground pork	⅓	cup pistachio nuts (optional)
½	cup chopped parsley or ¼ cup chopped lovage	3	hard-cooked eggs

Wash and stem the spinach, and blanch it in a large pot of boiling water for 2 minutes. Immediately place the pot under cold running water, and let the water run into the pot until the spinach is cool. Drain the spinach, squeeze it dry, and set it aside.

Prick the sausages all over with a fork, and parboil, in enough water to cover, for 5 to 10 minutes. Rinse and cool the sausages. Remove the casings, keeping the sausages intact. Set aside.

In a large frying pan melt the butter, and sauté over medium heat the garlic, onions, zucchini, and sweet red or frying peppers for about 5 minutes, or until they are cooked through but not wilted. Chop the spinach and add to the pan. Sauté rapidly over medium-high heat, stirring constantly, until all moisture is gone from the spinach. Remove the zucchini and set the other vegetables aside.

Soak the bread in the milk while you bone the chicken.

Bone the chicken (see page 96 for directions, except do not remove the wings). Remove the meat from the thigh and leg bones. Grind this meat to use for the forcemeat stuffing. The easiest way to do this is in a food processor. Process until smooth.

Add the bread and milk and ground pork to the ground chicken. Process for a few seconds with stop and start pulses of the machine. Add the parsley or lovage, basil, sweet marjoram, lemon juice, allspice, and mace or nutmeg. Process for just 1 second. Add the reserved zucchini and process until finely chopped.

Combine the chicken mixture with the egg and the cheeses. Stir in the reserved vegetables and the peas and pistachios (if used).

Preheat the oven to 325°F.

Fit the chicken skin into a buttered 9 × 5-inch loaf pan, with the meat side up. The skin will not fit exactly but it should extend up the sides with some overlap. Put ⅓ of the chicken mixture on the bottom. Add the sausages, placed in 2 parallel rows extending lengthwise with the pan. Add the second ⅓ of the chicken mixture. Top with the hard-cooked eggs, arranged in a row along the center of the pan. Press down on the eggs so they almost hit the sausages. (If you had a cross section of a slice, the 2 rows of sausages would be on the bottom, surrounded by the chicken mixture, and then the row of eggs would be immediately above in the center.) Add the remaining chicken mixture and fold over any skin hanging over the top of the pan. It may be necessary to mound the stuffing mixture slightly.

Cover the pan with foil. Crimp the edges up near the top, or water could seep into the *cima*. Place the loaf pan in a large roasting pan, and pour boiling water into the roasting pan to halfway up the sides of the loaf pan.

Bake the *cima* for 1¼ to 1½ hours. When the *cima* is done, the juices will run clean when tested with a knife and the surface will feel firm when you press down upon it.

Remove the *cima* from the oven, pour off any juices, and let it cool in the pan for at least 2 hours. Chill the *cima* or serve warm, cut into thin slices.

The *cima* will keep in good condition for at least 1 week if wrapped in foil and stored in the refrigerator.

Makes 1 loaf

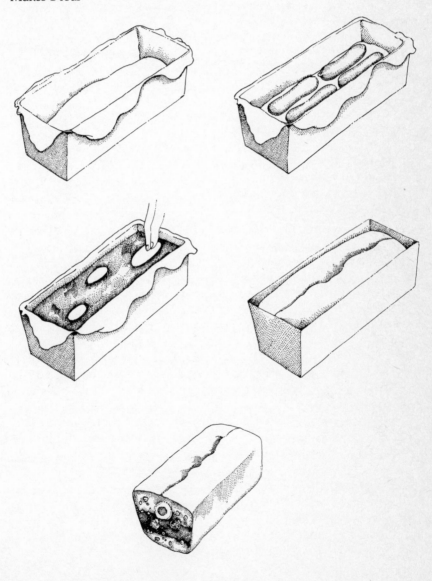

Beer Cake

This snack "cake," filled with vegetables and sausage, traditionally is served with beer. Jeanette Burhop of Michigan, who shared her recipe with me, uses diced salami, ham, and bacon for this hearty meal-in-one. Although this is popular in Michigan, Jeanette says the recipe originated in Tennessee. As the texture is heavy, slice the cake into thin pieces.

3	tablespoons vegetable oil	½	pound Cheddar cheese, shredded (about 2 cups)
1½	pounds sweet Italian sausages	12	eggs
1	cup minced sweet green peppers	2½	cups whole wheat flour
½	cup minced scallions, white parts only	1	tablespoon Dijon mustard
½	cup minced roasted sweet red peppers or pimentos	2 to 3	tablespoons chopped basil
½	pound Munster cheese, shredded (about 2 cups)		

Heat the oil in a large frying pan, and sauté the sausages over medium heat until partially cooked. Remove the sausages, let cool, then discard the casings and crumble the sausage. (You can crumble the sausage before cooking, but I think the meat tends to dry out and become overcooked that way.)

In the oil remaining in the pan, sauté the sweet green peppers, scallions, and sweet red peppers or pimentos for 5 minutes, until cooked through but not browned. Remove the vegetables with a slotted spoon, and add to the sausage. Cool slightly, then toss with the cheeses.

Preheat the oven to 325°F. Grease a tube pan.

Beat the eggs, then add the flour and mustard. Combine with the sausage mixture, making sure the meat and vegetables are coated with the batter. Stir in the basil.

Spoon the mixture into the pan. Bake for 1¼ hours, or until a knife inserted in the center comes out clean.

Cool in the pan before unmolding. The sausage releases more fat during baking, so blot the top of the cake with cotton toweling the minute it comes out of the oven.

If stored in foil, the beer cake stays in good condition in the refrigerator, for up to 2 weeks and in the freezer for up to 2 months.

Serves 10 to 20

Easy Torta Rustica

We first tasted a *torta rustica* when we exchanged houses with a family in Courmayer, Italy—a resort town at the foot of Mont Blanc. The grocery stores sold several versions, but they all featured an omelet layer and ham.

1	pound trimmed kale, spinach, or Swiss chard leaves	¼	pound cooked beef or chicken, thinly sliced
2	cloves garlic, minced	1	recipe Whole Wheat Pie Crust (see page 191)
2	tablespoons butter		
3	eggs	½	cup chopped mozzarella cheese
½	cup grated Parmesan cheese		
½	cup ricotta cheese		
3	tablespoons chopped basil		

Blanch the greens, drain, and squeeze them dry. Coarsely chop them. Sauté the greens and the garlic in the butter until all the moisture is evaporated; set aside.

Beat the eggs. Stir in the Parmesan and ricotta cheeses and the basil. Cut the beef or chicken into 1-inch-wide strips.

Roll out the dough to ¼ inch thick. Gently fit it into a 7- to 8-inch soufflé dish. The dough will extend over the sides of the dish.

Fill the dough, starting with the meat strips. Arrange ⅓ of the meat on the bottom, then ½ the mozzarella cheese, followed by ½ the greens and ½ the egg mixture. Repeat the layering once. Top with the remaining meat and fold the dough over toward the center. The pastry edges will not quite meet (this is to allow any steam to escape) and will probably look untidy—which doesn't matter, as it will form the bottom when served.

Preheat the oven to 400°F.

Bake the torta for 45 minutes, or until a knife inserted in the center comes out clean and the pastry is lightly browned. Remove from the oven, let sit in the pan for a few minutes, and then invert the torta. Serve either warm or cold, cut into wedges.

The torta will keep for at least 1 week in the refrigerator if wrapped in foil.

Makes 1 torta

Italian Torta Rustica

Here is another torta, a bit more complicated than the one above, but I think the extra work is well worth it. For yet another torta, this time a vegetarian version, see page 38.

½ pound trimmed spinach
5 tablespoons olive oil
2½ cups coarsely chopped red onions
2 cloves garlic, minced
¼ cup sliced mushrooms (optional)
5 eggs
1 tablespoon chopped basil or sweet marjoram
5 tablespoons grated Parmesan cheese
2 to 3 tablespoons butter
½ pound boneless pork cutlets taken from the loin

whole wheat flour
¾ cup ricotta cheese
freshly ground black pepper
1 recipe Whole Wheat Pie Crust (see page 191
½ pound mozzarella cheese, shredded (about 2 cups)
2 sweet red peppers, broiled, peeled, and thinly sliced
⅓ cup Tomato Sauce (see page 268)

Blanch the spinach in a large pot of boiling water for 2 to 3 minutes, or until limp and barely cooked through. Immediately run the spinach under cold water to stop the cooking process, drain, and squeeze it dry. Coarsely chop the spinach and set it aside.

Heat 3 tablespoons oil in a frying pan, add the onions and garlic, and sauté until wilted and cooked through, about 5 minutes. Remove the onions with a slotted spoon and set aside. In the oil remaining in the pan, sauté the mushrooms until they have released their juices and then become dry. Set them aside.

Beat 4 eggs and stir in the basil or sweet marjoram and 2 tablespoons Parmesan cheese. Heat 1 tablespoon butter in an 8-inch frying pan, and add ½ the egg mixture. Cook it without stirring for about 1 minute, or until the mixture is cooked through. Remove it from the pan. If necessary, add 1 tablespoon butter to the pan, and cook the rest of the egg mixture. You should end up with 2 flat omelets. Set them aside.

Pound the pork until it is as thin as possible. Dip into the flour, then shake off any excess flour. Sauté in 2 tablespoons oil until barely cooked through. Immediately dip into 2 tablespoons Parmesan cheese and set aside.

Beat the remaining egg and add the ricotta cheese, spinach, and pepper to taste. Set aside.

Preheat the oven to 400°F.

Roll out the dough to fit an 8-inch-square pan. Fit it in the pan, molding it up the sides of the pan, and crimp the top.

Sprinkle ½ the mozzarella cheese on the bottom of the pan. Cut 1 of the omelets into shapes that will conform to the pan, and line the pan with the omelet. Arrange ½ the sweet red peppers on top. Spoon on the tomato sauce, then top with the pork. Add ½ the spinach mixture. Sprinkle with the mushrooms, garlic, onions, and the remaining peppers. Cover with the second omelet, cut into pieces to fit the pan. Add the remaining mozzarella cheese and smooth over the remaining spinach mixture. Sprinkle with the remaining Parmesan cheese and dot with 1 tablespoon butter.

Bake the torta for 35 minutes, or until completely cooked through.

The torta can be eaten warm, but it has a more complex flavor the next day, after the flavors have had a chance to meld.

If the torta is wrapped in foil and stored in the refrigerator, it should keep for at least 1 week.

Makes 1 torta

Russian-Style Turnovers

These flavorful turnovers were inspired by the Russian *piroshki*, little turnovers often served with borscht. If you have any leftover filling, use it to stuff an omelet.

Dough

1	cup whole wheat flour	½	cup grated Swiss cheese
½	cup rye flakes	⅓	cup cold water, plus 2 tablespoons if necessary
½	cup rye flour		
1	teaspoon dry mustard		
⅔	cup butter		

Filling

2	tablespoons butter	2	tablespoons minced dillweed
1	onion, minced	2	tablespoons minced parsley
½	cup finely shredded cabbage		black pepper
¾	pound ground beef	2	eggs, beaten
¼	teaspoon cayenne pepper		
½	cup cooked wheat berries		

Make the Dough

Combine the whole wheat flour, rye flakes, rye flour, and mustard. Cut in the butter until the mixture resembles coarse cornmeal. Mix in the cheese. Slowly add the water, tossing constantly with a fork. The mixture should not be completely mixed at this point. Pour the mixture into a plastic bag, and knead it in the bag just enough so the dough adheres to itself. Place in the refrigerator for at least 30 minutes while you make the filling.

Make the Filling

Melt the butter in a large frying pan, add the onion and cook, stirring occasionally, for 4 minutes, or until the onion has wilted but has not browned. Stir in the cabbage and cook for 2 minutes longer. Add the ground beef and cook, stirring frequently, for 4 minutes, or until it is cooked through and only lightly browned.

Stir in the cayenne, wheat berries, dillweed, and parsley. Add pepper to taste.

Drain the filling in a colander to remove excess moisture and fat. When the filling has cooled, stir in the eggs.

Assemble the Turnovers

Divide the dough into quarters. Roll out 1 section to ⅛ inch thick. Cut rounds 4½ to 5 inches in diameter. I find the easiest way to do this is to invert a saucer and use it as a guide. Continue forming the rounds until all the dough is used up.

Preheat the oven to 400°F.

Line up the rounds on the counter. Place a heaping tablespoon of the filling on each round. Fold the dough over the filling, shaping each round into a half-moon. Press the edges firmly together and crimp.

Place the turnovers on greased baking sheets, and bake for 25 to 30 minutes, or until cooked through and lightly browned. Serve with sour cream on the side if you wish.

Although the cooked turnovers stay in good condition for several days in the refrigerator, I would suggest assembling them just before baking. Both the dough and the filling will last for at least 4 days in the refrigerator.

To freeze, assemble the turnovers and wrap in foil. They will keep in the freezer for up to 3 months. To serve, loosely unwrap and heat in the oven. Do not thaw first.

Makes 13 turnovers

Gyros

Gyros (hēē´rōs) are handy snacks to have around, particularly if you have teenagers who are always hungry. They're based on the Greek American compressed lamb dish that is spit roasted, sliced, and served in pita bread with onions, tomatoes, and Garlic Yogurt Sauce (see page 248).

1	teaspoon fennel seeds	1	teaspoon cumin powder
2	tablespoons boiling water	⅛	teaspoon cayenne pepper
1	tablespoon chopped (very fresh) garlic	2½	pounds ground lamb, at least ⅙ fat by weight
2	onions, chopped		
½	cup dry whole wheat bread crumbs	½	pound ground beef
2	eggs	½	cup minced parsley
¼	teaspoon dried thyme	¼	pound fresh pork fat
1	teaspoon dried sweet marjoram		pita bread
¼	teaspoon ground cinnamon		

Slightly crush the fennel seeds, and soak in the boiling water for 15 minutes.

Process the garlic and onions together in a food processor or blender. Add the bread crumbs and eggs and mix just until combined. Add the fennel seeds and water, thyme, sweet marjoram, cinnamon, cumin, and cayenne, and blend for 1 minute.

Combine the garlic mixture with the ground lamb, ground beef, and parsley. Mix until thoroughly combined but do not overmix. Fry a small amount to check the seasonings, and add more if necessary.

Preheat the oven to 350°F.

Thinly slice the pork fat, and place a single layer on the bottom of a 9 × 5-inch loaf pan. Spoon in the meat mixture and top with another layer of pork fat. Cover the pan with foil. Crimp it near the top, or water could seep into the loaf.

Place the loaf pan in a roasting pan. Pour boiling water into the roasting pan to halfway up the sides of the loaf pan. Do not let the loaf pan float. Bake for 1½ to 1¾ hours, or until cooked through but not dry.

Remove the pork fat slices on top. Do not drain the fat that forms around the loaf, as it helps to preserve the meat. Replace the foil and set another loaf pan, right side up, on top of the loaf. Weight it by putting several cans, or a large peanut butter jar filled with water, in the empty loaf pan. Weight the loaf for 2 to 3 hours, then remove the weights.

Refrigerate, then unmold when chilled. Wrap in foil and store in the refrigerator.

To serve, thinly slice the meat and broil until the edges are crisped. Some of the fat will melt out. Stuff into pita bread.

The gyros loaf will keep in good condition for up to 1 week if wrapped in foil and stored in the refrigerator. It may also be frozen for up to 3 months.

Makes 1 loaf

Making Sausages

Anyone who is concerned about the amount of preservatives contained in commercial meat products should make sausages from scratch. Homemade sausages will not last as long as the commercial versions (for obvious reasons), but most will stay in good condition for 3 or 4 days in the refrigerator, as long as you start with absolutely fresh meat. They can also be frozen for up to 3 months.

There's nothing complicated about making sausages: they're merely ground meats and fats seasoned to taste with spices or herbs. Pork is a traditional favorite for sausage making because its bland yet rich flavor is an excellent foil to a variety of spices and herbs, but you can use any meat. (Fish sausages also can be quite delicious, but they don't keep, so I haven't included any in this book.)

Sausages should have a high proportion of fat to meat, to keep them juicy and moist. An ideal proportion would be 2 parts meat to 1 part fat, but I've cut down on the fats considerably in the sausage recipes that follow. These sausages taste fine and are easier to digest than fattier versions, although their texture is denser.

I grind the fat and meat in an electric meat grinder, but you can also use a food processor or an old-fashioned meat grinder that fastens onto a counter top. Some butchers will grind both meat and fat for you, which saves time.

If you plan to make sausages frequently and to use casings to hold the meat in place, I would suggest you buy a sausage-stuffing attachment for your meat grinder. Instead, you can make cheesecloth casings or form the sausages into patties: both of these methods work well when you're using sausage meat as an ingredient in other recipes and don't care whether it retains a sausage shape. If you're terribly coordinated, you can also stuff casings with a funnel, but frankly, I wouldn't recommend it. Making sausages is a messy enough proposition as it is.

Natural sausage casings, made from cleaned animal intestines, can be special-ordered at most butcher shops and can sometimes be purchased from butcher supply stores. Usually you'll be given hog casings packed in salt. Before you can use them, you will have to soak the casings in water for 1 hour. I always test the casings, to make sure there are no holes, by fitting an end around the water tap and running warm water through it. The casings come in various lengths: I find it easiest to work with 3-foot lengths.

While the casings are soaking, you should mix together the ground meat, fat, and seasonings. (The *Quatre Épices* spice mixture, page 266, is an excellent flavoring for a plain pork sausage.) Check the flavor of the sausage by sautéeing a patty and tasting it. Do *not* taste raw sausage! The flavors will meld while the sausage ripens overnight, but salt-free sausages should be highly seasoned because they tend to taste extra bland unless they are seasoned carefully.

Set up the sausage-stuffing attachment on your grinder, and attach 1 length of the casing to it, leaving about 3 inches at the end. Stuff the casing with the sausage mixture, holding the casing horizontally to minimize any air bubbles. Karl Engel, a professional sausage maker, told me he presses down on air bubbles with the back of a knife to remove them. Don't fill the casing too tightly.

Remove the stuffed casing from the machine, and twist it to form individual sausages, then tie them with white string at each end if you wish.

Ripen the sausages in the refrigerator overnight, loosely covered with waxed paper. Most sausages will keep for 3 or 4 days in the refrigerator; or freeze them for longer storage.

Breakfast Sausage

1 pound ground pork	½ teaspoon ground sage
½ pound ground beef	1 teaspoon black pepper
¼ pound ground fresh pork fat	1 teaspoon dried sweet marjoram
¼ teaspoon dried thyme	⅛ teaspoon ground coriander
⅛ teaspoon cayenne pepper	

Thoroughly mix the ground pork, ground beef, and ground pork fat. Stir together the thyme, cayenne, sage, pepper, sweet marjoram, and coriander. Combine with the meat. I find the easiest way to do this is with my hands, but if you prefer, use a spoon. Fry a small amount to check the seasonings, and correct if necessary.

Moisten your hands with cold water, and form the meat mixture into 2½-inch patties. Layer them in a bowl, separated by waxed paper. Cover the bowl and let sit for 6 hours or overnight to allow the flavors to mingle.

Cook the patties in a skillet for about 10 minutes. Drain on paper toweling.

If prepared with freshly ground pork, these sausages will keep in good condition in the refrigerator for up to 3 days. Freeze them for up to 3 months.

Makes 12 to 15 sausages

Sicilian Sausages with Cheese

I buy a pork butt, bone it, grind the meat for this recipe, then simmer the bone in water to make a stock. Any leftover stock makes a flavorful base for Italian tomato sauces. If you don't want to bother with this step, use beef or chicken stock.

¾ pound coarsely ground pork butt	1 teaspoon freshly ground black pepper
¼ pound coarsely ground fresh pork fat	1 tablespoon chopped Italian parsley
¾ cup chopped provolone cheese	1 tablespoon chopped lovage or basil
1 tablespoon grated Parmesan cheese (optional)	1 teaspoon chopped sweet marjoram
1 teaspoon fennel seeds	2 to 3 strands hog casings (2 to 3 feet, see page 111 for preparation directions)
½ cup pork, beef, or chicken stock	

Mix together the ground pork, ground pork fat, the cheeses, fennel seeds, stock, pepper, parsley, lovage or basil, and sweet marjoram.

Stuff the prepared casings (see page 111 for directions).

Loosely cover the sausages and refrigerate. They should keep in good condition for up to 5 days. Freeze for longer storage, up to 3 months.

Makes 1¾ pounds

Cajun Pork Sausages

Susan Harnett was given this recipe by her father's school chum, Inez Laborde, who lives in Avoyelles parish in Louisiana. Inez uses ¼ cup salt in this recipe, but Susan has omitted it here. In a Cajun household this sausage would often be boiled and served with grits for breakfast, particularly on a day when the men are duck hunting. You can also fry the sausages.

This recipe makes a lot of sausage; should you wish to make less, see the variation for 5 pounds meat.

20 pounds boneless Boston butt pork shoulder
10 large onions, finely chopped
5 large sweet green peppers, finely chopped
¼ cup chopped celery
¼ cup cayenne pepper
1 tablespoon ground paprika
1 tablespoon garlic powder
vegetable oil
hog casings (see page 111 for preparation directions)

Coarsely grind the pork and mix it with the onions, sweet green peppers, celery, cayenne, paprika, and garlic powder. Sauté a small amount of the sausage in a little oil to check for seasoning. Taste, remembering that the flavors will meld as the sausages sit in the refrigerator. Add additional seasonings if necessary.

Stuff the prepared casings (see page 111 for directions). Then place the sausages in the refrigerator, and let them sit for at least 1 day before serving. Freeze most of the sausages, leaving out only what you can use up in a few days.

The sausages will keep in good condition for at least 4 days in the refrigerator and for up to 4 months in the freezer.

Makes about 21 pounds

Variation
• For an alternative seasoning for 5 pounds meat, substitute 3 tablespoons *Quatre Épices* (see page 266), 1 teaspoon chopped (fresh) sage, and 2 teaspoons ground paprika for the seasonings in the recipe, and mix with only 5 pounds boneless Boston butt pork shoulder.

Italian Fennel Sausages

Refrigerate the sausages for 1 day before serving, to meld the flavors. The sausages are easy to make using a meat grinder with a sausage-stuffing attachment. If you have a meat grinder, attach the coarse strainer to the machine, otherwise the texture will be too fine.

2	pounds coarsely ground pork	1	tablespoon white vinegar
½	pound coarsely ground fresh pork fat		hot pepper flakes (optional)
2	teaspoons freshly ground black pepper	2 to 3	strands hog casings (about 4 feet, see page 111 for preparation directions)
1	tablespoon plus 1 teaspoon fennel seeds or aniseed		

Combine the ground pork, ground pork fat, pepper, fennel seeds or aniseed, vinegar, and hot pepper flakes (if used) to taste.

Stuff the prepared casings (see page 111 for directions).

Loosely wrap the sausages so that air can circulate around them. Treated this way, the sausages should stay in good condition for up to 5 days. Freeze them for longer storage, but use within 3 months.

Makes 2½ pounds

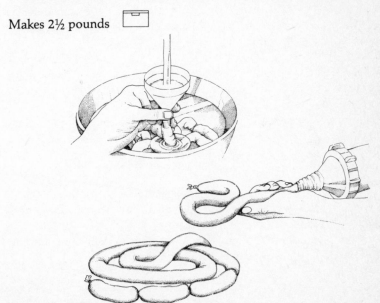

Polish Sausage

Karl Engel makes some of the best German sausage in the Northeast in his Sausage Factory in Saugus, Massachusetts. He prepares sausages similar to those his father made in his butcher shop in Saxony, Germany. Karl uses pork butt in this recipe, and he also uses salt when he makes it. When his wife Regina prepares these sausages at home, she simmers them for 20 to 30 minutes in water and does not prick the skins. "I like the sausages to stay together," she says.

6¼	pounds boneless pork	2½	teaspoons coarsely ground black pepper
2¼	teaspoons ground nutmeg		
2¼	teaspoons ground ginger		hog casings (see page 111 for preparation directions)
3¾	teaspoons ground coriander		

Coarsely grind the pork. Add the nutmeg, ginger, coriander, and pepper. Grind again.

Stuff the filling into prepared casings (see page 111 for directions).

Loosely cover the sausage and store in the refrigerator for up to 5 days. Freeze for longer storage, but use within 3 months.

Makes 6¼ pounds

Coarse Bratwurst

The bratwurst seasoning in this recipe of Karl Engel's can be difficult to find. It's available in large quantities from butchers' supply houses. A good substitute is a mixture of black pepper, sweet marjoram, nutmeg, ginger, allspice, and cloves. Panfry the bratwurst slowly for about 30 minutes, covering the pan toward the end of the cooking period. They are good served with mustard, mashed potatoes, and vegetables.

6¼   pounds boneless pork
½   teaspoon ground caraway seeds
⅓   cup bratwurst seasoning, or the following mixture:

2	teaspoons black pepper	2½	teaspoons ground ginger
3	tablespoons dried sweet marjoram	¼	teaspoon ground allspice
2½	teaspoons ground nutmeg		pinch ground cloves

hog casings (see page 111 for preparation directions)

Coarsely grind the pork. Sprinkle with the ground caraway seeds and bratwurst seasoning, then regrind the mixture to mix thoroughly.

Stuff the prepared casings (see page 111 for directions).

Loosely wrap the bratwurst and refrigerate. They should stay in good condition for up to 5 days. Freeze for longer storage, but use within 3 months.

Makes 6¼ pounds

Scrapple

Sometimes when I'm busy and don't feel like any serious cooking, I'll brown a pork shoulder and braise it for 2 to 3 hours in milk. The milk (which I keep adding because it reduces down as the pork braises) cooks down into a clotted gravy that is delicious over mashed potatoes. I then convert any leftover pork and gravy into breakfast scrapple with the help of a food processor. You can also make scrapple with a leftover roast pork simmered in stock or water until it is fork tender. Scrapple is a Pennsylvania Dutch mush, originally developed to use up the scraps from butchering. My version has a less solid consistency than the scrapple I buy in Pennsylvania, so if you want a firmer version, just increase the amount of cornmeal. Scrapple recipes vary depending upon the area: some scrapple is made from sausage, while other versions have buckwheat and lots of liver. If sweet marjoram is out of season, substitute dried sweet marjoram—just don't use dried sage. Sage is one herb that tastes palatable only when fresh: dried it has a musty, unpleasant aftertaste.

2	cups pork or beef stock or leftover pork gravy	¼	teaspoon cumin powder (optional)
1½	cups water	1	tablespoon chopped (fresh) sage
1¼	cups cornmeal	2	tablespoons minced parsley or combined parsley and lovage
¼	pound chicken livers, trimmed of membranes		
1	onion	1	tablespoon chopped sweet marjoram (or 1 teaspoon dried)
1½	cups finely shredded cooked pork		
	freshly ground black pepper		hot pepper sauce
1	teaspoon Worcestershire sauce		butter

Bring the stock or gravy and water to a boil and add the cornmeal. Lower the heat to the point where the cornmeal is bubbling but not boiling furiously, and cook, stirring frequently, for 15 minutes.

Purée the chicken livers in a food processor, add the onion, and coarsely chop it. Stir the liver-onion mixture into the cornmeal, and cook, stirring constantly, for 10 minutes. Add the pork, pepper to taste, Worcestershire sauce, cumin (if used), sage, parsley and lovage (if used), sweet marjoram, and a dash of hot pepper sauce. By now the mixture should be quite thick. Cook for another 5 to 10 minutes, stirring constantly.

Do not let the cornmeal burn. (A slight crust will form on the bottom of the pan because of the liver).

Remove the pan from the heat, and melt a little butter in a frying pan. Make a patty and fry it to check for seasonings. Remember that the flavor will become stronger after the scrapple has sat in the refrigerator 1 day. Adjust the seasonings to suit your taste.

Spoon the scrapple into a buttered 9 × 5-inch loaf pan and smooth out the surface. Cover the pan and refrigerate the scrapple until firm. To serve, slice the scrapple into ½-inch pieces, and panfry them in a little butter until heated through and browned.

If the scrapple is covered and stored in the refrigerator, it should stay in good condition for at least 1 week. Or freeze for up to 3 months.

Makes 1 loaf

Fish

Fish are difficult to store because they're so perishable. Add to that the fact that by the time they reach the consumer, several days may have elapsed from the time the fish were caught, and you can see why it's worth spending the time to locate a fishmonger who takes pride in the quality of his products.

There's no way to disguise poor-quality fish. If you have a fisherman in the family, you probably know what fresh fish look like: the inside of the gills will be a pinkish red, and the flesh will be firm when you press down on it. The eyes are bright and transparent and are not sunken into the sockets. (If the eyes are white, watch out, because the more opaque the eyes, the older the fish.) The fish should not smell like ammonia. I prefer to buy whole fish that usually haven't been treated with preservatives—the fishmonger fillets the fish, and I made stock or chowder out of the frames after removing the gills and eyes.

I realize you may live in a town where it's impossible to find fresh fish. If you must buy frozen fish, try to find fish that have been flash-frozen (rapidly frozen at a very low temperature), because that method best preserves the texture of the fish. The fish should be tightly wrapped, with no sign of hardened patches that indicate freezer burn. Always ask the supermarket staff whether the fish are fresh or defrosted (usually they're willing to tell you). Also, be suspicious of any fish sitting in a pool of water, because they've probably been defrosted.

The best way to defrost fish is in the refrigerator because slow defrosting retains the moisture of the fish, while defrosting at room temperature causes the fish to dry out. If you don't think there's much difference, defrost 1 pound of fish at room temperature and 1 pound in the refrigerator. The fish defrosted at room temperature will be swimming in fish juices, while there will be only 1 or 2 tablespoons of juice around the refrigerated fish.

When you cook fish, ignore suggestions for cooking until the flesh flakes when tested with a fork. If you cook a fish that long, it's overdone. When a fish is almost done, it will have lost most of its translucency and will have turned opaque. If just a small amount of the center of a fish is translucent, remove it from the pan because it will continue to cook after it's removed from the heat. This rule applies to all the ways of cooking fish. (By the way, I broil only oily fish because broiling tends to dry out and toughen the flesh of fish.) For baking, poaching, or steaming fish, I use the method devised by the Canadian Bureau of Fisheries for estimating cooking time: measure a fish at its thickest point, and plan on 10 minutes per inch. So if you were baking a 3-inch-thick bass, you would bake it for about 30 minutes. This is merely a rule of thumb, and you should start testing about 5 minutes before you think the fish will be ready, but it generally works well.

In another chapter I've given you a recipe for Fish Stock (see page 263), which is invaluable for making fish sauces or for poaching fish. If you ask for non-oily white fleshed fish scraps, usually your fishmonger will give them to you or sell them to you cheaply. Once you have fish stock, you can reduce it similar to the way you reduce meat stock. Then use it in butter sauce, stir it into hollandaise or a white sauce, or combine it with the pan juices along with a little garlic, parsley, and lemon juice. Or add 1 or 2 tablespoons to fish sauces for a more complex flavor. If you have leftover clam or mussel broth, strain and save it as a base for fish stews or chowders, or reduce it to add flavor to sauces. I usually freeze fish stock in ½-cup amounts.

Because fish are so perishable, people tend to overlook the marinades, pastes, terrines, and stews that make it possible to preserve fish for at least 1 week. Americans tend to deep fry, bake, or broil their fish, but in Europe marinated fish are common specialties. For example, the Belgians marinate their cooked fresh pike or pickerel in an onion-carrot mixture, the Swedes fry smelts and then cover them with a dill-onion marinade, while the French marinate sautéed mackerel in a white wine or mustard sauce.

As most marinated fish will keep for at least 1 week in the refrigerator, you'll find a number of marinated fish recipes in this chapter. You'll notice I use mackerel, which is an oily fish that spoils quickly when raw but stays in good condition when cooked. One caution: these dishes are good cool—but not chilled. When fish are served too cold, the flavors tend to become dull, and the nice fresh taste dissipates.

Fish pastes and butters are good keepers—if they're sealed tightly with melted butter. The food processor has removed the work from grinding fish, so if you have leftover fish or shellfish, it's an easy process to turn them into pastes. I've experimented with different proportions of seasoning, and I've opted to go light so that I can retain the delicate tastes of the fish. If you prefer, increase the seasonings in the pastes, but taste them first. As with other recipes in this book, the fish pastes gain flavor after 1 day in the refrigerator: what might taste a little bland on the first day will be just right by the second.

I love fish terrines but the most delicious ones are made with a binder of egg whites and heavy cream, which means that they're delicately flavored but loaded with calories—so I save them for special occasions. I have experimented, however, with terrines that use less cream, and I offer one of my most successful experiments here—Sole Scallop Terrine. It has only ½ cup heavy cream and it uses tofu, a low-calorie, no-cholesterol soybean "cheese," as the binder. The tofu, which has a very delicate flavor and texture, recedes into the background, and the flavors that come through are the sole, scallops, and basil. It's delicious with a fresh herb mayonnaise or a cucumber sauce.

You'll also find recipes from a couple of creative Massachusetts restaurant chefs: Scallop Terrine developed by Nitzi Rabin of Chillingsworth restaurant on Cape Cod, and Bluefish Spread from Marian Morash of the Straight Wharf restaurant on Nantucket.

The other unusual recipes you'll find here are some fish recipes given to me by Susan Harnett, who is a fine Cajun cook. They include Fish Creole and Shrimp Chicken Gumbo.

Layered Mackerel

2	cups water	2	cups ½-inch strips Bermuda onions
½	cup lemon juice	2	cloves garlic, minced
1	clove garlic, sliced	1	cup sliced mushrooms
4	peppercorns	2	pounds (very fresh) mackerel fillets with skin
½	cup olive oil		cornmeal
5	tablespoons vegetable oil		
2	cups ½-inch strips sweet red and green peppers		

Place the water, lemon juice, sliced garlic, peppercorns, and olive oil in an enameled or stainless steel saucepan and bring to a boil. Simmer slowly, covered, for 30 minutes, then strain. Set aside and keep warm.

While the marinade is simmering, heat 2 tablespoons vegetable oil and sauté the sweet peppers, onions, and minced garlic until cooked through, about 3 minutes. Stir in the mushrooms and cook for another minute until they are wilted. Remove from the heat and reserve.

Dip the mackerel fillets in the cornmeal, and shake to remove any excess. Heat the remaining vegetable oil and cook the fillets for 2 to 4 minutes on each side, or until they are lightly browned and cooked through. Set aside.

To assemble the dish, place a layer of vegetables in the bottom of a deep casserole large enough to hold ½ the fillets in 1 layer. (I use a round glazed earthenware dish.) Pour ⅓ of the marinade over the vegetables, then top with ½ the fillets, skin side down. Cover with the remaining vegetables. Pour the second ⅓ of the marinade over the vegetables, and top with the remaining mackerel. Cover with the remaining marinade.

Let the dish marinate in the refrigerator for at least 24 hours before serving. As the dish sits, the oil may float to the top, so stir the marinade before serving. Serve at room temperature.

The mackerel keeps with no loss of quality for up to 1 week in the refrigerator.

Serves 8

Bluefish Spread

When guests sit down to dinner at the Straight Wharf restaurant in Nantucket, Massachusetts, they are given this delicious spread to eat with French bread melba toast while they peruse the menu. Marian Morash, the chef at the Straight Wharf and author of *The Victory Garden Cookbook*, points out that the bluefish must be very fresh, because older bluefish has an oily taste.

1½ pounds bluefish fillets with skin	⅓ cup lemon juice
1 pound cream cheese, softened	Worcestershire sauce
½ cup finely chopped parsley	hot pepper sauce
½ cup finely chopped onions	cayenne pepper
	freshly ground black pepper

Preheat the oven to 400°F.

Place the bluefish in a stainless steel or glass baking dish. Barely cover with boiling water. Top with foil and poach for 15 to 25 minutes, or until the bluefish is just cooked through. The cooking time depends upon the thickness of the fillets.

Remove the bluefish from the oven, drain off the liquid, and cool the bluefish. Skin the fillets and check for bones. Flake the bluefish into a mixing bowl. Beat in the cream cheese until combined. Mix in the parsley, onions, and lemon juice. Season with 1 or 2 dashes of the Worcestershire and hot pepper sauces. Add cayenne and pepper to taste. Taste, and correct the seasonings if necessary.

Place the spread in a glass bowl, cover, and store it in the refrigerator, where it will stay in good condition for up to 1 week. Bring the spread to room temperature before serving.

Makes 3½ cups

Salmon Spread

Many fish markets in the Boston area sell fresh salmon scraps, which reduces the cost of this spread considerably. You may wish to look for a similar price break. If you are inland, of course, salmon will be more expensive—but this rich spread goes a long way, and it makes an attractive appetizer mounded in a bowl and garnished with lemon twists and fresh herbs. I like to let the flavors meld for 1 day before serving, although there's usually a lot of snitching the minute this goes into the refrigerator. For a special occasion you may wish to put the spread through a fine sieve, which gives it a velvety texture.

One caution: be sure to remove the salmon from the poaching liquid the minute it is done, for if the salmon cooks too long, it loses a great deal of flavor and texture.

1½	pounds salmon, poached, boned, and skinned		hot pepper sauce
		⅛	teaspoon ground mace or nutmeg
¾	pound butter	⅛	teaspoon curry powder
½	teaspoon Worcestershire sauce	1	tablespoon onion juice
1½	tablespoons Dijon mustard	½	cup minced herbs (such as basil, lovage, or sweet marjoram)
1	teaspoon catsup		
¼	cup lemon juice		

Purée the salmon in a food processor with the butter. Add the Worcestershire sauce, mustard, catsup, lemon juice, a dash of hot pepper sauce, the mace or nutmeg, curry, and onion juice. (I make the onion juice by squeezing an onion on my juicer. You don't want any pulp. You could also purée the onion in a food processor and strain out the pulp to get the juice.)

Process the spread by on and off pulses of the food processor until all the ingredients are blended. Add the herbs and run the machine for a few seconds longer.

Taste the mixture and add a little more Worcestershire sauce, hot pepper sauce, lemon juice, and mustard if necessary.

Store in a covered glass jar in the refrigerator, where it will keep for up to 1 week. For longer storage, freeze for up to 1 month.

Makes about 3 cups

Scallop Terrine

Nitzi Rabin suggests that scallops are an excellent choice for fish terrines because their lack of fiber easily makes for a fine-textured result. The salt is necessary; it reacts chemically with the mixture and makes the texture denser. Divide up the scallops, salt, egg whites, and cream, and process them in 3 batches for the best texture. It's important to hold the scallops and cream over bowls of ice, and the egg whites should also be cold, not at room temperature. Nitzi uses a Quick Temp oven thermometer for testing whether the terrine is done and considers it a great convenience when making terrines. The particular size mold specified in this recipe is sold at restaurant supply stores, but Nitzi says you can also bake the terrine in individual buttered custard cups.

2	pounds scallops		1 to 2	teaspoons salt
⅛	teaspoon dry mustard		1½	cups heavy cream
¾ to 1	teaspoon white pepper			
1	cup egg whites (from about 8 eggs)			

Butter a loaf pan that's about 2¾ inches high, 4 inches wide, and 12 inches long. Then completely line it with buttered waxed paper that is wide enough on the sides to fold over the top of the pan. The waxed paper makes the terrine easy to remove.

Place ⅓ of the scallops in a food processor and add the mustard and pepper, then process until combined. Gradually add ⅓ of the egg whites until the mixture has a medium-runny consistency and is lump-free. Add ⅓ of the salt and ½ cup cream and process until it is incorporated. Repeat this process twice with the remaining scallops, egg whites, salt, and cream, then stir the ingredients together thoroughly so the spices are evenly distributed.

Preheat the oven to 350°F.

Spoon the mixture into the prepared pan, fold over the buttered waxed paper, and rap the pan on the counter to remove any air bubbles. Place the pan in a high-sided roasting pan, then pour boiling water into the roasting pan to halfway up the sides of the loaf pan. Top the terrine with a tent of foil so the top doesn't brown, and cook for 1¼ to 1½ hours, or until the internal temperature reads 140°F with a Quick Temp thermometer.

The terrine can be served immediately or can be stored and served with a cream sauce. (A recipe for the sauce is given in the variations.) The terrine should keep for up to 1 week in the refrigerator if wrapped tightly.

Makes 25 slices

Variations

• Nitzi uses this as a base for several terrines. Sometimes he mixes in pieces of scallops, lobsters, shrimp, and julienne spinach before baking, or he'll turn it into an herb terrine with fresh tarragon or basil. He also likes cubes of sole or chunks of fresh salmon added in.

• Low-Sodium Variation: Nitzi has found that the salt has a chemical reaction with the scallops that results in a firm-textured terrine. For a terrine without the salt, he suggests adding 1 whole egg with the scallops, then the whites, and a generous amount of tarragon, basil, or chives to make up for the loss of flavor.

• Because the terrine makes an ample amount, Nitzi suggests reheating slices in a cream sauce. To do this, finely chop a shallot, cover it with water, and cook it in a frying pan until the water almost disappears. Then add the juice of 1 lemon and about 1½ cups heavy cream (about 2½ ounces per portion). Simmer the cream until it reduces slightly and begins to thicken. Slice the fish terrine, gently put the slices in the pan, and turn down the heat. Once the slices are reheated, remove them and place them on a warm platter. Then add chopped basil or tarragon to the pan, taste, add more lemon juice if necessary, and pour the sauce over the slices.

Sole Scallop Terrine

This terrine takes about 3 minutes to make in the food processor. Wait to sample it, however, until the terrine has chilled overnight, because the tofu dominates when the terrine is warm but becomes almost unnoticeable as it chills. Use either basil or dillweed, but adjust the amount to suit your taste—too much of either herb will overpower the delicate flavor of the sole and scallops. Substitute parsley for the most delicate flavor. If you are fortunate enough to find bay scallops, leave them whole; the larger sea scallops should be quartered.

2	pounds sole (or any lean, white fleshed fish) fillets	2	egg whites
1	pound soft tofu	1	pound scallops
¼	cup lime juice	1 to 1½	tablespoons chopped basil or dillweed
½	cup heavy cream	1	tablespoon butter

Butter a 9 × 5-inch loaf pan. Preheat the oven to 350°F.

Purée the sole with the tofu in 2 batches. Add the lime juice, cream, and egg whites to the second batch, and purée until combined. Add ¼ of the scallops to the mixture and purée again. Place the rest of the sole-tofu mixture in the food processor, and process until the mixture is thoroughly combined. Add the basil or dillweed and purée for 1 second.

Place the mixture in a large bowl and stir in the remaining scallops. You want them to be evenly distributed throughout the mixture.

Spoon the mixture into the loaf pan, and dot with the butter. Cover with a piece of foil, tightly crimped along the top of the pan. Do not let the foil extend down the pan, or water could seep into the terrine.

Place the pan in a deep roasting pan, and pour boiling water halfway up the sides of the loaf pan. Bake for 1½ hours, or until the terrine is cooked through. Cool, and drain off any liquid before refrigerating.

Let the terrine sit for at least 1 day before serving. Serve with a Cucumber Basil Sauce (see page 237).

If it is covered tightly and drained so the juices don't sour, the terrine should keep in good condition for at least 5 days.

Makes 1 loaf

Variation
• Substitute parsley for the basil or dillweed, add ¼ pound drained and flaked crab meat, and reduce the sole to 1¾ pounds.

Pickled Mussels

This recipe was inspired by mussels we tasted years ago at a hotel in Cavalière on the French Riviera, where—more often than not—mussels were a favored appetizer choice. It's important to cook the mussels only to the point where they open, because mussels become flavorless and tough if they are overcooked.

3½	pounds mussels	1	large onion, sliced
1 to 1⅓	cups Lemon Mint Vinegar (see page 6)	4	cloves garlic, crushed
		4	basil sprigs

Clean the mussels. Put 1 inch of water in the bottom of an enameled or stainless steel pot, add the mussels, and steam them just until opened. Discard any mussels that remain closed. Reserve the mussel broth. Remove the mussels from their shells and set aside.

Over high heat boil the mussel broth until it is reduced by at least ⅓ (to ¾ cup) and the flavor is concentrated. Strain it through coffee filters, and set aside to cool.

Combine the broth and vinegar. Layer the mussels and onions in a large glass jar. Tuck in the garlic and basil, and pour the vinegar over all. The mussels should be covered with the marinade. If they are not, lightly press them down and add a mixture of equal parts vinegar and water.

Cover the jar and marinate the mussels for at least 3 days before serving. The mussels should stay in good condition for up to 1 week without spoiling, as long as they are covered with the marinade.

Makes about 4 cups

Profile

Susan Harnett

Thirty-four-year-old Susan Harnett and her husband, Tony, own some of the most attractive supermarkets in the Boston area. Visiting one of the Bread and Circus stores is like shopping at an expanded gourmet shop: the produce is beautifully displayed, with locally grown, fresh carrots next to exotic black peppers from Holland and fresh *shitaki* mushrooms; cheeses from the provinces of France sit near English Stiltons and Cheddars from Wisconsin and Vermont; while freshly made butter from Maine tempts you in a case nearby.

But Bread and Circus isn't your average gourmet shop. Walk along the aisles and you'll notice grains, nuts, and tofu—all stock items in a natural food store. In the 9 years the Harnetts have owned the business, it has grown to be one of the largest independently owned natural food chains in the country.

As owner of a natural food business, Susan Harnett samples many of the new products that come onto the market. She's always looking for good-tasting products to use in her own Cajun and Southern-style cooking. Susan was delighted to find a rice syrup ideal for making pecan pies (which she makes with whole wheat pastry) and a natural Worcestershire sauce to perk up stews and soups.

"I think it's much easier being a good natural food cook today than it used to be," Susan told me. "The industry has changed dramatically in the years we have been running the stores. Now we're getting good-quality gourmet foods without the preservatives and additives, and ethnic foods from various cultures are becoming popular. People are going back to their roots and digging up family recipes, just like I do with Cajun cooking, and they're manufacturing these foods for the natural food industry.

"Recently a black manufacturer decided that natural foods were not spicy enough, so he came up with natural barbecue and Worcestershire sauces that were popular items the minute they hit the shelves. You can buy brands of *salsas* in various consistencies, along with whole grain corn chips to go with them. Also, more and more manufacturers are developing the kind of sauces that grandmother made in the fall and canned in mason jars. People who don't have the time to prepare them at home can now buy a wide variety of condiments," Susan pointed out.

Susan attributes her interest in cooking healthful foods to her diet while she was growing up. "I was raised on a very good diet of basic foods in Louisiana. We ate lots of wild game, fresh vegetables . . . home-grown things. Everything was made from scratch. We ate fish from the lakes and shellfish from the gulf, and rice every day."

Susan's parents are both good cooks: her father, who was raised in the bayous west of New Orleans by French-speaking relatives, cooks Cajun-style, while her mother was brought up with the Creole foods of New Orleans. "It wasn't until I was 19 and moved to New York City that I realized I had been living in a unique culture, that not everyone ate the way we did," she explained.

Susan favors the Cajun cooking from her father's side of the family. Cajun cooks turn simple ingredients, coupled with lots of vegetables and flavorings, into meals that many people consider to be the most interesting regional foods in America.

The Cajuns live in the swampy waterways west and southwest of New Orleans, where fish and shellfish—including the tiny lobsterlike crawfish—can be found in abundance. Pork is the favorite meat of Cajun cooks. One of Susan's fondest memories of growing up in a Cajun household is the *boucherie*, a time when all the neighbors get together to slaughter a pig and make sausages. The blood is saved for the blood *boudin noir* sausages, and the intestines are recycled for sausage casings. Huge caldrons are used to render fat for cracklings. This is all delicious but, Susan says, much too fatty. "One of my dreams is to write a cookbook showing how you can cut down on the fat and still have good-tasting Cajun food," she said.

I talked with Susan about how she cooks Cajun food the natural way and her suggestions for seasoning without salt. "I use lots of herbs and spices, which probably comes from my ethnic heritage. Northern cooking tastes very bland to me," Susan explained. She favors cayenne pepper, which she thinks has medicinal qualities and a special flavor, and she shuns black pepper, which she thinks is hard to digest.

"In Louisiana we use lots of Worcestershire and hot pepper sauces. However, I only add hot pepper sauce at the very end of the cooking time; otherwise the flavor cooks away.

"Garlic and onions are basic ingredients in all Cajun cooking, as is a vegetable seasoning. My grandmother's basic vegetable seasoning is chopped onions, scallions, celery, green bell peppers, parsley, and garlic. If a Cajun cook were making pork sausage, you'd find this vegetable mixture as a basic ingredient. Bay leaves are always included in stews and gumbos," she added.

Susan substitutes an unrefined, unfiltered sesame oil for the lard, butter, or shortening traditional in Cajun cooking: she even makes a flour-based roux with sesame oil. "I like sesame oil because it's a living oil; it bubbles when it cooks and imparts a deep, rich flavor to the foods, giving them a depth I find is lacking in many natural foods," Susan commented.

Many Cajun specialties are excellent keepers because the longer they sit, the better they taste. There's no single way to fix these specialties, Susan explained, because every family has its own version. You'll find Susan's Shrimp Chicken Gumbo in this chapter, along with Crawfish *Étouffe* and Fish Creole.

Shrimp Chicken Gumbo

This is an authentic Cajun gumbo from Susan Harnett.

2	cups chopped okra	1	cup Roux (see page 255)
4	tablespoons sesame oil		
1	large onion, chopped	2	quarts water
2	stalks celery, chopped	1	4-pound chicken, cut up
½	sweet green pepper, chopped	¼	teaspoon cayenne pepper
½	bunch parsley (with stems), chopped (1 cup)	4	bay leaves
		½	teaspoon dried thyme
8 to 10	scallions, chopped	¾	pound shelled shrimp
4	cloves garlic, crushed and minced		

Sauté the okra in 2 tablespoons oil until the soft and ropy texture is gone, 10 to 15 minutes. Set it aside.

In a large saucepan heat the remaining oil and sauté the onions, celery, sweet green peppers, parsley, scallions, and garlic until wilted and softened, about 7 minutes.

Add the roux and water. Bring the mixture to a boil, stirring constantly, then add the okra, chicken, cayenne, bay leaves, and thyme. Lower the heat and simmer the mixture for at least 1 hour. Fifteen minutes before serving, add the shrimp. Remove the bay leaves and serve the gumbo over brown rice.

The gumbo should keep for up to 1 week in the refrigerator if stored in a covered pot.

Serves 6 to 8

Fish Creole

Susan Harnett serves this fish stew over brown rice.

¼	cup olive oil		½ to 1	cup water or Fish Stock (see page 263)
1	onion, finely chopped		2	bay leaves
½	sweet green pepper, finely chopped		1	pound non-oily white fleshed fish scraps (monkfish is nice), cut into large bite-size chunks
1	stalk celery, finely chopped			
¼	cup chopped parsley			hot pepper sauce
2	cloves garlic, crushed			cayenne pepper
1	16-ounce can tomato purée			

Heat the oil in a large pot, and sauté the onions, sweet green peppers, celery, parsley, and garlic until wilted and cooked through, about 10 minutes. Add the tomato purée, ½ cup water or stock, and the bay leaves. Simmer for 20 minutes, add the fish and remaining water or stock, if necessary, and cook for 15 minutes longer, or until the fish flakes when tested with a fork. Add hot pepper sauce and cayenne to taste.

The fish will keep in good condition for up to 1 week if stored in a covered dish in the refrigerator.

Makes 4 cups

Crawfish Étouffe

Susan Harnett's father, Ellis Guillory, who is a talented Cajun cook, says the longer this stew sits, the better it gets. As the scallions keep poorly in the stew, be sure to add them just before serving. The crawfish must be very fresh if you plan to keep this for a full week in the refrigerator.

1 stalk celery, finely chopped
1 large onion, finely chopped
1 medium-large sweet green pepper, finely chopped
½ cup finely chopped parsley (including stems)
½ cup butter or ⅓ cup sesame oil
2 to 3 tablespoons whole wheat pastry flour
2 tablespoons tomato purée

1 cup water
1 large clove garlic, crushed
cayenne pepper
soy sauce (optional)
Worcestershire sauce (optional)
1 pound crawfish tails, shelled, or 1½ pounds medium-size or small shrimp, shelled
¼ cup chopped scallions hot pepper sauce (optional)

Sauté the celery, onions, sweet green peppers, and parsley in the butter or sesame oil for about 20 minutes over medium heat. Add the flour and stir until lightly browned. Add the tomato purée and water and stir for 5 minutes over a low flame.

Stir in the garlic, a pinch of cayenne, and a dash each of soy sauce and Worcestershire sauce if you wish. Add the crawfish tails or shrimp and simmer for 20 minutes. Just before serving, stir in the scallions, and a dash of hot pepper sauce if you wish.

Serve hot over brown rice. The *étouffe* will keep for up to 1 week in the refrigerator.

Serves 4

Fish with Citrus Juice

This recipe adapts well to almost any kind of firm fleshed fish. I've made it with scrod, bluefish, and mackerel—with delicious results each time, although scrod produces the most delicately flavored result. It's also fun to vary the citrus juices—sometimes I use tangerine juice rather than orange juice, or I'll make it with lime and tangelo juice. (Tangelos, a cross between tangerines and grapefruit, are in season during midwinter.) It is important, however, to use freshly squeezed juice because refrigerated packaged juice will destroy the fresh taste of the marinade.

2 pounds scrod, bluefish, or mackerel fillets with skin	1 hot red pepper, thinly sliced into rings
cumin powder	3 tablespoons sweet green or red peppers cut into matchstick pieces
whole wheat flour	
¾ to 1 cup olive oil	
½ cup freshly squeezed lime juice	1 tablespoon finely chopped garlic
¾ cup freshly squeezed orange, tangerine, or tangelo juice	3 tablespoons chopped basil or 2 tablespoons chopped coriander or mint
¼ teaspoon cayenne pepper	
2 onions, chopped	

Cut the fillets into 2-inch-wide pieces. Lightly sprinkle them with cumin, and dust with flour. Heat ¼ to ½ cup oil in a large frying pan, and cook the fillets on both sides until browned. (The amount of oil depends upon the number of fish pieces.) Drain them on paper bags.

Combine the lime juice, orange, tangerine, or tangelo juice, cayenne, ½ cup of the remaining oil, the onions, all the peppers, the garlic, and the herbs. Place the fish in a deep glass or earthenware serving dish, and cover with the marinade. It may be necessary to layer the fish. If this is the case, pour some of the marinade over each layer. This amount of marinade should be sufficient to cover the fish. If it is not, press down lightly on the fish, and add a little more lime and orange juice.

Chill at least overnight before serving. The fish will keep in good condition for up to 1 week if stored in the refrigerator in a dish covered with foil.

Makes 2 pounds

Shrimp Scallop Paste

This delicately flavored paste should be served with thinly sliced French bread or with bland crackers that won't overwhelm the flavor. The paste also makes a delicious stuffing for rolled fillets of sole or flounder: wrap the fish around 1 or 2 tablespoons paste and some chopped parsley or tarragon, dot the fish with butter, and bake it in the oven, or oven poach it in Fish Stock (see page 263). You can substitute the larger sea scallops for the bay scallops)—cook them longer and purée all of the scallops with the shrimp.

¾	pound butter		Worcestershire sauce
1	pound shelled shrimp		hot pepper sauce
½	pound bay scallops	¹⁄₁₆ to ⅛	teaspoon curry
3	cloves garlic, minced		powder
1	onion, minced	¼	pound butter
⅓ to ½	cup lemon juice		(optional)

Melt ¾ pound butter in a large frying pan and add the shrimp. Gently cook them in the butter until cooked through, 2 to 3 minutes. Remove the shrimp with a slotted spoon and set aside. Halve 3 shrimp lengthwise and set aside.

In the same butter cook the scallops. They will cook through in about 2 minutes. Set them aside.

Add the garlic and onions to the butter remaining in the pan, and cook, stirring until the onions are wilted, for about 3 minutes.

Place the shrimp in the food processor and add the butter and lemon juice. Process the shrimp with on and off bursts until puréed.

Reserve ½ cup of the scallops. Process the remaining scallops with the shrimp purée. Don't overprocess: the mixture should have some texture.

Add a dash each of Worcestershire sauce and hot pepper sauce and the curry. You may wish to increase the amount of seasoning, but do so only after tasting each addition. The flavor is subtle and you want to taste the seafood, not the seasonings. Stir in the reserved scallops.

Spoon the mixture into a glass or pottery bowl, and arrange the halved shrimp around the edge of the bowl. Garnish with minced parsley in the center.

Omit the parsley if you are planning to store the paste. Melt ¼ pound butter and use it to seal the top. The butter seal should keep the paste in good condition for at least 1 week.

Makes 3½ cups

Variations
- Tarragon Mustard Variation: Add 2 teaspoons chopped tarragon and 2 teaspoons Dijon mustard.
- Stuffed Mushrooms: Sauté mushroom caps in butter until cooked through, then stuff with the paste mixed with cream cheese to taste. Serve cold.
- Stuffed Cherry Tomatoes: Hollow out cherry tomatoes and stuff with the shrimp scallop paste.
- Stuffed Hard-Cooked Eggs: Mix some of the paste with the mashed yolks of the hard-cooked eggs, mayonnaise, and a touch of tomato paste, and stuff into the sliced egg whites.

English Potted Shrimp

My first choice for this dish would be the tiny, delicately flavored Maine shrimp. However, they're hard to find and have a short season. Regular shrimp—or rock shrimp—cut into ½-inch pieces would be a good second choice. When reheating the shrimp to coat them with the butter and spices, cook them for just a minute—otherwise they will be tough. Serve with toast.

2	cups shelled, cooked shrimp	¼	teaspoon ground nutmeg
1	cup butter		
⅛	teaspoon cayenne pepper		

Dry the shrimp. In a large frying pan melt ½ cup butter and add the cayenne and nutmeg. Stir in the shrimp and toss over low heat until they are coated with butter.

Spoon the shrimp into a small, deep container. In a clean pan melt the remaining butter and clarify it (see page 254 for directions). Pour the clarified butter over the shrimp to seal them.

The shrimp will keep in good condition for up to 1½ weeks in the refrigerator, as long as the butter seal is unbroken.

Makes about 2¾ cups

Variations
- Add 2 teaspoons chopped dillweed, or a combination of chopped dillweed and lovage, and 2 teaspoons Dijon mustard.

Pickled Shrimp and Fennel

Pickled shrimp is a delicious party dish that improves as it marinates in the refrigerator. Be sure the shrimp you buy, however, have been quick-frozen and never thawed. Sometimes supermarkets will sell shrimp that have been frozen, thawed, and refrozen: these shrimp always have a terrible texture and an old taste. (If the shrimp are defrosted, smell them, and if in doubt, don't buy them.) Florence fennel can be hard to find unless you have an Italian market nearby, but it's worth tracking down because its crisp texture and slight anise flavor are pleasant foils to the shrimp. Remove the shrimp and vegetables from the marinade before serving them, otherwise they will drip all over people as they eat. Given the price of shrimp, this dish deserves a beautiful presentation. I like to serve it in a deep glass bowl, or I line a platter with Boston lettuce or shredded Chinese cabbage, mound the shrimp and vegetables in the center, and garnish them with lemon twists.

4 quarts water	freshly ground black pepper
2 to 3 stalks celery or lovage	¼ cup chopped sweet marjoram, parsley, or sweet cicely
¼ cup mixed pickling spices	
2½ pounds shrimp (2 pounds shelled)	1 pound Florence fennel (including leaves), thinly sliced
2¼ cups vegetable oil	
1½ cups rice wine or white wine vinegar	1 sweet red pepper, seeded and thinly sliced into rings
⅓ cup lemon juice	
1 teaspoon minced lemon rind	1 hot red pepper, seeded and thinly sliced into rings (optional)
2 teaspoons celery seed	
2 tablespoons Dijon mustard	3 large onions, sliced into rings
4 cloves garlic, minced	
½ teaspoon dry mustard hot pepper sauce	

Bring the water to a boil, add the celery or lovage stalks and pickling spices, and boil for 2 minutes. Add the shrimp. When the water comes to a boil again, lower the heat to a slow boil, and cook only until the shrimp are curled and pink, 1 to 3 minutes depending upon their size. Immediately drain the shrimp, peel, and cool them. (If you have cooked shelled shrimp, rinse off the pickling spices.)

Mix together the oil, vinegar, lemon juice, lemon rind, celery seed, Dijon mustard, garlic, dry mustard, a dash of hot pepper sauce, a generous amount of pepper, and the sweet marjoram, parsley, or sweet cicely.

Place the shrimp in a large bowl, and toss them with the fennel, all the peppers, and the onions. Stir the marinade and toss it with the shrimp and vegetables. Tightly pack the shrimp and vegetables in a deep 3-quart glass container. Pour the marinade over them. Cover the container, refrigerate, and let the shrimp marinate for at least 24 hours before serving.

If the shrimp remain covered with marinade, they will stay in good condition for at least 1 week in the refrigerator.

Makes about 3 quarts

Portuguese Pickled Fish

This is a colorful addition to a party buffet.

¾	cup combined olive and vegetable oils	5	carrots, grated
2½	pounds cod, haddock, or halibut steaks (about ¾ inch thick)	1	cup white wine vinegar
		1	bay leaf, crumbled
3	large onions, sliced and separated into rings	3	teaspoons minced garlic
			freshly ground black pepper
2	sweet red peppers, cut into rings		lemon juice (optional)
		¼	cup minced parsley

Heat ¼ cup oil in a large, heavy skillet until hot. Blot the fish steaks dry with paper toweling, and fry them for 3 to 5 minutes on each side, depending on the thickness of the steaks. When they are a golden brown and cooked through, place them on paper bags to drain.

Clean the frying pan and heat the remaining oil. Add the onions and cook for 3 minutes, then add the sweet red peppers and cook for another 2 minutes, stirring occasionally. Stir in the carrots, vinegar, bay leaf, garlic, and pepper to taste. Cook for 5 minutes longer. Taste the mixture. If it seems bland, add lemon juice to taste. Stir in the parsley.

Place the fish in the bottom of an enameled or glass dish. Cover with the vegetables, and then pour the remaining marinade over all. Refrigerate for at least 2 days before serving.

If the fish is covered with the marinade, it should stay in good condition for up to 1 week in the refrigerator. Tip the dish and spoon the marinade over the fish occasionally to keep the oil from separating from the vinegar.

Serves 8 to 10

Marinated Swordfish and Peppers

Serve this either as a cold buffet main course or as an appetizer. I prefer to use a mild vinegar such as rice wine vinegar, mixed with a little sherry vinegar when I can find it.

2 tablespoons butter
2 tablespoons plus 1 to 1⅓ cups vegetable oil
3 cloves garlic
1 pound swordfish chunks, cut into 1½ × ½-inch pieces
1⅓ cups vinegar hot pepper sauce
1 tablespoon Dijon mustard
¼ teaspoon ground sweet Hungarian paprika

1 teaspoon good-quality curry powder
½ teaspoon Worcestershire sauce
1 tablespoon minced sweet marjoram or basil
3 small onions, sliced into rings
3 red frying peppers, sliced into rings freshly ground black pepper

Heat the butter, 2 tablespoons oil, and 1 clove sliced garlic in a large frying pan. Dry the swordfish and quickly sauté it until it is cooked through. Set aside.

Beat together the vinegar, the remaining oil, a dash of hot pepper sauce, the mustard, paprika, curry, and Worcestershire sauce. Stir in the sweet marjoram or basil.

Layer the swordfish, onions, frying peppers, and the remaining garlic (cut into slivers) in a tall glass jar or a bowl. Sprinkle each swordfish layer with the pepper. Press down lightly, then pour the marinade over all; the marinade should cover the ingredients. If it does not, mix in a little water. Cover the container and store it in the refrigerator. The swordfish will keep in good condition for up to 1 week if kept well chilled and covered.

Makes 4 to 5 cups

Variation
• Add blanched broccoli and cauliflower florets.

Cheeses

Cheese making can be as simple or complex as you wish. You can prepare a farmer's pot cheese in a few hours or make a mold ripened blue cheese that needs special hothouse conditions to succeed and takes several months to age. You can use cow's milk, goat's milk—or even sheep's milk—to provide an enormous variety of soft and hard cheeses.

When I first started working on this book, I had visions of developing several types of hard cheese that would be easy to make at home. Cheeses, after all, are ideal pantry foods: some varieties of Parmesan, for example, age for 4 years or longer.

I started out by visiting the Freeman Farm at the Old Sturbridge Village museum complex in Sturbridge, Massachusetts, where they make cheeses the way farmers did at home 150 years ago. (It wasn't until the 1850s that cheeses were made in factories and large scale cheese production started in this country.)

Cheese making at Sturbridge Village starts in the spring, when they produce a year's supply of rennet from a young calf's stomach (the younger the calf, the higher the concentration of rennet). The Freeman Farm has a traditional cool spring room, where the cheeses age, and a large outdoors cheese press for pressing each cheese.

A cheese is usually made with a mixture of both the evening and morning milkings, which gives a mix of bacteria and, some people think, a better flavor to the cheese. The milk is heated, rennet is added, and the cheese sits until the curds form. Curds are the solidified form of the milk, and the whey is the liquid by-product. The curds are cut, the whey is drained, and then the cheese is pressed and formed into a wheel.

It's important that the cheese be pressed sufficiently and have a smooth surface, because mold grows in the ridges and cracks and is hard to remove.

The cheese is stored in the spring room, where it is rubbed down with lard every day for 1 week to help form a rind. Then it is wrapped and aged.

Obviously, there are easier ways to make hard cheeses today than there were 150 years ago, but many of the basic techniques remain the same.

After visiting the Freeman Farm and talking with experienced cheese makers, I decided that, for most of us, making hard or aged cheeses at home is impractical. Although making cheeses is a traditional way of using up surplus milk, this works only if you have a dairy animal; otherwise it's prohibitively expensive to buy the large volume of milk necessary to produce even a small volume of cheese. And there's a long wait before you can sample your labors: most hard cheeses age for at least 60 days. Finally, if you want to make Cheddar or other hard cheeses, you'll also need to invest in a cheese press (or make one yourself) and other basic equipment.

On the other hand, should you choose to make soft, fresh cheeses, you can produce a great variety of delicious cheeses to eat immediately, with almost no expenditure for equipment. The flavor of homemade cheeses is a vast improvement over most store-bought varieties. Compare a standard cream cheese, with its gummy texture, bland flavor, additives, and preservatives, with the soft texture and rich flavor of a homemade cream cheese that contains no additives. Almost all of the homemade soft cheeses can be turned into herb cheeses. You can add spices or minced vegetables to vary the cheeses further.

In this chapter you'll find a range of easy soft cheeses to make. You can try several recipes without investing in any equipment at all, while others require an equipment investment of less than $25. The only ingredient in the Buttermilk Pot Cheese is a good-quality commercial buttermilk. As this milk is heated to 200°F, you can use a candy thermometer rather than the dairy thermometer necessary for cheeses made with milk heated to a lower temperature.

Yogurt cheese is equally easy to make, because all you do is drain yogurt until it thickens into a cheeselike consistency. The special cheese-cloth used in cheese making is unnecessary; coffee filters work just as well. A Lebanese friend, who taught me the recipe, shapes the cheese into balls, layers it in olive oil, and stores it in the refrigerator, where it keeps for months.

Crème Fraîche, in the Basics chapter (see page 256), and Soft Cream Cheese, which you'll find in this chapter, form the base for many other recipes. Unlike cream, Crème Fraîche doesn't curdle, and its slightly sour taste is delicious in sauces or spooned over fresh fruit.

Cheeses made with rennet and cheese starter are slightly more complicated. Robert Carroll, owner of the New England Cheesemaking Supply Company in western Massachusetts, gave me basic information about cheese making and contributed soft cheese recipes from the British Isles, France, and the United States that he thinks are particularly appropriate for beginning cheese makers. The Rodale Test Kitchen also has been experimenting with cheese making, and Debra Deis there has perfected a Ricotta-Style Cheese that uses ingredients you can find at any supermarket.

A note about rennet: Rennet tablets and liquid rennet have different strengths and are not interchangeable in recipes. Robert Carroll says, however, that ¼ to ½ teaspoon liquid rennet is roughly equivalent to ¼ rennet tablet. He warns that too much rennet in a recipe can give a bitter, metallic taste to your cheese. As a rule of thumb, ¼ teaspoon liquid rennet will set ½ gallon milk warmed to 86°F in 30 to 45 minutes.

Junket tablets, a form of rennet but not a substitute for rennet tablets, are sold in the pudding mix section of supermarkets. If you have trouble finding a local source for rennet, New England Cheesemaking Supply Company (P.O. Box 85, Ashfield, MA 01330) will mail both the tablets and the liquid to you.

Do try these recipes. They have different levels of complexity—but they don't require a vast expenditure in cheese-making equipment and are delicious alternatives to store-bought cheese. If you want to progress to more complicated, hard cheeses once you've mastered these, there are several excellent recipes in *The Complete Dairy Foods Cookbook*, published by Rodale, and in Robert Carroll's *Cheesemaking Made Easy*, published by Garden Way.

Buttermilk Pot Cheese

This cheese has become a staple food at our house because it is flavorful, low in calories, and exceptionally easy to make. The flavor of the cheese can vary, depending upon the quality of buttermilk you use, so it's worth locating a source for high-quality buttermilk. You can make any amount of cheese; just remember the ratio of buttermilk to cheese is about 4 to 1.

    1   gallon commercial
            buttermilk

Place the buttermilk in an 8-quart heavy enameled or stainless steel pan. Slowly heat it, without stirring, until it reaches the temperature of 200°F. (You can use a candy thermometer.) Do not let the buttermilk boil or the cheese will be tough. Heating the buttermilk will take about 1 hour.

Remove the pot from the heat, cover it, and let stand for 2 hours so the curds and whey will be completely separated.

Line a colander with dampened coffee filters or cheesecloth, and set it in a deep bowl or pot. Pour in the buttermilk mixture. The whey will pour through, leaving the pot cheese.

Let the cheese drip for 2 to 3 hours or overnight before serving. This cheese will keep for up to 1 week in the refrigerator.

Makes about 5 cups

Cheese Spread

Once you have made the first batch of spread, you can add to it every few days, blending in shredded cheese or butter and cream cheese as needed. I use whatever firm cheese I have on hand, such as Cheddar or Swiss—and sometimes some Parmesan for flavor. Recently I filled a crock with Swiss, Parmesan, and Blarney (an Irish Cheddar-type cheese). Cheddar, however, is always a good choice.

    4   cups shredded cheese   1   tablespoon olive oil
            (such as Cheddar)   ⅛   teaspoon hot pepper
    4   ounces cream cheese   sauce
    ¼   cup butter   1   tablespoon mushroom
    1   tablespoon plus 1   soy sauce (optional)
            teaspoon prepared
            horseradish

Hold the shredded cheese at room temperature until it is soft. Combine with the cream cheese, butter, horseradish, oil, hot pepper sauce, and soy sauce (if used). Process until smooth. (This is easiest in a food processor.)

Pack into a crock, cover with plastic wrap, and let it age in the refrigerator for at least 2 days before serving. If you replenish the cheese—and the flavorings—the crock will last indefinitely. It will keep for up to 3 months without replenishing.

Makes about 2 cups

Homemade Yogurt

For a less-creamy yogurt make this with skim milk. You'll need commercial yogurt for the first batch; after that, save yogurt from each batch to start the next.

1½   quarts milk
1   cup dry milk
3   tablespoons yogurt

Place the milk in a large stainless steel pan, and heat it to barely warm. Whisk in the dry milk and the yogurt.

Cover the pan and place it in a warm spot such as on the back of a gas stove or on the floor of the oven of a gas stove (both with only the pilot light on) or over a heating pad set on low. Check after a few hours to make sure the yogurt culture is working.

The yogurt should be ready after 8 hours. Being careful not to jiggle it (which will upset the curd and make the yogurt lumpy), cover it and store in the refrigerator, where the yogurt should stay in good condition for at least 1 week.

If you are using this yogurt as a starter for the next batch, use the starter when the yogurt is no more than 5 days old; it loses more of its friendly bacteria the older it gets. If in doubt with older yogurt, play it safe and use 4 tablespoons yogurt as a starter.

Makes 6 cups

Pesto Cheese

This year the chic item at Boston's gourmet food shops is an Italian cheese torta with basil, which retails for a whopping $12 per pound. The torta, made in a loaf shape, has a buttery *muscarpone* cheese layered with basil and pine nuts. Although the torta is interesting, it's far too rich for my taste, so I have come up with this soft-textured version with a base of yogurt cheese to add tartness. It's important to drain the yogurt and soft cream cheeses thoroughly before you combine them, because the torta should be as dry as possible. The olive oil topping helps preserve the torta and prevents the basil from turning black when it's exposed to the air. Be sure to note the variation, as the cheese makes an excellent topping for pasta.

2½ cups well-drained Yogurt Cheese (see page 157)	2 teaspoons chopped garlic olive oil
2 cups Soft Cream Cheese (see page 158)	3 tablespoons pine nuts (optional)
2 cups tightly packed basil	½ cup grated Parmesan cheese

Combine the yogurt cheese with the soft cream cheese, and let drain overnight in a colander lined with coffee filters. Although you have previously drained both cheeses, they will exude additional liquid if you drain them again.

Place the basil and garlic in a food processor or blender, and process for a few seconds. Add ⅓ cup oil, the pine nuts (if used), and the Parmesan cheese. Process just long enough to combine the ingredients and chop the pine nuts. Place the basil mixture, or pesto, in a mixing bowl, and add oil, a tablespoon at a time, until it has a spreading consistency. It should not be necessary to add more than 2 or 3 tablespoons oil. Set the pesto aside, covered.

Oil a 6-cup mold. I use a Pyrex bowl but a deep square dish would work even better. Starting and ending with the cheese, alternate layers of cheese and the pesto base. You should have about 6 layers of cheese and 5 of pesto. This step can get a little messy—I just smooth off each layer with a rubber spatula and wash my hands frequently.

Smooth out the top surface and cover with at least ½ inch of olive oil. Seal with foil or plastic wrap, and store in the refrigerator overnight before serving, to allow the flavors time to meld. The cheese can be unmolded or served from its dish. Serve with thinly sliced French bread or toasted pita bread. It is also delicious on halved plum or cherry tomatoes.

The cheese will keep in good condition for at least 2 weeks, as long as the surface is kept covered with oil.

Makes about 5 cups

Variations
- Pasta Topping: Boil pasta, drain it, but do not let it cool. Coat with a spoonful of the olive oil that seals the cheese, and then stir in pesto cheese to taste. The cheese melts, giving a creamy topping to the pasta. One-half pound dry pasta will need 1 scant cup cheese or less, depending upon your taste.
- For an impressive presentation layer the pesto and the cheese on a dish rather than in a bowl. It's more work but when you're finished, you have a cheese square that will set off any buffet table beautifully.

    Begin by making sure that the cheese has been drained completely and that there is no moisture left to drain; the cheesecloth or coffee filters should be dry.

    Then remove the cheese and place it between two long sheets of waxed paper. Roll out the cheese with a rolling pin until it is about ¼ inch thick. You should now have a "sheet" of cheese between the waxed paper that is large enough that you can cut 6 5-inch squares from it. The easiest way to do this is to cut the squares right through the waxed paper.

    Take 1 cheese square, peel off the bottom layer of waxed paper, and place it in the center of your serving dish. Then peel off the top layer of paper. Spread on a layer of pesto, then repeat with a layer of cheese. Repeat this layering until you've used up all the cheese and pesto and you have a top layer of cheese.

    Garnish with basil leaves and a few pine nuts.

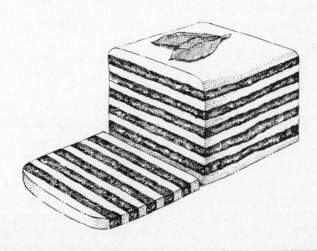

Profile

Robert Carroll

Ten years ago, when a friend talked Robert Carroll into buying two registered dairy goats for $75 apiece, he was interested only in the challenge of raising the goats and having them thrive on his 4 acres in rural Massachusetts. Thrive they did, so much so that they soon produced far more milk than the Carrolls could use.

Robert figured that the only way to use up the surplus milk was to make cheeses. He headed over to the University of Massachusetts, where he once studied animal science, to research small-scale cheese making. He found a dearth of information, but he did track down a few 18th century recipes. He and his wife, Ricki, experimented with them to produce their first cheeses.

When he went searching for supplies, Robert discovered that most American cheese-making supply houses are set up for large commercial operations, not for home-scale setups. Europe, on the other hand, has many small-scale operations, and he eventually began importing equipment from there. He later visited home cheese makers in England, France, and Holland to learn how to make specialty cheeses.

Today the Carrolls' life is centered around cheese: they own the New England Cheesemaking Supply Company in Ashfield, Massachusetts; they publish a bimonthly newsletter, the *Cheesemakers' Journal*; and they have written a book, *Cheesemaking Made Easy*, which gives instructions for making 60 cheese varieties.

As Robert has spent many years teaching home cheese-making workshops, I asked him what his advice would be for someone just starting out.

"Start with something simple that takes an insignificant amount of time and needs an insignificant amount of supplies," Robert told me.

While people come to his workshops all set to make hard, aged cheeses, he talks them into starting with soft, fresh cheeses and mastering these before progressing to aged cheeses, which require a greater investment of time and equipment.

The only supplies you need to make soft cheeses are a stainless steel or enameled pan, cheesecloth, a starter culture, rennet, and a dairy thermometer. (Candy thermometers don't work because they start recording at too high a temperature.) Everything that comes into contact with the milk must be made of glass or stainless steel or be enameled. That's because during cheese making the milk becomes acidic, and metallic salts from aluminum or cast-iron pans can be absorbed by the curds.

The cheesecloth used for cheese making bears no resemblance to the cheesecloth sold at hardware stores. The cheesecloth you need is really butter muslin and is sold at fabric stores or through cheese-making supply companies. If you keep the cheesecloth clean, Robert explained, you should be able to use it over and over again for months.

Cheese making is simple once you master a few rules. "It is really just taking milk and removing a large portion of the water so that the protein and fat stay in a preservable, edible, and attractive condition. Essentially, cheese making is a form of dehydration," Robert explained to me.

I asked him exactly what the rennet and starter culture do and why they are necessary for cheese making.

"Rennet is what makes milk coagulate and turn into a junket like custard. It's an enzyme that's extracted from the stomach of calves—but there are also nonanimal sources of rennet. All the rennet does is make the protein and fat become solid, and the water drains away. You don't even need rennet for some kinds of cheese making.

"The starter culture is what develops the acidity in the milk. The acidity aids in preservation and also develops flavor," Robert pointed out.

You start out with a dried culture from a cheese-making supply house. As long as you keep it alive, you can keep a culture going for months. Keeping a cheese culture is like keeping a yogurt culture going; you reserve about 2 ounces starter in a clean, covered container to make the next batch of cheese.

Cheeses can be made from either homogenized, pasteurized, supermarket milk or raw milk. Supermarket milk should be as fresh as possible; if it has an off taste or is sour, it should be discarded. Raw milk should be pasteurized unless you are sure it is free from pathogens. Robert recommends pasteurizing raw milk at 145°F (measured with a dairy thermometer) for 30 minutes in a double boiler, then immediately cooling it down by placing the top of the double boiler, containing the milk, in a pan of cold water or ice slush.

"People need to be aware of details. I suggest making a diary of what you do. Be aware of temperatures. For example, your kitchen shouldn't be too cold. If it's comfortable for you, the cheese will love it. A temperature of 68 to 72°F is ideal. The lower the temperature, the slower the cheese drains. If it gets real hot in the summer, that's definitely a problem because you can end up with gas-producing bacteria, and the cheese will grow out of the mold," he said. During the hot summer days of July and August, don't make cheeses unless you have an air-conditioned kitchen.

I was interested to learn that you should never make breads in the same area where you're making cheeses, because the yeasts from the breads will get into the cheeses, and the cheeses will end up rising. For the same reason Robert also pointed out that you should not use the same utensils for breads as for cheeses: never use your bread board, for example, as a cheese draining board.

Above all, Robert cautioned, it is essential to keep your surfaces and utensils clean. "Remember that milk has living bacteria in it. You want to raise only the right creatures in the milk—it's like raising a herd of pedigree animals; you don't want any mongrels in there. So you aim for a limited possibility of contamination. Have everything well scrubbed. Put your utensils in boiling water, and take ordinary precautions."

Although Robert makes dozens of different cheeses, he has chosen 7 recipes that are good for beginners. Some date from his trips to England.

Lactic Acid Cheese

Beginning cheese makers should start with this tasty, easy-to-make cheese recipe from Robert Carroll. It's a versatile cheese—equally good as a cheese spread with herbs or as a cream cheese substitute in recipes for cheesecake or other desserts. The cheese starter culture bacteria consume the milk sugar over a 24-hour period, producing in the process, with help from the rennet, enough lactic acid to coagulate the milk. This cheese is also known as acid-curd cheese or bag cheese.

1	gallon milk	1	drop liquid rennet
½	cup cheese starter culture or commercial buttermilk	2	tablespoons cool water

Place the milk in a stainless steel or enameled pan, and heat it to 72°F. Stir in the cheese starter culture or buttermilk and the rennet dissolved in the cool water. Mix thoroughly. Cover the pan and let it sit. The room temperature should be about 72°F. The milk should have coagulated into a soft curd after 24 hours.

Line a colander with fine-mesh cheesecloth, and pour the curds into it. Tie the corners of the cheesecloth into a knot, and hang the bag of curds to drain for 4 to 8 hours. The longer you drain the cheese, the drier the cheese will be.

Wrap the cheese and store it in the refrigerator, where it will stay in good condition for up to 2 weeks.

Makes 1½ to 2 pounds

Variation
• Once the cheese is drained, add herbs and spices. Robert Carroll mixes it in a food processor, using the plastic blade. His favorite seasoning mixture is freshly ground black pepper, freshly chopped garlic, chopped chives, and ground paprika to taste. He also likes freshly chopped dillweed.

Cup Cheese

Robert Carroll says this very mild Pennsylvania Dutch cheese has been made by the Amish and Mennonites for generations.

1	gallon milk	½	teaspoon baking soda
1	cup commercial buttermilk	3	tablespoons butter
1	drop liquid rennet	1	cup heavy cream
2	tablespoons cool water	1	egg, beaten

Place the milk in an enameled or stainless steel pan, and heat it to 72°F. Add the buttermilk and the rennet dissolved in the cool water. Stir thoroughly. Cover the pot and let the milk stand at room temperature (68 to 72°F). After 12 hours a soft curd should have formed.

Slowly cut the curd into ½-inch cubes. Do this carefully because the curd is delicate. Place the pot back on the stove, and warm the curds to 115°F. Occasionally stir the mixture gently while it is reheating.

Pour the warm curds into a cheesecloth lined colander, and drain for 12 hours.

Crumble the drained curds into the top of a stainless steel double boiler, and stir in the baking soda and butter. Let the mixture stand for 5 hours.

Heat the curds in the double boiler until they melt. Add the cream and mix until smooth, then stir in the egg. Bring the mixture to a boil. Pour the cheese into dishes—or cups—and refrigerate them.

Serve the cheese cool. The cheese will keep in good condition for at least 1 week if refrigerated.

Makes 1¾ to 2 pounds

Coulommiers Cheese

Although Coulommiers cheese originated in France, it has been made in English farm houses for many years. An English Coulommiers is a soft, creamy cheese that can be eaten fresh or aged for several weeks in the refrigerator. It may become covered with a soft, white mold, which some people like to eat; you can scrape it off if it isn't to your liking. Cheese-making equipment is essential for this recipe.

2 quarts milk	3 drops liquid rennet
1 tablespoon cheese starter culture or 2 tablespoons commercial buttermilk	2 tablespoons cool water

Place the milk in a stainless steel or enameled pan, and warm it to 90°F. Stir in the cheese starter culture or buttermilk and cover the pan. Let it sit for 30 minutes.

Rewarm the milk to 90°F. Combine the rennet and the cool water and stir it into the milk. Gently stir the mixture for 1 minute in an up and down motion.

Cover the pan and let the milk sit for 45 minutes or longer. It should coagulate. The curd has formed correctly when it breaks cleanly around an inserted finger.

Meanwhile, sterilize 1 Coulommiers mold, 2 reed cheese mats, and 2 hardwood cheese boards in boiling water.

Place a cheese board in a pan, where it can drain the whey, and cover with a mat. Place the mold on top of the mat. The mold has 2 stainless steel hoops, one fitting inside the other; make sure that the bottom section of the mold rests on the mat.

When the milk has set into a solid curd, ladle thin slices of the curd out of the pot, and gently lower these slices into the mold. Steady the mold with your hand so the curd doesn't escape. The thinner the curd is sliced, the better it drains in the mold. Continue to add slices of the curd until the mold is filled. If there is remaining curd, add it to the mold as the curd sinks.

When the mold is filled, cover the top with a mat, and place a cheese board on the mat. Drain the cheese for 8 to 10 hours in a kitchen where the temperature is between 68 and 76°F.

After the cheese has drained, the curd should be below the level of the top mold section. Carefully remove the top piece of mold. Place the mat and cheese board on the remaining mold section, and swiftly flip the mold upside down.

Gently remove the mat from the top of the mold and clean it. Replace it and the cheese board over the mold.

Repeat this process of flipping the cheese several times daily for the next 2 days.

Once the cheese is firm to the touch, has pulled away from the sides of the mold, and is 1 to 1½ inches high, it may be removed from the mold.

The cheese may be air dried in the refrigerator for several hours until the surface is no longer wet, then it should be wrapped in plastic wrap. The cheese may be eaten fresh or aged in the refrigerator for several weeks.

Makes ¾ to 1 pound

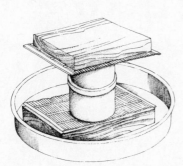

Cambridge Cheese

This soft cheese, sold in the streets of Cambridge, England, is traditionally made in a rectangular shape, but Robert Carroll uses a round Coulommiers mold. The cheese has a layer of yellow curd sandwiched between 2 layers of white curd.

2	quarts milk	⅛	cheese color tablet
¼	cup commercial		cool water
	buttermilk	3	drops liquid rennet

Place the milk in an enameled or stainless steel pan, and heat it to 90°F. Add the buttermilk and stir thoroughly. Remove the milk from the stove, and let it stand for 30 minutes, covered.

Dissolve ⅛ cheese color tablet in ⅛ cup cool water. Stir this mixture into 3 cups of the milk. Place this milk in an enameled or stainless steel pan, and warm it to 90°F. Combine 1 drop rennet with 2 tablespoons cool water, and stir it into the milk. Cover the milk for 45 minutes to allow time for it to coagulate.

Reheat the remaining milk to 90°F in a stainless steel or enameled pan, and add 2 drops rennet dissolved in 4 tablespoons cool water. Stir the mixture thoroughly, cover, and let sit for 45 to 90 minutes to allow for it to coagulate.

Sterilize a Coulommiers cheese mold, 2 reed cheese mats, and 2 cheese boards in boiling water. Place the mold on a mat on top of a cheese board. Ladle thin layers of the uncolored curd into the mold until you have used up ½ the uncolored curd. Ladle in all the colored curd in thin layers. Ladle the remaining uncolored curd into the mold. Cover the mold with a mat and cheese board.

Drain the cheese in the mold for 2 to 3 days at room temperature (68 to 72°F) until it is firm.

Carefully remove the cheese from the mold. Let it stand, uncovered, for several hours to dry, or pat it dry with paper toweling before refrigerating.

Wrap the cheese in plastic wrap, and store it in the refrigerator for up to 2 weeks.

Makes ¾ to 1 pound

Crowdie Cheese

Robert Carroll learned to make this traditional Scottish cheese in Great Britain. It is also known as "cruddy butter" because often butter is added to the fresh curd. The cheese has a creamy, buttery taste that's particularly pleasant for breakfast or as a foil for fresh herbs.

2	quarts milk	¼	cup cool water
2	tablespoons cheese starter culture or ¼ cup commercial buttermilk	1	cup heavy cream
		3	tablespoons butter, softened and creamed
⅛	rennet tablet or ⅛ teaspoon liquid rennet		

Warm the milk to 90°F in a stainless steel or enameled pan. Add the cheese starter culture or buttermilk and stir thoroughly. Dissolve the rennet in the cool water. Add the solution to the milk and stir thoroughly. Cover the milk and let it stand. After 2 hours it should have formed a firm curd.

Cut the curd into 1-inch cubes. Stir the mixture gently so you don't damage the curds. Reheat the curds to 90°F. Stir them gently. Remove the curds from the heat, and let them stand, covered, for 1 hour.

Line a colander with cheesecloth. Ladle the curds and whey into the colander. Place the colander in a sink so the whey drains away. Or if you wish to save the whey for cooking, drain the curds into a bowl. Drain the curds for 2 hours.

Place the drained curds in a bowl. Add the cream and butter. Mix in thoroughly until the cheese has a pastelike consistency. Store the cheese in covered containers and refrigerate immediately. The cheese will keep in good condition for several weeks.

Makes about 1 pound

Variation
• Make an herb cheese by adding chopped fresh herbs to taste, along with the heavy cream and butter. Robert Carroll particularly likes fresh dillweed.

Colwick Cheese

This traditional soft cheese is often served for dessert in England. Robert Carroll suggests presenting it with fruit and filling the depression in the center, which is characteristic of this cheese, with whipped cream. You'll need cheese-making equipment to make Colwick cheese.

2	quarts milk	½	teaspoon liquid rennet
2	tablespoons commercial buttermilk	¼	cup cool water

Heat the milk to 90°F in an enameled or stainless steel pan. Stir in the buttermilk. Dilute the rennet in the water, add to the milk, and gently stir for 1 minute.

Remove the pan from the stove, and let the milk stand for 1 hour until it coagulates.

Sterilize a Coulommiers cheese mold, 2 reed cheese mats, 2 cheese boards, and cheesecloth in boiling water. Line the mold with the cheesecloth, and place it on a mat and cheese board.

Ladle the curd into the cheesecloth-lined mold, and top with the second mat and cheese board. Drain the cheese for 1 hour.

Pull the sides of the cheesecloth upward and inward away from the sides of the mold. Repeat this step twice an hour for the next 6 hours. This process will give the cheese a depressed center and curled edges.

Drain the cheese for 24 to 36 hours, or until it is firm enough to hold its shape when removed from the mold.

Remove it from the mold, and carefully peel away the cheesecloth. Cover the cheese and refrigerate it. It will keep in good condition for up to 2 weeks.

Makes ¾ to 1 pound

Queso Blanco

This bland Latin American cheese has a somewhat sweet flavor. Robert Carroll suggests substituting it for tofu in recipes, including stir-fried dishes. Even if deep fried, the cheese does not melt. You can buy the citric acid in wine-making supply stores, or you can substitute vinegar for the citric acid and water.

1	gallon milk	¼	cup cool water
2	teaspoons granulated citric acid or ⅜ cup vinegar		

Place the milk in the top of a stainless steel double boiler, and heat it to 180°F (this will take perhaps 1½ hours). Dissolve the citric acid (if used) in the cool water, and stir it or the vinegar into the hot milk. Stir slowly; the milk will form curds almost immediately. Stir the curds for several minutes.

Pour the hot curds and whey into a cheesecloth lined colander. Drain the cheese for several hours.

Remove the cheese from the colander, and cut it into ¼- to ½-inch cubes. Store the cheese in a covered container in the refrigerator, where it will keep for up to 2 weeks.

Makes abouts 2 pounds

Robert Carroll

Yogurt Cheese

For years I bought yogurt cheese until a Lebanese friend demonstrated how easy it is to make. All that is necessary is to drain yogurt until it becomes firm. Serve it plain or stir in chopped garlic and mint. My friend drains his yogurt through cheesecloth, but I find coffee filters work just as well and cost less.

2   pounds yogurt

Spoon the yogurt into a colander lined with a single layer of dampened coffee filter. Place over a deep bowl to drain. Let sit for at least 12 hours. The longer the yogurt drains, the denser it becomes. If you want a dense cheese to spread on pita bread or crackers, let it drain for 24 hours. However, if you plan to serve the yogurt cheese with chopped cucumbers as a salad appetizer, drain only until the yogurt forms a cheeselike consistency, about 4 hours.

Yogurt cheese will keep for up to 2 weeks in the refrigerator if kept covered.

Makes about 1⅓ cups if drained for 24 hours

Variation
• Form the cheese into walnut-size balls, and place in a clean glass jar. Add several cloves of garlic if you wish. Cover with oil, seal, and store in the refrigerator, where the cheese will last for months.

Soft Cream Cheese

This rich, slightly sour cheese is delicious with bagels or as the base for an appetizer herb cheese. It is expensive to make unless you have a ready source of cream, but it is worth making for a treat, because it is so much better than commercial cream cheese. On cold days I put the bowl on the floor of my gas oven, where the pilot light provides the right temperature to create the cheese.

  1 cup sour cream
  2 cups heavy cream

Mix together the sour cream and cream, and place in a bowl. Cover with plastic wrap. If the room temperature is more than 80°F, as it might be during the summer, keep the mixture at room temperature for 24 hours. It will thicken, forming a crème fraîche. If it is cooler, try the floor of the oven if you have a gas stove, or place it for a while on a heating pad set at the lowest possible temperature.

Line a colander with coffee filters or cheesecloth, and drain the cheese for 24 hours. Spoon it into a bowl and mix thoroughly.

Cover the cheese and store it in a glass jar in the refrigerator. It should keep for up to 1 week.

Makes about 2¼ cups

Soft French-Style Cheese

This delicate, soft-textured cheese is excellent served with fresh raspberries or strawberries—or other summer fruits. You can whip the cream separately and fold it in, but it is easier to whip the cheese and cream together until the cream thickens.

  2 cups Buttermilk Pot
       Cheese (see page
       144)
  ½ cup sour cream
  1 cup heavy cream
  ⅓ cup egg whites (3 or 4)

Beat together the pot cheese, sour cream, and cream until the cream whips and the mixture thickens. (Do not overbeat or the cream will turn to butter.) Set aside.

Whip the egg whites until they form soft peaks. Gently mix them into the cheese mixture. Place the cheese in a cheesecloth lined coeur à la crème mold or colander, and let drain for 24 to 36 hours before serving. If you do not drain the cheese sufficiently, it will spoil faster.

This cheese keeps for up to 6 days, depending upon how fresh the pot cheese and cream are.

Makes about 3 cups

Ricotta-Style Cheese

On one of my visits to the Rodale Test Kitchen, I tasted this cheese that Debra Deis was making and asked her for the recipe. It's not a true ricotta, which is made from a nonacidic sweet whey, but it has a smooth, creamy flavor. Junket tablets are sold in the pudding mix section of supermarkets.

1	gallon milk	½	Junket tablet
½	cup yogurt	2	tablespoons water

Pour the milk into a clean, large stainless steel or enameled pot. Set this pot on a rack inside a still larger pot. Fill the outside pot with hot water. Warm on the stove over low heat until the milk reaches 85°F.

Stir the yogurt into the milk with a whisk. Cover with a clean towel. Let the milk stand at a warm room temperature (72 to 85°F) until the milk is lightly curdled, 6 to 8 hours. It will have a softer, more delicate texture than yogurt.

Crush the Junket in the water, and stir it gently into the milk, combining thoroughly. After 2 to 3 hours the curd will become firm and will be ready to be heat-set.

Heat ½ gallon water in a large pot to 180°F.

Dip off and discard as much excess whey from the cheese as possible.

Place a cheesecloth lined colander in a large bowl, and set it beside the pot of hot water. Using a slotted spoon, ladle the curds into and out of the hot water to rinse them off, and then place them immediately in the colander. This will make the curds firmer. Do not worry if some of the curds fall apart. Continue this process until all the curds have been processed in the hot water. Drain the hot water gently through the cheesecloth to retrieve any curds that you left there.

Rinse the cheese briefly with cool water, stirring the curds with your fingers. Tie the ends of the cheesecloth together, hang it up, and let drain for 45 minutes. (The faucet above the kitchen sink is a good spot to hang the cheese.)

Refrigerate the cheese in a covered glass bowl. The cheese will keep for up to 2 weeks in the refrigerator.

Makes 4 cups

Pastas, Breads, and Pastries

I have eaten some very bad whole wheat pastas in the name of natural food. This is inexcusable because whole wheat pastas, properly prepared, are every bit as good as pastas made with white flour. The secret is to roll them as thinly as possible and to use a sufficient number of eggs to keep the pastas tender. All you need to succeed is a food processor and a hand-cranked pasta machine. (You can make fine pastas without the food processor, but a pasta machine is a must for the paper-thin pastas I suggest.)

Immediately after cutting a pasta, I dry it on toweling stretched out on the kitchen counter. When it is absolutely dry (usually overnight), I store the pasta in shoe or gift boxes on the pantry shelf. Some people prefer to freeze pastas, but that's not necessary, because the drying method works so well. Pastas dried in this manner will keep for 6 months or longer, but try not to jostle the box, because dried pastas are brittle and will break.

In case you don't have a pasta machine but would still like to make pastas from scratch, I have also given you a pasta recipe for manicotti that's cooked in a frying pan on top of the stove, similar to the way you would make crêpes. My friend Marie Caratelli, a fine Italian cook from Maine, gave me the recipe. Marie fills the manicotti with ricotta and Romano cheeses and tops them with tomato sauce and mozzarella cheese.

When I was teaching cooking, my students always wanted to know how to make crêpes, so we would stand around the stove making crêpes until everyone had made one successfully. The key is to work quickly and to make sure the batter completely covers the bottom of the pan. It may take a while before you have perfected the arm motion, but if you swirl the batter around in the pan rapidly, you should have no problem forming crêpes.

Leftovers are easily converted into company dishes when you put them in a puff pastry casing. I like whole wheat puff pastry: I think it has more flavor than white flour puff pastry, and I prefer it for certain recipes. Especially around the holidays it's helpful to have a supply of puff pastry on hand. I've given you both the quick and the classic versions.

Just like whole wheat pastas, there are whole grain breads—and then there are whole grain breads. Many cooks, who always end up with dry, heavy breads, have resigned themselves to such loaves because they think that's just how breads made with whole grain flours turn out. That's not so. If you need convincing (and even if you don't), read what pastry chef Ingrid Lysgaard Motsis has to say in this chapter about bread making, and try her breads as well as her flaky Whole Wheat Danish Pastry and Whole Wheat Croissants.

In the pages that follow, you'll find pasta, crêpe, tortilla, and pastry recipes along with recipes for Ingrid's breads and for some unusual yogurt breads and quick breads.

Whole Wheat Pasta

Commercial whole wheat pasta will always be thicker than home-made pasta, because extra-thin pasta is brittle and too fragile to ship. By making your own pasta, you end up with a far superior product—at ¼ the price. Making pasta sounds intimidating, but anyone who has a food processor and a hand-cranked pasta machine can make tender pasta without fuss. I like whole wheat pasta that's rolled out to be as thin as possible, but you might prefer a thicker dough. This dough can be rolled quite thin without breaking. Be sure to let the dough rest for at least 30 minutes before rolling it, to allow the gluten time to relax.

2⅓	cups whole wheat flour	4 eggs
		1 tablespoon olive oil

Place 2 cups flour, the eggs, and the oil in a food processor. Process until the dough forms a ball. Add the remaining flour, 1 tablespoon at a time, and process the dough for about 30 seconds, or until it is smooth. Lightly flour the dough, wrap it in plastic wrap, and let it rest in the refrigerator for 30 minutes.

Set up the pasta machine and place the rollers at the thickest setting. Divide the dough into 4 portions, and cover with a towel. Take 1 portion of the dough, lightly flour it, and put it through the rollers. Flour it lightly again, fold into thirds, and put it through the rollers a second time. Repeat the folding and rolling at least 10 more times, or until the dough is soft and smooth.

Place the rollers on the next thinnest setting. If necessary, flour the dough lightly, but do not fold it. Put the dough through the machine. Continue rolling the dough, setting the machine at progressively thinner settings until the dough is as thin as you wish. My machine goes from numbers 1 to 6 (the thinnest setting). I find the dough easiest to handle if I divide it in half at about setting 4 and again at setting 6. Your machine may be different, but the important point is to keep the dough from becoming too long and unwieldy. As you feed the dough through the rollers, stretch it slightly.

Lay the dough out on kitchen towels to dry for a few minutes. (Towels made from flour sacking are ideal.) This step is essential because if you try to cut the dough immediately after rolling, it will stick together and you will have a gummy mess on your hands. Aim for dough that has just slightly dried out and has started to stiffen but is not yet dry. Once the dough has slightly dried out—usually 15 minutes drying time is sufficient—roll it through the cutting blades at the setting you prefer. At this point it can be used as is, frozen, or dried for later use by drying it on a pasta rack or draping it over a broom handle suspended between 2 chairs.

Continue rolling the remaining dough while the first batch is drying. Alternate rolling and cutting the dough until it is used up.

When the pasta is completely dry, store it in a shoe box or tin on the pantry shelf, where it will keep almost indefinitely. The pasta also freezes well and will keep frozen for up to 3 months. See the note for freezing directions.

Makes about 1⅓ pounds

Note

To Freeze Fresh Pasta: Prepare and roll the pasta as in the recipe directions. However, after you roll it through the thinnest setting of a pasta machine, sprinkle it with cornstarch rather than wheat flour.

Then cut the pasta and lay it in a single layer on waxed paper. Fold to a manageable length, keeping waxed paper in between the layers of pasta. Place in freezer bags, push out as much air as possible, and freeze.

To cook, thaw the pasta briefly on a counter until it is flexible, about 10 minutes. If unfolded while still stiff, it will break. Unfold, then drop into boiling water. Stir once and cook at a moderate boil until the pasta is tender, about 4 minutes. (Fresh pasta cooks much more quickly than dried pasta.)

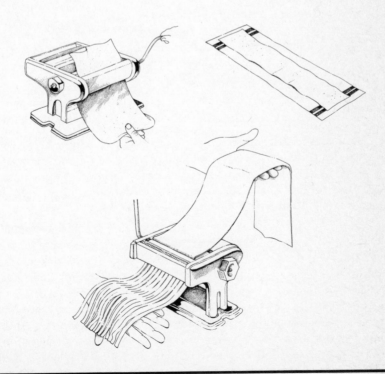

Red Pepper Pasta

Specialty pasta shops sell red pepper pasta at hefty prices for a good reason: red pepper purée takes a while to make. I prefer to serve this pasta plain, with just a touch of butter to highlight the pepper flavor, but it's also nice tossed with matchstick pieces of zucchini in a pesto sauce.

3	large sweet red peppers (about ¾ pound)	2½	cups whole wheat flour
2	eggs	1	tablespoon olive oil

Broil the peppers, turning them frequently until they are blackened all over, then remove from the oven. Place the peppers in a paper bag for 10 minutes. Peel, seed, and drain the peppers. You should end up with ¼ pound pulp.

Purée the peppers in a food processor. Add the eggs, 2 cups flour, and the oil. Process until the dough forms a ball. Add the remaining flour, 1 tablespoon at a time, and process the dough until it is smooth. It will be softer than a regular pasta dough. Wrap the dough in plastic wrap, and let rest in the refrigerator for at least 1 hour.

Roll out and cut the dough (see page 162 for directions). As this dough has a softer, wetter texture than regular pasta dough, you should lightly flour it 3 or 4 times while rolling it out.

Dry the pasta, then store in a covered tin in the pantry. Or sprinkle it with cornmeal so it doesn't stick together and freeze it (see page 163 for directions). The pasta will keep for several months either dried or frozen.

Makes about 1⅓ pounds

Spinach Pasta

The beautiful true green color of this pasta is achieved by using blanched fresh spinach. (Of all the methods of cooking spinach, blanching best preserves the color.) Blanch the stemmed spinach leaves in a pot of boiling water, immediately run them under cold water, and squeeze the spinach dry before chopping and measuring it. Use the pasta as you would any spinach pasta—with Parmesan cheese, sliced mushrooms, and cream; cut into wide strips for lasagne; or cut into fettuccine widths for a cold pasta salad with spring vegetables and seafood.

½	cup tightly packed spinach (about ½ pound before stemming and trimming), blanched	2	eggs
		1	egg yolk
		2	tablespoons olive oil
		2	cups whole wheat flour

Place the spinach in a food processor, and process it until minced. Add the whole eggs and process until the spinach is puréed. Add the egg yolk, oil, and flour, and process until the dough clumps together. This is a heavy dough, which may be hard for the machine to knead, so if the processor seems to be overworking, take the dough out and knead it a few times by hand until it forms a ball. Dust the dough with flour, wrap it in plastic wrap, and place it in the refrigerator for 1 hour.

Roll out and cut the dough (see page 162 for directions). After the initial flouring of the dough, you should not have to add any additional flour, because the dough is exceptionally easy to roll out.

Dry the pasta and store it in a covered tin or box in the pantry, or sprinkle it with cornmeal and freeze it (see page 163 for directions). The pasta will keep either way for several months.

Makes 1¼ pounds

Basil Pasta

When we exchanged houses one summer in Courmayer, Italy, I discovered a basil pasta at one of the pasta shops. This whole wheat version, flecked with basil, has a subtle flavor that's delicious with a fettuccine Alfredo sauce of cream and Parmesan cheese or in a lasagne made with sausage, tomato sauce, and Parmesan and ricotta cheeses.

1 cup packed basil leaves without stems	2½ cups whole wheat flour
4 eggs	1 tablespoon olive oil

Purée the basil in a food processor. Add the eggs and process just for 1 second to combine. Pour in 2¼ cups flour and the oil. Process until the dough forms a ball. Add the remaining flour, 1 tablespoon at a time, and process the dough for about 30 seconds, or until it is smooth. Lightly flour the dough, wrap it in plastic wrap, and let rest in the refrigerator for at least 30 minutes.

Roll out and cut the dough (see page 162 for directions).

Dry the pasta completely before storing in a covered tin in the pantry, or freeze it (see page 163 for directions). The pasta will keep for several months in either the freezer or the pantry.

Makes about 1⅓ pounds

Variations
• Sweet Marjoram, Parsley, or Lovage Pasta: Substitute 1 cup sweet marjoram or parsley leaves for the basil, but substitute only ¾ cup lovage leaves.

Carrot Onion Pasta

This flavorful pasta is a good choice to accompany a pot roast or pork casserole or to serve alone. The carrots add color and a hint of sweetness, while the onion juice contributes a more complex taste. Because you'll be working with a moister pasta dough than most, it's important to dust it with flour several times as you roll it out. I make the onion juice by squeezing an onion on a juicer, which gives me the onion flavor without the fiber.

⅔	cup cooked sliced carrots (about 2 medium-size), cooled	2 to 3	dashes hot pepper sauce
3	eggs	1	tablespoon olive oil
1	tablespoon onion juice	2¼	cups whole wheat flour

Purée the carrots in a food processor until minced, then add the eggs and process until puréed. Add the onion juice, hot pepper sauce, and oil, and combine with on and off bursts of the processor.

Add 2 cups flour and process until the dough forms a ball. Add the remaining flour, 1 tablespoon at a time, and process the dough until it is smooth. The dough will be softer and wetter than a regular pasta dough. Do not add more flour. Dust the dough with flour, wrap in plastic wrap, and let it rest in the refrigerator for about 1 hour.

Roll out and cut the dough (see page 162 for directions). As this dough has a softer, wetter texture than regular pasta dough, you will need to lightly flour it 4 or 5 times while rolling it out. I dust it with flour at the beginning, add almost no flour until I get to settings 4 through 6 on the pasta machine, and then I very lightly dust it for each setting.

After the pasta is rolled, let it dry for about 4 to 5 minutes before cutting it.

Dry the pasta and store it in a covered tin or shoe box in the pantry, or freeze it (see page 163 for directions). The pasta will keep for several months.

Makes about 1½ pounds

Variation
• Omit the onion juice and use the pasta as a base for noodle puddings.

Egg Noodles

Years ago a woman in one of my cooking classes asked me to teach her an easy way to make pasta by hand. I experimented with several traditional pasta recipes—all of which required a lot of muscle power to roll out correctly—and finally settled upon a dough with extra egg yolks to guarantee a tender texture. These noodles follow the same principle. The yolks give the pasta a beautiful golden tint and a rich flavor. If you have never prepared homemade pasta, start with this recipe because it's exceptionally easy to handle.

2¼ cups whole wheat flour
3 eggs

3 egg yolks
1 tablespoon olive oil

Place 2 cups flour, the eggs, egg yolks, and oil in a food processor. Process the mixture until it forms a ball. Add the remaining flour, 1 tablespoon at a time, only as long as the dough ball easily absorbs the flour. How much flour the dough absorbs really depends upon the amount of bran in the flour: I've made these noodles with 2 cups flour plus 1 tablespoon—and also with 2¼ cups flour. It's better to have the dough a little wet than too dry, because you can always add more flour. If necessary, remove the dough from the processor and knead it briefly. Flour the dough lightly, place it in a plastic bag so that it doesn't dry out, and let the dough rest for at least 1 hour in the refrigerator.

Roll out the dough using a hand-cranked pasta machine (see page 162 for directions), or roll it out by hand, then cut it into wide noodles. One way to tell if you are rolling the dough out evenly is to compare the color in the center of the pasta with the edges. If the center has a more intense color, the dough is thicker there and you should stretch the dough until it has a uniform thickness and color.

To cut the dough by hand, start with dough that is pliable but has slightly dried out. Loosely fold it into a flat roll about 3 inches wide, then with a sharp knife cut it into ½-inch slices. Don't saw at the dough but press down evenly, then unroll the noodles and place them on kitchen towels to dry out completely.

Store the noodles in a covered tin or a shoe box on the pantry shelf. Or wrap and freeze them fresh (see page 163 for directions). The noodles will keep for several months in either the pantry or the freezer.

Makes about 1¼ pounds

Banana Prune Tea Bread

This bread should appeal to people who find most banana breads too cloying and sweet. It's delicious served with cream cheese or sweet (unsalted) fresh butter.

2	large bananas	⅓	cup butter
2	eggs	½	cup honey
1	teaspoon ground cinnamon	1¾	cups whole wheat or rye flour
¼	teaspoon ground cardamom	1¼	cups rolled oats
½	teaspoon ground nutmeg	2	teaspoons baking soda
1	teaspoon vanilla extract	½	cup chopped walnuts
½	cup milk	½	cup finely chopped dried prunes

Preheat the oven to 350°F. Butter a 8¼ × 4½-inch loaf pan.

In a food processor or blender purée the bananas, add the eggs, and blend thoroughly. Add the cinnamon, cardamom, nutmeg, and vanilla. Combine with the milk.

In a mixing bowl cream the butter, add the honey, and beat together until combined. Stir in the banana mixture.

Mix together the flour, rolled oats, and baking soda. Stir the dry mixture into the wet ingredients, but do not overmix or the bread will be tough. Mix in the walnuts and prunes.

Spoon the mixture into the loaf pan. Bake for 45 minutes, cover, and return it to the oven for 15 minutes more, or until a knife inserted in the center comes out clean.

Cool in the pan for 2 minutes, then remove from the pan and place on a rack; completely cool before serving.

Wrap in foil and store at room temperature or in a bread box. Refrigerate the bread during hot weather. The bread will stay fresh for up to 5 days at room temperature and for up to 3 weeks in the refrigerator. You can also freeze it for up to 3 months.

Makes 1 loaf

Cracked Wheat
Yogurt Bread

This filling bread makes delicious sandwiches or breakfast toast.

1	cup cracked wheat	2	tablespoons honey
2½	cups water	1	cup yogurt
2	teaspoons dry yeast	2	tablespoons corn oil
1	cup cornmeal	¼	cup butter, softened
3 to 4	cups whole wheat flour		

Place the cracked wheat in a mixing bowl, add 1½ cups water, and let stand for at least 1½ hours or up to 24 hours.

Dissolve the yeast in the remaining water. Mix together the cornmeal and 3 cups flour. Add the yeast mixture, honey, yogurt, oil, and butter.

Knead for 10 minutes, or until the surface of the dough has become satiny. You may need to add up to 1 cup more flour.

Place the dough in a buttered bowl, turn the dough so the buttered side is up, and cover with a kitchen towel. Let the dough double in bulk (about 1 hour). Punch it down. (At this point you may refrigerate it overnight if you wish.)

Squeeze the cracked wheat dry and knead it into the dough. Let the dough rise until doubled in bulk. Punch it down, form into 2 loaves, and place in 2 buttered 8 × 4-inch loaf pans. Let the dough rise again. It will not quite double in bulk.

Preheat the oven to 425°F.

Bake the loaves for 30 minutes. Remove the loaves from the pans, and cool on a rack before slicing.

If the bread is wrapped in plastic bags or foil and stored in the refrigerator or a bread box, it should keep in good condition for at least 4 days. You can freeze the bread for up to 3 months.

Makes 2 loaves

Walnut Spiral Bread

This middle European classic bread is a fine choice for an afternoon tea.

Dough

½	cup milk	¼	cup warm water
2	tablespoons honey	2	egg yolks
½	cup butter	2¾ to 3	cups whole wheat flour
2	teaspoons dry yeast		

Filling

½	cup honey	½	teaspoon grated lemon zest
½	cup heavy cream		
3	cups coarsely ground walnuts	1	teaspoon vanilla extract
¼	cup chopped dried prunes		

½ to 1   teaspoon butter

Make the Dough

In a quart saucepan heat the milk, stir in the honey and butter, and continue stirring until the butter is melted. Cool the milk until just warm.

Soften the yeast in the water, then add it to the milk mixture along with the egg yolks. Combine the liquid ingredients with the flour. Knead the dough on a lightly floured counter for about 10 minutes, or until smooth. You may need to add additional flour, but do it little by little because this should stay a rich dough with a slightly soft texture. Form the dough into a 6-inch square, wrap it in plastic wrap or foil, and store it in the refrigerator for at least 2 hours or overnight.

Let the dough come to room temperature while you make the filling.

Make the Filling

In a heavy saucepan boil the honey and cream together for 2 to 3 minutes, or until they are combined and slightly reduced. Add the walnuts, prunes, and lemon zest, and cook, stirring constantly, for another 2 to 3 minutes, or until the mixture is thick. Watch closely because the honey burns easily. Add the vanilla and cool the filling.

Assemble the Bread

Roll out the dough on a lightly floured surface to a 14 × 18-inch rectangle. Lightly butter the dough to within 1 inch of the borders, then spread the filling over the buttered part of the dough. Moisten the borders with water. Roll up the dough, starting with the long side, then pinch the ends and tuck them under to seal. You will have a long tubelike form.

Place the roll on a buttered baking sheet, and arrange it in a U shape. Cover the dough with a kitchen towel, and let it rise for 30 minutes; the dough will rise only slightly.

Preheat the oven to 350°F.

With a skewer or fruit knife evenly pierce the top of the bread to allow the steam to escape. Bake for 35 to 40 minutes, or until cooked through. Brush the surface with butter the moment the bread emerges from the oven. Cool before serving in thin slices.

Wrap the bread in foil, and store in the refrigerator, where it will stay in good condition for up to 1 week. You can freeze it for up to 3 months.

Makes 1 loaf

Variations
• Substitute pecans or filberts for the walnuts, and dates or raisins for the prunes.

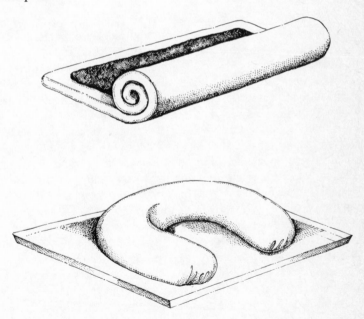

Profile

Ingrid Lysgaard Motsis

Ingrid Lysgaard Motsis is one of the most talented bread and pastry chefs in Boston. She not only makes light and flaky croissants, delicious breads and coffee cakes, and irresistible Danish pastries, but she also understands the chemistry involved in baking breads and has developed several foolproof, easy recipes to use in her teaching demonstrations.

Ingrid was born and raised in the small town of Holstebrö, part of the Danish province of Jutland, about 1 hour from the North Sea. Her father was a professional baker who owned one of the bakery shops in town. Ingrid often helped out in the shop, washing up after her father and his assistants. "I was always watching how my father worked, but I never realized how much I learned from him until later in life," Ingrid told me.

She earned her master's degree in education, then came to Boston in 1965, planning to teach. Instead, she ended up training as a chef and soon was giving baking demonstrations. Now she is a baking chef–instructor at one of the local junior colleges.

Because Ingrid has years of experience teaching people how to make breads and pastries, I asked her to talk with me about some of the most common mistakes inexperienced bakers make. In the process she also passed on some tips about baking breads without white flour.

People who are used to baking with white flour have to become familiar with different textures when they start baking with whole grains. Ingrid says the most frequent mistake they make is adding too much flour in an attempt to get a dough that is as dry as normal white flour dough. "The whole grain dough should be soft enough to work. Whole wheat is somewhat stickier than white flour, and when you start working with rye flour, it's very, very sticky," Ingrid pointed out.

"I'm always looking for a sticky dough . . . sticky is fine; it's when you have a wet dough that you have to add flour. The more you work your dough, the more the liquid gets absorbed. You should be careful to work the dough sufficiently before you decide to add more flour," she explained.

Although people sometimes think a whole wheat dough takes longer to knead, Ingrid said that's not true. "You don't have to work it any longer than a white flour dough. It just seems longer because it's a messier process. The dough will loosen up, but the texture will always be different. It will never be as elastic as a white flour bread dough; it will feel heavier, look heavier, and will rise more slowly."

Ingrid also thinks that whole grain breads should not be allowed to rise as high as white flour breads. "A whole wheat dough would come up higher than a rye dough because it has gluten in it, but either way you would not let the bread rise until doubled in bulk unless you have a very rich dough with lots of eggs, honey, and butter," she said. Ingrid usually lets her breads rise to a little less than double in bulk.

I asked Ingrid about typical bread-baking mistakes. She said the first problem is getting the water the wrong temperature for proofing the yeast. She recommends lukewarm water, at a temperature of 100 to 110°F, and she suggests testing for lukewarm by running the water against the inside of your wrist, similar to testing the milk in a baby's bottle. "If the water is too cool, it takes forever to get the dough going, and if it's too hot, it will actually kill off the yeast," Ingrid pointed out.

"Most people also don't know how to knead. First they put too much flour in the dough. Then they just press down on the dough or push it out, rather than kneading it. You have to push down and out with a smooth motion so the dough moves on the surface. This develops the gluten in the flour. Beginners often hold the dough in place with one hand and push out with the other, which breaks the gluten strands instead of stretching them, and the texture is affected.

"Next, they don't allow enough time for the dough to rise, particularly with rye bread, which takes longer to rise because it lacks gluten."

When a loaf of bread has a crust separated from the top, this usually means the bread has overrisen. Although the bread probably tastes all right, the texture is different.

Ingrid said she was once a judge at a baking contest and realized that many of the contestants were baking their breads at the wrong temperatures. "If the temperature is too low, it dries out the bread, and it takes a long time to get the color it should have. If the temperature is too high, the crust is formed before the bread has risen to its maximum in the oven, and you run the risk of a doughy texture," she pointed out.

I asked Ingrid how you could tell whether a bread recipe called for the correct baking temperature. She told me that a "lean" dough, such as a flour and water dough for French or Italian bread, should be baked at a high temperature such as 400 or 450°F, while a "rich" dough, with eggs and butter, should be baked at a lower temperature. The richer and heavier the dough, the lower the temperature, is Ingrid's rule of thumb. "I bake most breads at around 375°F. One exception might be a banana bread that should bake for a long time at 325°F."

It's also important to know your oven and be able to tell when the temperature needs turning down. Uusually if the bread takes on color in the first 10 minutes, the oven is too hot. "Often I turn the oven down 25° later on in the baking, after the bread has risen to its maximum. This is called 'oven spring'—the point after the yeast is killed and the gasses are released. I don't recommend turning down your oven until that point," Ingrid advised.

Ingrid is amazed at the number of people who cut bread with a regular knife. "People hack away at their bread with a little knife, and it ruins the texture and presses the dough together. Let the bread sit for at least ½ hour before cutting into it with a serrated bread knife. The bread will still be warm, but you won't ruin the texture," she explained.

Many of Ingrid's recipes call for a "starter" sponge. Ingrid thinks this method gives the dough a lighter texture and gives the yeast a chance to work and be fully developed before it goes into the dough. "In the old days they used a starter to make sure the yeast was good, but that's not why I use it. I use it for lightness," she said.

Another hallmark of Ingrid's recipes is that often the dough "ripens" in the refrigerator before being baked. This technique, which develops a more complex flavor in baking goods, is especially useful for salt-free breads. She also thinks the ripening period makes the pastries lighter in texture. It's important, however, to occasionally push down on the dough while it's ripening, to retard the growth of the yeast. Ingrid also likes to freeze Danish pastry and croissant doughs because she thinks freezing makes the pastries flakier.

Ingrid doesn't knead the dough when she makes croissants or Danish pastries. This was a new technique for me: I have made Danish pastry for 20 years, have eaten my fill of pastries in Denmark, and once made pastry from scratch for 450 people. Although the recipe I use is delicious, you have to be an experienced baker for it to turn out well. Last year Ingrid invited me to one of her classes, and I decided her method was far superior to the one I used.

She starts with a sponge, which she then incorporates into the dough. Then, instead of kneading the dough, she literally throws, or "crashes," it onto the counter. "If you knead the dough, you make it too tough, and it will be harder to roll in the butter. When the products are baked, there will be a tendency for the butter to ooze out if the gluten strands are too developed," she explained.

Whatever the reason, crashing the dough makes the dough exceptionally easy to handle, as you'll find out by making Ingrid's Whole Wheat Danish Pastry and Whole Wheat Croissants—certainly the least bothersome pastry recipes I've ever tried. You'll find the recipes in this chapter, along with other breads Ingrid developed especially for use with whole grains.

Danish Rye Bread

Danish country bread is usually made of rye, a major crop of Denmark. Ingrid Lysgaard Motsis's recipe makes wonderful Danish open-faced sandwiches. Ingrid suggests spreading the bread with a thick coating of butter, then topping it with herring or mackerel in tomato sauce, hard-cooked eggs with tomato, pâté garnished with fried onions . . . or whatever you wish. Ingrid says it's important to bake the bread in pans of the size she suggests. You can sometimes find pans of this size sold for making fruitcakes.

3	tablespoons dry yeast	2 to 2½	cups whole wheat flour
½	cup warm water	¼	cup bran flakes (unprocessed bran)
1½	cups warm buttermilk		
¼	cup butter, softened		
2	cups rye flour		

Dissolve the yeast in the water in a large bowl. Add the buttermilk, butter, and rye flour. Stir in 2 cups whole wheat flour. Gradually add the remaining whole wheat flour if necessary to make a soft dough. The dough should be soft enough to stir with a wooden spoon; do not add more flour than the recipe calls for.

Briskly stir the dough with a spoon for 2 minutes. Cover the bowl with a kitchen towel, and let the dough rise for 6 hours.

Stir down the dough and knead it with a wooden spoon for 30 seconds. The dough will be very sticky.

Divide the dough in half, and spoon it into 2 small, buttered loaf pans, about 6 × 3 × 3 inches. Sprinkle very lightly with the bran flakes, and press down to flatten the tops. Cover the pans and let the dough rise for about 1½ hours.

Preheat the oven to 350°F.

Bake the loaves for 50 to 60 minutes. The top may crack on the loaves while they are baking.

The bread should be served thinly sliced, which is easier to do after 1 or 2 days.

If the bread is wrapped and stored in a bread box, it should last for up to 2 weeks, developing flavor as it ages. Or freeze it for up to 3 months.

Makes 2 loaves

Whole Wheat Croissants

One of Ingrid Lysgaard Motsis's most popular lessons in her cooking classes is croissant making. Ingrid developed this version especially for this book.

Starter

½	cup whole wheat flour	2 to 3	tablespoons warm water
1	tablespoon dry yeast	2	tablespoons honey

Dough

1½	cups whole wheat flour	⅜	cup cold water
¼	cup milk	1	cup butter cornstarch

Make the Starter

Mix together the flour, yeast, water, and honey. You should have a soft ball. Cut a cross in the top of the ball to make the surface area larger. Immerse the ball in a deep bowl of warm water (about 100 to 110°F), and let it rise to the top of the water. This will take less than 15 minutes.

Make the Dough

Place the flour in a bowl or on the counter. Add the starter, along with the milk and ¼ cup cold water. Mix together lightly and add the remaining water if necessary to make the dough soft enough to crash against the counter (see page 174). Crash it on the counter, then pick up the ball of dough and crash again 12 to 15 times to mix the dough well. Do not knead it; kneading would make the dough tough. Then rest the dough on the counter for 10 minutes.

Meanwhile, work the butter with a rolling pin until it has the same consistency as the dough. Form it into a square, and coat it on all sides with cornstarch. Pat the dough into an 8-inch square. Place the butter in the middle and enclose it. Let the dough rest for 5 minutes.

Fold the dough in turns. With long, even strokes roll the dough out into a rectangle of about 4 × 9 inches and ⅓-inch thick. Fold the dough in thirds as if you were folding a letter. Give the dough a ¼ turn, and roll the dough out again, along the fold, into a rectangle the same size as before. Fold it again in thirds. You have now made 2 turns. Wrap the dough and let it rest in the refrigerator for 45 minutes.

Repeat the 2 turns twice, resting the dough in the refrigerator between rolling, so that the dough receives 6 turns. Wrap the dough in plastic wrap, and let it ripen in the refrigerator for 2 to 3 days before shaping the croissants. At least once a day unwrap the dough and lightly press down to retard the action of the yeast, then rewrap the dough and return to the refrigerator.

Assemble the Croissants

To shape the dough, halve it lengthwise. Put ½ the dough in the refrigerator while you shape the rest.

Roll the dough out into a long rectangle of 16 × 5 inches. Cut the dough into 6 triangles. Starting from the wide end, roll them up tightly and form them into crescent shapes. Repeat the shaping with the remaining dough.

Place the croissants seam-side down on a lightly buttered baking sheet. Let them rise until doubled in bulk.

Preheat the oven to 375°F.

Bake the croissants until done, 15 to 18 minutes.

You can freeze the croissants after shaping, defrost them in the refrigerator overnight, then let them sit at room temperature until they are slightly puffy before baking. Then wrap in foil and bake in a preheated 350°F oven for 15 to 20 minutes.

Makes 12 croissants

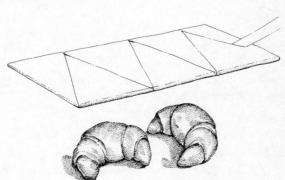

Whole Wheat Danish Pastry

This pastry is adapted from a delicious recipe Ingrid Lysgaard Motsis teaches in her baking classes. It is easiest to work the dough with a wooden pastry scraper. The fillings *Remonce* and Almond Paste, will keep for several weeks in the refrigerator, so make up full recipes even though you probably won't use them up immediately.

Starter

2	tablespoons dry yeast	2	cups whole wheat flour
½	cup warm water	2	tablespoons honey

Dough

3	cups whole wheat flour	3	eggs
¼	cup cornstarch	½	cup milk, at room temperature
1	teaspoon grated orange zest	1	pound butter
1	teaspoon ground cardamom		

Make the Starter

Dissolve the yeast in the water, then add the flour and honey. Don't work it too much. Ingrid scrapes it together with a wooden pastry scraper. The mixture should stick together but not be too wet. Cut a cross in the top, and immerse the starter in 110°F water for about 10 minutes. The starter will rise to the top of the water when it is ready.

Make the Dough

Meanwhile, prepare the dough. Mix together the flour, cornstarch, orange zest, and cardamom. Place the dry ingredients in a mound on the counter, and make a well in the center. Break in the eggs and pour in the milk. Cut in the eggs and milk with a wooden pastry scraper.

When the starter comes to the top of the water, place it on top of the dough, and cut the two together until completely incorporated. The dough will still be very moist. Crash the dough a few times on the counter (see page 174), and cover with plastic wrap so it doesn't dry out. Do not knead the dough.

Lightly flour the butter, then knead it until it has the same consistency as the dough. Wrap the dough around the butter, and let rest for 5 minutes.

Flour the counter and roll out the dough into a 20 × 17 × ⅓-inch rectangle. Do not press down on the dough; just place the rolling pin in the middle of the dough and gently roll it out. Fold the rectangle in thirds as if you were folding a letter. (See Classic Puff Pastry, page 188, for illustrations of folding and rolling.) Give it a quarter turn and roll it out again along the fold. Fold again in thirds. Wrap the dough and let rest, refrigerated, for no more than 45 minutes.

Repeat the turns, wrap the dough, and let it rest for 45 minutes.

Finally, repeat the turns again. Lightly flour the dough, wrap it in foil, and store it in the crisper of the refrigerator before shaping. For best flavor leave the finished dough tightly wrapped in the refrigerator for 3 to 4 days. Or freeze the dough (Ingrid thinks freezing improves the flavor).

Assemble the Pastry

Divide the dough into quarters, and shape only a quarter at a time.

Roll out the dough to about ⅛ inch thick. Each ¼ batch will yield 6 to 9 pastries. As you are shaping the pastries, brush off any excess flour with a pastry brush.

Once you have the basic pastry dough, there are any number of variations you can make. I will describe 2 shapings. (The best description I have seen for shaping pastries is in *The Cooking of Scandinavia*, one of the titles in the Time-Life Foods of the World series. The book gives step-by-step instructions for shaping 5 pastries.)

You can fill the pastries with sieved apricot, peach, or raspberry preserves. Ingrid uses pastry cream or *Remonce* and an Almond Paste, recipes for which follow.

Bow Ties: Use either Almond Paste or apricot preserves with this recipe. To prepare the apricot preserves, rub ½ cup through a sieve, then cook in an enameled saucepan until the preserves have reduced to about ⅜ cup. Set aside to cool. (If I'm busy, I don't bother with this step but the preserves are a little lumpy.)

Roll the ¼ of the dough into a 10 × 18-inch rectangle. Trim any ragged edges. Spread the apricot preserves or Almond Paste over ½ the dough lengthwise. Fold over the rest of the dough to form a long envelope. Press down lightly on the dough to press in the filling.

Preheat the oven to 400°F. Butter a baking sheet.

Cut through the dough at 2-inch intervals, making 9 pastries 2 × 5 inches in size. Make a 3-inch slit in the center of each pastry. Curve one end of the rectangle through the slit, and straighten it out to make a bow-tie shape.

Set the pastries on the baking sheet, and bake them for 10 minutes. Reduce the heat to 350°F, and bake for another 15 minutes. Cool on a rack before serving.

Continue this step until all the dough is formed. Do not let the pastries rise before you bake them.

Makes 24 to 36 pastries

Cock's Combs: Flour the counter and roll out ¼ of the dough to form a 10 × 15-inch rectangle. Trim the ragged edges. Spread a thin layer of *Remonce* along 1 long side of the dough. Then spread the other side with a thin layer of the Almond Paste. Fold the sides together as if you were closing a book. Press down lightly. Seal the edges with your fingers, and cut the dough into 2½-inch-wide strips.

Preheat the oven to 400°F. Butter a baking sheet.

Place the strips so that their long edges are parallel to the counter edge. Cut 3 slits on each pastry, perpendicular to the counter edge, ¾ of the way through. Bend the pastries slightly to form crescents. Put the pastries on the baking sheet, and bake for 10 minutes. Reduce the heat to 350°F, and bake for another 10 minutes. Remove from the oven, and let the pastries cool before serving.

Continue this step until all the dough is formed. Do not let the pastries rise before you bake them.

Makes 24 to 36 pastries

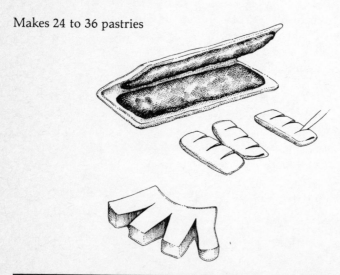

Remonce

½ cup butter, softened   1 teaspoon vanilla
¼ cup honey   extract

Cream the butter and honey together until they are light and fluffy. It may take 15 minutes. Add the vanilla and cream the mixture for another moment to incorporate it.

Store the *remonce* in the refrigerator in a covered jar, and bring to room temperature before using. The *remonce* will keep for several weeks.

Makes about ½ cup

Almond Paste

6   ounces blanched   1   teaspoon almond
     almonds   extract
¼ cup honey   2 to 2½ egg whites

In a food processor or blender chop the almonds until pulverized. Place in a small bowl, and mix in the honey, almond extract, and enough egg whites to make the mixture spreadable.

Store in a covered container in the refrigerator, where the paste will stay in good condition for up to 1 month.

Makes about 1½ cups

Whole Wheat Dinner Rolls

Letting the dough ripen in the refrigerator adds extra flavor to these rolls developed by Ingrid Lysgaard Motsis and helps compensate for the lack of salt. The dough also makes an excellent bread loaf (see the variation).

Starter

½	cup whole wheat flour	3 to 4	tablespoons warm water
1	tablespoon dry yeast	2	tablespoons honey

Dough

2	cups whole wheat flour	½	cup butter, softened
3	large eggs	½	teaspoon ground cardamom
¼	cup cold water		

Make the Starter

Mix together the flour, yeast, water, and honey until the mixture forms a soft ball. With a knife, cut a cross in the top, and immerse the dough in a small, deep bowl of warm water that is between 110 and 120°F. Let the ball rise to the top of the water. This should take about 15 minutes.

Make the Dough

Just before the starter is done, start making the dough. Place the flour in a bowl or on the counter. Lightly beat the eggs with the water, and add them to the flour along with the butter and the cardamom. Gently mix the ingredients together. Add the risen starter. Instead of standard kneading, this dough is developed by literally crashing it against the counter top until it is smooth and elastic (see page 174). Do not add additional flour even if the dough is sticky.

Place the dough in a buttered bowl, and let it rise in a warm, draft-free place until it is almost doubled in bulk, about 1½ hours. Knead it for 6 to 7 minutes, and then let it rise again until almost doubled (30 to 50 minutes).

Knead the dough for about 30 seconds, just to remove the air bubbles. Place the dough in a buttered bowl, cover it carefully with plastic wrap, and place it in the refrigerator for at least 48 hours to develop flavor. You will need to remove the plastic wrap and press down on the dough at least twice to slow down the action of the yeast and prevent the dough from overrising.

If you wish, you can shape and bake the rolls before letting the dough ripen in the refrigerator, but the flavor will not be as complex.

Assemble the Rolls

Divide the dough into 18 pieces, and shape into rolls. Place the rolls on a buttered baking sheet, and let them rise until almost doubled in bulk.

As the dough is cold, it may take 1 to 2 hours for the rolls to rise, depending upon the temperature of the kitchen. The rolls do not rise much while baking, so make sure they have risen properly.

Preheat the oven to 350°F.

Bake the rolls for 20 to 25 minutes, or until done. The rolls will be golden brown and the outside edge will have pulled away from the baking sheet.

The rolls will stay in good condition for up to 5 days if wrapped and stored in a bread box or at room temperature. You can also freeze the dough before shaping the rolls, or freeze the baked rolls for up to 3 months.

Makes 18 rolls

Variation
• A Loaf of Bread: Shape the bread and bake in a preheated 375°F oven for 40 to 45 minutes.

Kugelhopf

Ingrid Lysgaard Motsis prepares this rich Austrian coffee cake in her pastry-making classes.

Sponge

1	tablespoon dry yeast	3	cups whole wheat flour
½	cup warm milk (about 110°F)		

Batter

½	cup warm water	1½	cups golden raisins
½	cup honey		boiling water
4	eggs, beaten	¼	cup cornstarch
½	cup butter, softened grated zest of 2 lemons (1¼ teaspoons)	½	cup blanched whole almonds

Make the Sponge

Dissolve the yeast in the warm milk in a large bowl. Stir in ½ cup flour and mix well. Sprinkle the remaining flour over the top. Cover the bowl and let the sponge sit until the yeast bubbles through the flour on top. This will take about 45 minutes.

Make the Batter

Stir the sponge and beat it vigorously with a wooden spoon. Gradually add the warm water, honey, eggs, ⅜ cup butter, and the lemon zest. Beat until a smooth batter forms. Cover the bowl and let the batter rise to 1½ times its original size.

Meanwhile, cover the raisins with the boiling water to plump them. Let the raisins sit for a few minutes, then drain them and pat dry with a kitchen towel. Toss the raisins with the cornstarch, and gently stir them into the risen batter.

Using the remaining butter, generously grease a 2-quart kugelhopf pan (or a tube pan). Arrange the almonds on the bottom and sides in an attractive pattern. Without disturbing the almonds, spoon the batter into the pan. Cover the pan and let the batter rise until almost doubled in bulk.

Preheat the oven to 350°F.

Bake the kugelhopf for 45 to 50 minutes. Test it with a skewer to see if it is cooked through. Let the kugelhopf sit in the pan for 5 minutes before unmolding onto a rack.

The kugelhopf will keep moist and in good condition for up to 1 week if wrapped and stored at room temperature. It may also be frozen for up to 3 months.

Makes 1 cake ⌐⌐

Ingrid Lysgaard Mathia

Whole Wheat Manicotti Rounds

All that's necessary to make these pasta rounds is an omelet or crêpe pan 4 to 6 inches in diameter. If the manicotti were made with white flour, the liquid would be ½ water, ½ milk—but using only milk tenderizes the whole wheat. Stuff the pasta with Ricotta Filling and top it with Tomato Sauce.

4	eggs	2	tablespoons water
1	cup milk		olive oil
1½	cups whole wheat flour		

Beat together the eggs, milk, and flour. Let the mixture rest for at least 1 hour.

Before cooking, check the pasta mixture and if it is thick, thin with the water. The consistency should be like heavy cream. How dense it becomes depends upon the amount of bran in the flour.

Coat a 4- to 6-inch frying pan with the oil. The size of the pan you use depends upon the desired size of the manicotti. Spoon 2 scant tablespoons of the mixture into the pan, and quickly smooth it out with a spoon. Cook for 30 seconds without browning. Flip over for 1 or 2 seconds. This side will be almost raw. (Sometimes the first piece of pasta sticks and has to be discarded.) If necessary, add more oil to the pan, and continue making the pasta until the dough mixture is gone. As you stack them, place pieces of waxed paper between the pasta rounds.

If you're not using them right away, wrap the pasta pieces in foil, and store in the refrigerator, where the pasta will keep for up to 1 week. Freeze for longer storage, up to 3 months.

You can fill the manicotti with Ricotta Filling, a recipe for which follows.

Makes 14 to 17 manicotti ⌐⌐

Ricotta Filling

The manicotti, above, may be filled with this ricotta cheese mixture and then covered with Tomato Sauce.

3 eggs
2¼ cups ricotta cheese
⅓ cup grated Romano or
    Parmesan cheese

½ cup shredded mozza-
    rella cheese
    Tomato Sauce (see
    page 268)

Preheat the oven to 350°F.
Beat together the eggs and the cheeses.
Use 1½ tablespoons of the filling to stuff each manicotti round. Place the manicotti, seam side down, in rows in a baking pan that has been lightly coated with a little of the tomato sauce. Then cover with tomato sauce. Sprinkle the manicotti with Romano and mozzarella cheeses if you like, and bake for 15 to 20 minutes, or until heated through.

Makes 2½ cups

Whole Wheat Zwieback

My friend Martina David-Ault, who contributed this recipe, calls these hard Swedish crackers "jawbreakers." They're good dunked in milk, and they have the virtue of keeping for weeks.

1 tablespoon dry yeast
½ cup warm water
¾ cup milk
3 tablespoons butter
1 teaspoon aniseed,
    ground

1 teaspoon fennel seeds,
    ground
3 to 4 cups whole wheat
    flour

Dissolve the yeast in the water. Warm the milk and melt the butter, and let cool to just warm. Add to it the yeast mixture, aniseed, fennel seeds, and flour. Work the dough until it loosens from the bowl. Let rise for 40 minutes.
Knead the dough on a floured table for about 7 minutes, then form into small balls, 2 inches in diameter. Place them on a greased baking sheet. Let rise for 30 minutes.
Preheat the oven to 450°F.

Bake for 7 minutes. Cool, and divide each zwieback with 2 forks. Place the zwieback on a buttered baking sheet, cut side up.

Brown the zwieback in a 425°F oven for 7 minutes. Remove from the oven, turn off the heat, and let the oven cool down. When it gets down to 200°F, place the zwieback back in the oven and let them dry out overnight.

Store the zwieback in an airtight, covered tin, where they will keep for up to 2 months.

Makes about 80 zwieback

Easy Puff Pastry

This pastry is amazingly flaky—considering how easy it is to make. The secret is sifting the flour through a fine sieve to remove the bran, which would make the pastry tough. (I save the bran and add it to bran muffins, crumb toppings, or whole wheat bread.) Measure the flour after you sieve out the bran.

Use this pastry to make Alsacian Appetizer Sticks (see page 26), as a casing for a chunky chicken à la king, or as a base for quiches or tartlets. This recipe was adapted from Marlene Sorosky's *Year-Round Holiday Cookbook*.

2 cups sieved whole wheat flour (measure after sieving)	½ cup plus 1 tablespoon sour cream
½ pound cold butter, cut into chunks	1 egg yolk

Place the flour and butter in a food processor. Pulse the machine on and off until the butter is in fine particles. Mix together the sour cream and egg yolk, and pour them over the flour mixture. Pulse the machine on and off just long enough to combine the ingredients. The minute the dough starts to form a ball, turn off the machine and shape the dough into a ball. Divide the dough in half, and flatten to form 2 rounds. Wrap in plastic wrap and refrigerate for 2 hours, or until cold enough to roll.

Regardless of what you decide to make, the dough should be rolled out to about ⅛ inch thick and baked at 400°F.

If the dough is wrapped tightly in plastic, it should stay in good condition in the refrigerator for at least 5 days. Freeze for up to 3 months.

Makes 3 9-inch pastry shells

Classic Puff Pastry

Puff pastry is not difficult to make, but it does require that you be around to do the turns every hour, so prepare the pastry on a day when you're sticking close to home. To make successful puff pastry, you must start with butter and flour mixtures that have the same consistency, and allow ample time for chilling and working the dough. If the dough is too warm as you're rolling the turns, the butter oozes out and the pastry becomes tough. Chilling the dough allows the gluten to relax, which makes it easier to use.

The principle is the same as that for Danish pastry: layers of dough are separated by thin layers of butter. As the pastry bakes, the layers swell—resulting in a light and flaky pastry. Once you know how to make puff pastry, you have the basis for main courses or desserts. You can fill a puff pastry shell with creamed chicken or fish—or use it as a casing for fruit or custard tarts. If you want to be really splashy, you can even surprise your friends with flaky whole wheat napoleons.

This is a rich dough with oodles of butter and cream. Don't substitute water for the cream in the dough—as you would in a puff pastry made with white flour—for the cream tenderizes the whole wheat.

1	pound butter, at cool room temperature	1¼ to 1⅓	cups heavy cream
3¾	cups whole wheat pastry flour	⅓	cup milk

Beat the butter with a mixer until smooth. Add ¼ cup flour and continue beating until it is completely mixed. Spoon the butter mixture onto a piece of waxed paper, and shape it into a square of about 6 × 6 inches. Wrap it up and chill it while you make the flour mixture. If it is a warm day, you may need to chill the butter for up to 1 hour so it will be the same consistency as the flour mixture.

Add the cream and milk to 3¼ cups flour, and mix just long enough so it is incorporated. Do not overmix. The dough should be firm enough to hold together yet soft enough to leave an indentation when pressed with a finger. If the dough is too sticky, work in the remaining flour. Press the dough into a ball, wrap in waxed paper, and chill for 15 minutes. Check the consistency of the butter to make sure it is cold enough to roll out without oozing.

On a lightly floured counter or pastry board, roll the dough into a rectangle of about 8 × 14 inches. Place the butter at one end of the rectangle, and fold the dough over, encasing the butter. Press the edges of the dough together to seal. Chill the dough for at least 30 minutes so the butter and dough are the same temperature.

Lightly flour the counter or pastry board, then roll out the dough into a long rectangle about ⅜ inch thick. Fold it in thirds, and turn the dough a ¼ turn so the open edge faces you. The dough should always have its open end facing you for rolling. Try to use as little extra flour as possible. As I make the turns, I always blow off any excess flour—or brush it away with a pastry brush.

Roll out the dough again and fold it in thirds. Wrap up the dough and chill it for at least 1 hour.

Repeat the chilling and rolling steps twice more. At this point the dough can be stored. Wrap it tightly in plastic wrap, and keep it in the refrigerator, where it will stay in good condition for at least 4 days.

Before you roll out the pastry, preheat the oven to 425°F.

Roll out the pastry to a thickness of ¼ to ½ inch. Shape the pastry, place it on a baking sheet lightly moistened with water, and bake until golden, 8 to 12 minutes.

Makes enough pastry for 3 8-inch tarts or 2 20 × 18-inch rectangles

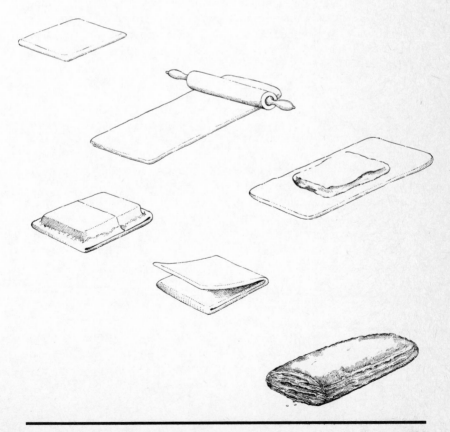

Wonton or Dumpling Wrappers

This egg dough recipe from Nina Simonds also makes Chinese egg noodles and Cantonese spring roll skins. As this is a stiff dough, using a pasta machine guarantees thin wrappers. The wrappers may be placed in plastic and frozen.

1⅓	cups whole wheat flour	1	egg, lightly beaten
		¼	cup cold water

Place the flour in a mixing bowl and add the egg and water. Using a wooden spoon, blend the mixture into a rough dough. Knead the dough for about 5 minutes on a lightly floured surface until smooth and elastic. If the dough is sticky, knead in a few tablespoons of flour. Cover the dough with a cloth or towel, and let it rest for 25 minutes.

Halve the dough. Using a pasta machine or a rolling pin, roll out each half to a paper-thin rectangle (about ¹⁄₁₆ inch thick). Cut out 3-inch squares for the wonton wrappers or 3-inch circles for the dumpling wrappers. Cover the wrappers with a cloth or towel to prevent them from drying out, and use immediately. Or separate them with waxed paper, wrap in plastic wrap, and freeze for up to 3 months. Thaw in the refrigerator before using.

Makes about 30 wrappers

Note
Fillings for Wontons: The wontons may be filled with any of many Chinese mixtures. Nina likes to fill them with different mixtures of chopped shrimp, water chestnut, or pork, seasoned with soy sauce, rice wine, sesame oil, minced scallions, and gingerroot.

Lightly beat an egg with a bit of water, and moisten the edges of the wonton wrappers with it. Center 1 tablespoon of filling on a wrapper, and crimp the wrapper up around the stuffing to make a little bundle. Press to make sure all the edges are sealed. Poach the wontons in a broth, or cook on a rack over steaming water.

Whole Wheat Pie Crust

I like the crunchy texture of a pie crust made with whole wheat flour, but many cooks prefer the softer texture that whole wheat pastry flour gives a crust. It's really a matter of personal taste, so I'll give you both versions. You can make this dough in a food processor, but be sure to process the dough only to the point at which it begins to clump. If you process it any longer, the dough will become tough. Whole wheat flours vary in the amount of bran they contain, so the amount of liquid needed also will vary. Remember that excess flour toughens the dough, so use a light hand when dusting the counter.

2 cups whole wheat flour

¾ cup cold butter, sliced into ½-inch-wide pieces

⅓ cup cold milk or ice water

Place the flour in a food processor, add the butter, and process with on and off bursts until the butter is in small particles. Add the milk or ice water and process until the dough begins to clump. If you need additional milk or water, add it 1 tablespoon at a time. The dough will be soft. Put the dough in a plastic bag, gently pat it into a ball, and refrigerate for at least 1 hour.

Cut the dough in half. Roll out each half on a lightly floured surface until it is the thickness you prefer, and place each half in an 8-inch pie plate. Bake according to the directions in individual recipes.

Makes 2 pie crusts

Variation
• Whole Wheat Pastry Flour Pie Crust: Use 2 cups whole wheat pastry flour, substitute ¼ cup milk for the ⅓ cup milk or ice water, and add 2 to 3 tablespoons sour cream. Proceed as above, adding the sour cream after the milk.

Whole Wheat Crêpes

1	cup cold water	2	cups whole wheat flour
1	cup cold milk	¼	cup plus 1 tablespoon
4	eggs		butter, melted

Whirl together the water, milk, eggs, flour, and butter in an electric blender for 1 minute. (Or use a mixer and strain through a fine sieve.) Refrigerate for at least 2 hours.

Grease a 6-inch frying pan and set over high heat until it almost begins to smoke. Immediately remove it from the heat, and pour a scant ¼ cup batter into the middle of the pan. Quickly tilt the pan in all directions to film the bottom of the pan with a thin layer of batter. (If the crêpe is too thick, cut down on the amount of batter you use.)

Immediately set the pan over high heat, and cook for about 1 minute. The crêpe is ready to be turned when you can shake and jerk it loose from the bottom of the pan: lift an edge to make sure it is cooked.

Turn the crêpe and cook for just a few seconds on the other side. This will be just a spotty brown and will be the side you fill. Flip the crêpe onto a rack, and continue cooking the remaining batter, greasing the pan lightly if necessary.

Cool the crêpes and stack between layers of waxed paper. Wrap in foil. Store in the refrigerator for up to 1 week before using or freeze the crêpes for up to 3 months.

Makes about 26 crêpes

Cornmeal Tortilla Crêpes

These crêpes are an amalgam, with the flavor of tortillas but the texture of crêpes. Their tender texture makes them an excellent choice for enchiladas.

2	eggs	½	cup cornmeal
¾	cup milk	¼	cup whole wheat
2	tablespoons corn oil		flour

Beat together the eggs, milk, oil, cornmeal, and flour until smooth.

Heat a 6-inch frying pan with sloping sides. Oil the pan slightly. Spoon in 3 scant tablespoons batter, immediately swirling the pan so the batter covers the pan bottom. Cook for about 30 seconds, or until that side is set. Turn, and cook for 1 or 2 seconds to set the other side.

Place on a towel. Continue making the tortilla crêpes until all the batter is gone. Add oil to the pan as necessary.

Cool. Stack between waxed paper, then wrap in foil. The tortilla crêpes will keep in good condition for up to 1 week in the refrigerator. Or freeze for up to 3 months.

Makes about 12 crêpes

Flour Tortillas

Traditional flour tortillas are made with lard rather than butter, so the flavor and texture of this version will be different.

2	cups whole wheat flour	¼ cup butter
		½ cup warm water

Place the flour in a large mixing bowl, and cut in the butter until the particles are fine. Gradually add the water, tossing with a fork constantly. Press into a ball and knead until smooth. Oil the surface of the dough, and refrigerate for at least 4 hours.

Bring the dough to room temperature before forming the tortillas. Divide the dough into 10 balls. Keep the dough covered with a damp cloth while you roll out each tortilla. Roll each ball of dough between waxed paper to an 8-inch diameter, adding flour as needed to keep the dough from sticking. Trim any ragged edges. The tortillas will shrink slightly as they are cooked.

Drop each tortilla onto a hot, ungreased fry pan or griddle. Cook until they are flecked with brown but are still white. This will take less than 30 seconds. Turn, and cook on the other side. Continue until all the tortillas are cooked.

Cool the tortillas, wrap, and refrigerate. They will keep in good condition for 1 week in the refrigerator. Freeze for longer storage, up to 6 months.

Makes about 10 tortillas

Sweets

The cookies, cakes, candies, and puddings in this chapter have a common characteristic: unlike most sweets they will stay in good condition for at least 1 week in storage. When I was testing the recipes and converting some old family favorites from white sugar and flour to honey and whole wheat flour, I couldn't help noticing how much longer these sweets lasted when made with honey rather than sugar. My mother's Cranberry Pudding, for example, stayed moist and fresh-tasting for at least twice as long as usual when prepared with honey.

The keeping quality of honey is certainly a bonus for the pantry cook, but it's of prime importance to locate the right kind of honey for baking. As I mentioned in the beginning of this book, I use a raspberry honey from Maine, but other honeys are good for cooking. When we're traveling, I'll usually search for local honeys: orange blossom honey from Florida, basswood honey from North Carolina, and an herb-flavored honey from Carcassonne, France, have found places on my pantry shelf in recent months. About the only honey I never use is buckwheat honey, which has such a strong flavor I find it overpowers any recipe in which it appears.

I hope you try the steamed puddings in this section. Puddings are great pantry foods because they stay moist and keep well for a considerable time. Many of the puddings, such as the Carrot Parsnip Pudding and the Cranberry Pudding, taste better when made with whole wheat flour and honey than when made with white flour and sugar. I suspect that if you convert standard steamed pudding recipes from sugar to honey (using about ½ as much honey as sugar), you will have equal luck.

You might not think of crème caramel as a pantry food, but when you go to the supermarkets in southern France, this custard is a standard packaged item, as is a rich egg custard in northern Spain. If you keep custards tightly wrapped, they will keep in good condition for at least 1 week.

Several of the cookie recipes call for nuts; I use them to reinforce the nutty flavor of whole wheat flour. I'm partial to filberts, but you can usually substitute walnuts for them. I've also varied the flours in the cookies to lighten up the taste of whole wheat flour: oat flour, rice flour, or potato starch are good choices. Rice flour and potato starch make the cookies short.

If you enjoy strudel and can't imagine making a whole wheat version, try Susan Hercek's recipe. I guarantee you'll be pleasantly surprised. Susan has developed a tissue-thin dough that makes a wonderful strudel—and any leftover dough can be frozen for noodles. Susan sometimes works in the Rodale Test Kitchen and is just one of the fine cooks I've met there.

Filbert Orange Cookies

1	egg	1	cup ground filberts
½	cup butter, melted	2	teaspoons minced orange zest
¼	cup honey		
1	teaspoon vanilla extract	1	cup brown rice flour

Beat together the egg, butter, honey, and vanilla. Stir in the filberts, orange zest, and flour.

Preheat the oven to 350°F. Butter baking sheets.

Drop the batter by scant teaspoons onto the baking sheets. Or roll into balls and flatten with the palm of your hand onto the baking sheets. Bake for 12 minutes.

Cool and store in a covered tin. The cookies will keep fresh for at least 1 week.

Makes about 40 cookies

Almond Party Cookies

These bite-size cookies with soft centers are an apt choice for a party dessert with a dish of homemade grapefruit or lemon sherbet.

½ cup butter, softened
¼ cup honey
1 cup ground toasted almonds or combined almonds and filberts

3 tablespoons whole wheat flour
2 tablespoons milk

Mix together the butter and honey. Stir in the nuts and flour. Add the milk.

Preheat the oven to 350°F. Butter and lightly flour baking sheets.

Scoop the batter into rounded ½ teaspoons, and drop onto the baking sheets. Bake for 8 to 10 minutes.

Let the cookies rest for 1 minute before cooling on a rack. Cool completely before storing in a covered tin, where they will soften but keep in good condition for up to 6 days.

Makes about 54 cookies

Gingersnaps

¾ cup butter
½ cup honey
½ cup molasses
1 egg
1 teaspoon vanilla extract
2½ cups whole wheat flour

1 tablespoon ground ginger
1 teaspoon ground cinnamon
2 teaspoons baking soda

Cream the butter, add the honey and molasses, and continue beating until they are combined. Beat in the egg and vanilla.

Mix together the flour, ginger, cinnamon, and baking soda. Add to the butter mixture. The dough will be slightly sticky. Refrigerate the dough for 1 hour before baking.

Preheat the oven to 350°F. Grease cookie sheets.

Form the dough into walnut-size balls. Flatten slightly with the palm of your hand and place on the baking sheets. Bake for 12 to 15 minutes, or until cooked through.

Store in a covered tin, the cookies will keep in good condition for up to 2 weeks.

Makes 48 cookies

Variation
• Press the individual dough balls into slivered almonds, then flatten a bit with the palm of your hand before baking.

Lemon Butter Cookies

The more lemon zest you use, the stronger the lemon flavor will be. The addition of cornmeal may seem a bit bizarre, but it adds texture and cuts the heavy taste of the whole wheat flour. The potato starch makes the cookies crumbly.

1	cup butter, softened	1	cup whole wheat flour
½	cup honey	¾	cup cornmeal
2	egg yolks	½	cup potato starch
1 to 1½	tablespoons finely minced lemon zest	1	teaspoon vanilla extract

Preheat the oven to 350°F.

Cream the butter and honey until light and completely blended. Mix in the egg yolks, then stir in the lemon zest, flour, cornmeal, potato starch, and vanilla.

Drop the cookies by rounded teaspoons onto ungreased baking sheets, and bake for 10 to 12 minutes.

The cookies will keep in good condition for at least 2 weeks if stored in a tin.

Makes about 40 cookies

Variations
• Chill the cookie dough until firm, roll into a long cylinder, and cut into rounds. Or roll it out and stamp out shapes with a cookie cutter.
• Add 1 cup chopped walnuts, pecans, or filberts to the dough.

Maple Syrup Cookies

These cookies are a favorite of Susan Harnett's family.

4	cups whole wheat pastry flour	½	teaspoon ground cloves
2	teaspoons baking powder	1	cup butter
2	teaspoons ground cinnamon	1¼	cups maple syrup
2	teaspoons ground ginger	1	egg, beaten
		1	cup pecan or walnut halves

Preheat the oven to 350°F.

Mix together the flour, baking powder, cinnamon, ginger, and cloves. Cream the butter with the maple syrup and mix in the egg. Stir in the flour mixture.

Place the dough in the refrigerator until chilled. Shape the cookies into 1½-inch balls, and place them 2 inches apart on baking sheets. Press a nut half into each cookie.

Bake until lightly browned, 10 to 15 minutes. They will be a little soft in the center, but if cooked longer, they get too dry and crumbly. To test whether they're done, break open a cookie. It should be just a little moist inside, not dry.

Store the cookies in a covered tin, where they will stay in good condition for at least 1 week.

Makes about 36 cookies

Scandinavian Ginger Cookies

These cookies have a better flavor if they're allowed to sit for 1 or 2 days before they're served.

2	egg yolks	1	teaspoon baking powder
¼	cup honey	2	tablespoons heavy cream
⅔	cup whole wheat flour	3	tablespoons butter, melted
¼	cup potato starch	1	teaspoon vanilla extract
2	tablespoons brown rice flour		
½	teaspoon ground ginger		

Beat together the egg yolks and honey. Mix the whole wheat flour, potato starch, brown rice flour, ginger, and baking powder. Add about ½ the flour mixture to the egg yolks. Add the cream and butter. Stir in the vanilla and the remaining flour mixture. Mix thoroughly.

Oil a baking sheet. Preheat the oven to 350°F.

You can either bake the dough immediately as drop cookies or chill the dough. Roll chilled dough into balls the size of jumbo olives, and place on the baking sheet. Flatten with the tines of a fork. Bake for about 10 minutes, or until cooked through.

Cool on a rack, then store in an airtight tin. The cookies will stay in good condition for at least 1 week.

Makes about 36 cookies

Orange Oatmeal Cookies

2½	cups rolled oats	1	cup butter, melted, or ½ cup melted butter plus ½ cup vegetable oil
⅔	cup chopped walnuts or filberts		
1½	cups whole wheat flour	3	tablespoons molasses
1	teaspoon baking soda	¼	cup orange juice
1	teaspoon ground cinnamon	1	teaspoon vanilla extract
¼	teaspoon ground nutmeg	2 to 3	teaspoons minced orange zest (from about ½ orange)
1	egg, lightly beaten		
½	cup honey		

Preheat the oven to 350°F. Lightly oil a baking sheet.

Process 1 cup rolled oats and ⅓ cup nuts in a blender or food processor. The mixture should be finely ground. Add this mixture to the flour, baking soda, cinnamon, and nutmeg, and mix until thoroughly combined. Stir in the egg, honey, butter and oil (if used), molasses, orange juice, vanilla, and orange zest. When mixed, fold in the remaining rolled oats and nuts.

Drop by rounded teaspoons onto the baking sheet. Bake for 12 to 15 minutes, or until the edges are browned.

These cookies keep moist and fresh-tasting for at least 1 week if stored in a covered tin.

Makes about 50 cookies

Tahini Oatmeal Cookies

These heavy, sweet cookies from Nesta Feldman are a filling choice for a cold winter day. Be sure to stir the tahini before measuring it, so it has the right consistency.

⅓ cup tahini (sesame seed paste)	¼ teaspoon vanilla extract
½ cup honey	½ cup chopped walnuts
½ teaspoon ground cinnamon	1½ cups rolled oats
	⅓ cup raisins

Butter a baking sheet. Preheat the oven to 350°F.

Beat together the tahini, honey, cinnamon, and vanilla. Stir in the walnuts, rolled oats, and raisins. The mixture will be thick and hard to stir.

Drop by rounded teaspoons onto the baking sheet. Bake for 10 to 12 minutes, or until lightly browned and cooked through.

Store the cookies in a covered tin, where they will stay in good condition for at least 1½ weeks.

Makes 30 to 36 cookies

Australian Sesame Seed Biscuits

My friend Isabella Frost recently returned from Australia, bringing back with her all her favorite recipes. These crumbly "biscuits"—as cookies are known in Australia—are a specialty at Bittern Cottage near Melbourne, where the owners sell crafts and serve teas.

1 cup rolled oats	¼ cup sesame seeds
1 cup unsweetened desiccated coconut	½ cup butter, melted
	¼ cup honey

Preheat the oven to 350°F. Butter and flour an 8-inch-square baking pan.

Combine the rolled oats, coconut, sesame seeds, and butter. Beat in the honey. Pat the cookie mixture into the baking pan.

Bake for 30 to 35 minutes, or until golden. Let cool for 30 minutes before cutting into squares.

Stored in a tin, these cookies will keep for at least 1 week.

Makes 1 pan

Greek Sesame Nut Candies

⅔ cup toasted sesame   1 cup honey
    seeds
⅔ cup chopped walnuts

Combine the sesame seeds, walnuts, and honey in a heavy saucepan. Slowly bring the mixture to the hard-ball stage (about 250°F on a candy thermometer). Stir frequently—it should take about 10 minutes. The honey will be a dark golden brown.

Pour the mixture onto a buttered jelly-roll pan, and immediately spread to a ¼-inch thickness. Cut into pieces of about 1½ × 2 inches, and remove from the pan.

Store the candies in a covered tin, where they will keep for several weeks, improving in flavor as they age.

Makes about 40 candies

Honey Nut Candy

Give this candy to your sugar-addicted friends. It has a better flavor than candy made with sugar and cooks up faster as well. The candy has a soft texture at first but hardens slightly as it cools.

1 cup chopped filberts,   ¾ cup honey
    toasted   ½ cup chopped dates
3 tablespoons sliced   finely chopped
    almonds   toasted filberts or
½ cup chopped walnuts   sesame seeds
½ cup butter   (optional)

Combine the filberts, almonds, walnuts, butter, and honey in a deep saucepan, and cook over low heat, stirring constantly, until a drop of the mixture makes a firm ball when dropped in cold water. This will take about 5 minutes.

Remove the mixture from the heat and stir in the dates. Pour the candy into a buttered pan. Cool slightly and, while still warm, take scant teaspoons of the mixture and form into balls.

Roll the balls in the filberts or sesame seeds or leave plain. Place the candy in a tin, where it will keep for several weeks.

Makes about 50 balls

Cream Pralines

Bring along some of this extra-rich chewy candy as a hostess gift, or prepare it as a holiday treat. You'll need a candy thermometer to gauge the soft-ball stage.

¾	cup honey	2	tablespoons butter
⅓	cup molasses (preferably light)	⅛	teaspoon ground nutmeg
1	cup heavy cream*	1⅔	cups chopped pecans

Combine the honey, molasses, cream, butter, and nutmeg in a 2-quart enameled or stainless steel saucepan. Bring the mixture to a boil, and cook over medium heat, stirring constantly, until the syrup reaches 220°F on a candy thermometer. Stir in the pecans. Continue cooking and stirring until the syrup reaches 240°F. (A little syrup dropped into cold water will form a soft ball.) The color will be deep golden brown. The total cooking time will be about 20 minutes.

Remove the syrup from the heat, and let it stand for 3 minutes. Beat the mixture by hand until it is stiff, about 3 minutes. Drop mounded teaspoons of the mixture onto foil or waxed paper. Place in the freezer, then remove once the pralines have hardened.

Store in a tin in the refrigerator, with waxed paper between the layers. The pralines will keep for several weeks.

*It is best not to use ultra-pasteurized cream in this recipe.

Makes 36 to 40 pralines

Filbert Yogurt Cheesecake

This unusual cheesecake uses a yogurt cheese as the base, which makes it less rich than a cheesecake made solely with cream cheese. (I've added a little cream cheese for texture.) Be sure to let the yogurt cheese drain for at least 1 day, otherwise the cake will be watery. I've also omitted a crust, which I think detracts from the flavor of the cheesecake. And I bake the cheesecake in a springform tube pan, which makes it easier to serve neat slices.

1½	cups filberts	1	teaspoon vanilla extract
1¼	pounds Yogurt Cheese (about 2 recipes, see page 157)	½	cup sour cream
8	ounces cream cheese	4	eggs
1	cup honey	2	egg yolks

Preheat the oven to 400°F.

Toast the filberts in the oven until golden and lightly browned. This will take 10 to 15 minutes. Immediately place the nuts on a kitchen towel laid out on the counter, fold the towel around the nuts, and rub back and forth to remove the skins. Cool the nuts, then grind them in a nut grinder or in a food processor. I like the textural contrast of coarsely ground nuts with the creamy cheesecake, but grind them finely if you prefer. Set the nuts aside.

Beat the yogurt cheese with a mixer until smooth. Add the cream cheese, honey, vanilla, sour cream, and 1 cup of the nuts, and continue beating for about 2 minutes. Add the eggs and egg yolks and beat until they are combined.

Butter a 10-inch springform tube pan, add the remaining nuts to the pan, and rotate the pan until the surface of the pan is lightly coated with nuts. Pour in the cheesecake batter.

Preheat the oven to 325°F.

Set the tube pan inside a large, deep pan, and pour boiling water into the large pan to a depth of 2 inches, forming a water bath. Place the pans in the oven, and bake the cheesecake for 1¼ to 1½ hours, or until it is set.

Remove the pans from the oven, and place the tube pan on a rack. Let the cheesecake cool in the pan for at least 2 hours. (Do not remove it before that time, or the cheesecake will fall apart.) Chill the cheesecake for at least 2 more hours before serving.

If the cheesecake is wrapped in foil and stored in the refrigerator, it will remain in good condition for at least 2 weeks.

Makes 1 cake

Carrot Cake

1¼	cups oat flour*		⅛	teaspoon ground cloves
2	cups whole wheat flour		1	cup honey
1	teaspoon baking soda		1¼	cups vegetable oil
1	teaspoon baking powder		4	eggs
2	teaspoons ground cinnamon		1	teaspoon minced orange zest
½	teaspoon ground nutmeg		3	cups grated carrots
			1	cup chopped nuts

Preheat the oven to 350°F. Butter a 10-inch tube pan.

Combine the oat flour with the whole wheat flour, baking soda, baking powder, cinnamon, nutmeg, and cloves. Set aside.

Beat together the honey, oil, and eggs. Slowly mix in the flour mixture. Stir in the orange zest, carrots, and nuts. Spoon the batter into the tube pan.

Bake for 50 to 60 minutes, or until the cake is cooked through. Cool in the pan for 10 minutes, then invert onto a rack to cool completely.

The cake will keep moist for up to 1 week in the refrigerator if wrapped in foil. It will keep for up to 3 months in the freezer.

*To make oat flour, process rolled oats in a blender or food processor until it has a flourlike consistency.

Makes 1 cake

Ginger Cake

1	cup butter		2	teaspoons ground ginger
½	cup honey		1	teaspoon ground cinnamon
¾	cup molasses		½	teaspoon ground cloves
3	eggs		¼	teaspoon ground mace or nutmeg
3	cups whole wheat flour		1	cup boiling water
1	teaspoon baking powder			
1	teaspoon baking soda			

Preheat the oven to 325°F. Butter a 9 × 13-inch baking pan.

Cream the butter for 2 minutes. Add the honey and molasses, and cream the mixture for 2 minutes longer. Beat in the eggs one by one. Mix together the flour, baking powder, baking soda, ginger, cinnamon, cloves, and mace or nutmeg until thoroughly combined. Stir this mixture into the butter alternately with the boiling water. Stir only until smooth.

Pour the batter into the pan, smooth out, and bake for 40 to 45 minutes, or until the top springs back when touched with your finger.

Cool, then store, wrapped in foil, or place in a covered tin. The cake should stay in good condition for several days. If it dries out, use the cake as the base for a ginger trifle with a fresh custard sauce.

Makes 1 cake

Nova Scotia Raisin Cake

There's no fat in this sweet, heavy, sticky cake that's a specialty of my friend Sandra McKenzie. The cake, which falls halfway between a cake and a tea bread, is also good toasted for breakfast. I use a pan that's longer and narrower than a regular bread pan, and I find the cake cooks best in a pan that size.

2	cups whole wheat flour	1 to 2	tablespoons honey
1	teaspoon baking soda	1	cup buttermilk
½	cup molasses	½	cup raisins
		2	tablespoons hot water

Preheat the oven to 350°F.

Mix together the flour and baking soda. Pour in the molasses, honey, and buttermilk, and beat until all the ingredients are combined. Do not over-beat. Stir in the raisins and hot water and beat for a few seconds longer.

Spoon into a long, narrow 6-cup pan, and bake for 55 minutes, or until the cake tests clean when a straw is inserted in the center. Remove the cake from the pan, and cool on a rack.

Store, wrapped in foil, in the refrigerator—or if it's cool weather, store in a covered tin. The cake keeps in good condition for at least 1 week. You can also freeze it for up to 3 months.

Makes 1 cake

Parsnip Pecan Cake

1½ cups pecans (or filberts)
1½ cups finely grated
     parsnips
 1 cup fine, dry bread
     crumbs or ¾ cup
     whole wheat flour
 ½ teaspoon ground
     nutmeg

¼ teaspoon ground
    cloves
½ teaspoon ground
    cinnamon
6 eggs, separated
    juice of 1 lemon
½ to ¾ cup honey

Preheat the oven to 350°F. Grease and flour a 10-inch tube pan.

Grind the nuts with a food processor, electric blender, or hand grater until fine. Mix with the parsnips, bread crumbs or flour, nutmeg cloves, and cinnamon.

Beat the egg yolks with the lemon juice and honey until thick, and pale lemon yellow in color. Stir into the parsnip mixture.

Beat the egg whites until they form firm, shiny peaks; stir ⅓ of the whites into the parsnip mixture to lighten it, then fold in the rest. Spoon the batter into the pan.

Bake for 45 to 50 minutes, or until a toothpick inserted in the center of the cake comes out clean. Cool before removing from the pan. Frost with your favorite frosting before serving.

This moist cake will keep for at least 1 week wrapped in foil. For longer storage freeze it for up to 3 months.

Makes 1 cake

Maple Crème Caramel

This is the most requested dessert in my cooking classes, and the lovely thing about it is that it's really quite easy to make. In spite of its fragile appearance, crème caramel is a good keeper, best served ice cold. If you follow a few simple suggestions, your crème caramel will always turn out right: use absolutely fresh eggs; don't overcook the caramel syrup or it will be bitter; and cook the custard slowly so it ends up with a delicate texture. My technique of using a loaf pan for cooking both the syrup and the custard avoids the danger of burns from transferring a hot syrup into a dish, and this shape is attractive for serving as well.

¾ cup maple sugar or
    syrup
¼ teaspoon cream of tartar
 5 eggs

4 egg yolks
3¾ cups milk
1 teaspoon vanilla
    extract (optional)

Bring ¼ cup maple sugar or syrup, and the cream of tartar to a boil in a 9 × 5-inch loaf pan on top of the stove. Boil the mixture, stirring constantly, until the syrup starts to darken. It will stick to the spoon (about 5 minutes). Immediately remove from the heat, and rotate the pan until the bottom and sides are coated with the syrup. As the syrup cools, it hardens—at that point set the pan aside and make the custard.

Beat the eggs and egg yolks together until combined, then beat in the remaining maple sugar or syrup. Continue beating until the eggs increase in volume and the color lightens, 2 to 3 minutes.

Meanwhile, heat the milk to just below the boiling point, and also boil a large pot of water.

Preheat the oven to 325°F.

Stir the hot milk into the eggs, a little at a time, and then the vanilla (if used). Place the loaf pan in a large roasting pan, such as a turkey roaster. Strain the custard mixture through a fine sieve into the loaf pan to remove any stringy parts of the egg whites. The top may be foamy— if so, wait for a moment before adding all the custard mixture, or skim off the foam.

Pour the boiling water into the roasting pan to about ¾ of the way up the sides of the loaf pan. Place on the lowest shelf of the oven, and bake for 70 minutes, or until a knife inserted in the center comes out clean. Start checking after 1 hour because if you overcook the caramel, it develops little bubbles on the bottom and an unpleasant, slightly grainy texture.

Remove the bread pan to a rack, and let cool before refrigerating. Cover with foil or plastic wrap and place in the refrigerator, where the custard will stay in good condition for up to 1 week.

To unmold, run a knife around the edge of the custard, and place a plate over the pan. Invert so that the custard gently turns upside down onto the plate.

Serves 10 to 12

Variation
• Honey Crème Caramel: It is also possible to make the crème caramel using honey as a base. However, the caramel syrup will have a strong honey flavor, which is fine if you like the taste of honey. Substitute ¼ cup honey for the ¼ cup maple sugar or syrup in the caramel, and ⅓ cup honey for the ½ cup maple sugar or syrup in the custard.

Whole Wheat Strudel

When I first started working on this book, I mentioned that I wanted to locate someone who could make whole wheat strudel. As it turned out, I looked no further than the Rodale Test Kitchen, where Susan Hercek works occasionally. Susan, who is a fine natural food cook, has adapted many of her family's Slovak recipes to work with whole wheat flour and honey. On one of my trips to Emmaus, Susan taught me this recipe. I had never made strudel dough before, so I can testify that this recipe works and that making strudel is far easier than it sounds. Just remember to reserve enough time to make the strudel all at once, otherwise the dough might dry out.

Dough

1	egg	about 3	cups sieved whole wheat flour (reserve bran)
1 to 3	tablespoons vegetable oil		
1	cup warm water		

Filling

5	pounds Cortland or other firm fleshed apples, peeled and seeded	1	cup chopped walnuts
		¾	cup honey or combined maple syrup and honey
2	tablespoons lemon juice	¼	cup butter
1	cup raisins	2½	cups fine whole wheat bread crumbs

½ to ¾	pound butter
about ½	cup whole wheat flour
	ground cinnamon

Make the Dough

In a large mixing bowl beat the egg with a wire whip. Add the oil and water. Whisk in the flour 1 cup at a time. You can add the first 2 cups rapidly, but after that go slowly. Susan says that the amount of flour varies depending upon the type of flour and the humidity in the air. It's important to keep the dough as soft as you can but not sticky. If it is firm, you have added too much flour.

Place the dough on a board, and knead it like a bread dough. The bran remaining in the flour absorbs a lot of liquid, but it takes a while before this happens. For that reason Susan keeps the dough on the sticky side. The softer the dough is, the better it stretches. If necessary, add additional flour 1 tablespoon at a time.

Dust the top of the dough with flour, then cut it into 4 to 6 pieces, depending upon the finished size you wish the strudel pastry to be. It's easier for beginners to start with a small amount of dough. Form the dough into little balls without seams and lightly flour each ball. Place them on a floured surface, at least ½ inch apart. Cover the dough balls with an inverted bowl, and let them rest for 1 hour.

Make the Filling

Meanwhile, make the filling. Shred the apples on the coarse side of a grater, and place them in a large mixing bowl. Add the lemon juice, raisins, walnuts, and honey and maple syrup (if used) and set aside.

In a large frying pan melt ¼ cup butter. Add the bread crumbs and lightly brown them, stirring frequently so the crumbs don't burn. Stir in any bran that you have sieved from the flour. Stir ½ cup of the crumb mixture into the apple mixture. Place the remaining crumb mixture in a mixing bowl and set aside.

Assemble the Strudel

Melt ½ pound butter and set aside.

The strudel dough should be stretched on a table covered with a clean cloth. An old white tablecloth works well, but you can substitute a sheet. Whatever you use, however, it should be free from any wrinkles that could make folds in the strudel. Keep in mind that you will get butter stains on it.

Dust the cloth with the flour. Butter the strudel pans—jelly-roll pans work well in case any filling oozes out.

Using a pastry brush, brush the top of 1 of the dough balls with some of the melted butter, which should be warm but not hot. When you stretch the strudel dough, remember that you're making whole wheat strudel and you will end up with some holes because the flakes of bran tend to clump together, making it harder to stretch than a traditional white flour strudel.

Place the dough on a floured surface. Start forming the strudel sheet by buttering your fingers and stretching the dough along the outside, similar to the way you make a pizza. Stretch the dough into a 10-inch circle. Then place the dough on the floured tablecloth, buttered side up. Starting in the center, start stretching the strudel dough, walking around the table as you do. As you stretch, gently pull outward with both hands, making a fan shape. Be patient and don't try to stretch the dough too much in any one spot or you'll tear the dough.

If the dough starts to tear, don't try to patch it; just go on. It's important to keep the dough flat so it doesn't fold over itself. You are aiming for a 24-inch square if you have divided the dough into sixths. The size is not as important, however, as the thickness of the dough. It should be tissue-paper thin. Once the dough is at that stage, trim off the thick edges with a knife and set them aside. (You can form them into a ball and freeze them for noodles.)

Brush the dough with melted butter, starting in the center (which is the driest area) and brushing outward. Then lightly sprinkle the dough with some of the bread crumbs, and cut the dough in half. Lift ½ the dough and place it on top of the other half.

Take ⅙ of the filling, and mound it down one long side of the rectangle of dough in about a 2-inch strip, keeping it 1 to 2 inches away from the short ends. Sprinkle with cinnamon.

Fold in the 2 ends to partly enclose the filling. Using both hands, roll the strudel like a jelly roll, starting at the side with the filling. It may be helpful to use the tablecloth to roll the strudel. Place one of the buttered pans nearby. Spread your hands wide, get a nice even grip, and lift the strudel onto the pan, or lift the cloth and roll the strudel onto the pan. Brush with melted butter.

Continue making the strudels with the remaining dough and filling, buttering your hands each time you start a new sheet of strudel. You may need to melt additional butter.

Preheat the oven to 350°F.

Bake the strudels for 25 to 30 minutes, or until lightly browned and cooked through. Brush the strudels with butter when they come out of the oven.

The strudels will keep for several days, although the texture will soften in storage. For maximum storage freeze the strudels. The dough also freezes well and can be rolled out and filled once thawed.

Strudels are best served warm.

Makes 4 to 6 ⌷

Cranberry Pudding

My mother makes this steamed pudding every New Year's Eve, to be served with Honey Cream Sauce (below). It makes a wonderful gift.

2	cups cranberries	½	cup molasses
2	teaspoons baking soda	1½	cups whole wheat
½	cup boiling water		flour

Halve the cranberries and set aside. Dissolve the baking soda in the boiling water, and combine with the molasses. Stir in the flour and then the cranberries.

Spoon the mixture into 2 buttered 1-pound coffee cans. The cans will be about ½ full. Cover the tops of the cans with foil, crimping the sides of the foil near the tops of the cans to form tightly sealed lids.

Place the cans on a rack in a deep pot, and pour in boiling water to ⅔ of the way up their sides. Cover the pot and boil gently. Steam the puddings until completely cooked through, adding water to the pot as needed. The water level should be kept high, otherwise the tops of the puddings will be soggy and the sides will scorch. They will be done in about 1½ hours, when a knife inserted comes out clean and the puddings have pulled away from the sides of the cans. Remove the cans from the pot, and remove the foil lids to allow the steam to escape. Cool for 10 minutes, then unmold. Serve cold or at room temperature.

The puddings will keep for up to 1 week in the refrigerator, wrapped in foil, or for up to 3 months in the freezer.

Serves 6 to 8

Honey Cream Sauce

Serve this sauce with Cranberry Pudding or any other steamed pudding.

½ cup honey	1 teaspoon vanilla
½ cup butter	extract
½ cup heavy cream	

Combine the honey, butter, cream, and vanilla in the top of a double boiler. Cook over simmering water, stirring frequently, for 10 to 15 minutes, or until the sauce coats a spoon. The sauce will be relatively thin but it will thicken when reheated.

Reheat before serving. The sauce will keep for at least 2 weeks.

Makes about 1¼ cups

Sweskasoppa or Swedish Tapioca-Fruit Pudding

Daphne Derven's Swedish grandmother, Ingeborg Dahlin Stott, makes *sweskasoppa* (swiss kǎ soup ǎ), a traditional pudding dish served either as a dessert or as a breakfast. The proportions vary depending upon the desired thickness, sweetness, and ratio of prunes to raisins.

1	cup apple juice	2	large cinnamon sticks, broken in half
3	cups water		
½	cup honey	1 to 2	oranges, sliced
2	cups unpitted prunes	2	tablespoons tapioca
3 to 4	cups raisins		

Bring the apple juice, water, and honey to a boil. Add the prunes, raisins, cinnamon, oranges, and tapioca.

Immediately lower the heat and cook slowly until the fruit is tender, about 15 minutes. Remove the cinnamon.

Serve either cold or at room temperature. If tightly covered, this will keep for several weeks in the refrigerator.

Serves 8 to 10

Prune, Date, and Nut Pudding

This pudding has a soft texture that becomes firmer in storage.

3	tablespoons whole wheat flour	3	eggs
½	teaspoon baking powder	1	cup milk
¾	teaspoon ground cinnamon	⅔	cup chopped dried prunes
¼	teaspoon ground nutmeg	⅓	cup chopped dates
⅓	cup butter, softened	1	cup chopped walnuts
⅓	cup plus 2 tablespoons honey	1	teaspoon vanilla extract

Preheat the oven to 350°F. Butter a 9-inch ceramic baking dish.

Combine the flour, baking powder, cinnamon, and nutmeg. Set aside.

Cream the butter; add the honey and then the eggs. When all are incorporated, gradually add the milk. Add the flour mixture. Stir in the prunes, dates, walnuts, and vanilla.

Pour into the baking dish, and bake for 40 minutes, or until a knife inserted in the center comes out clean. Serve with heavy cream to pour over the pudding or with a spoonful of whipped cream per serving.

The pudding keeps moist and flavorful for up to 1 week covered with foil and held in the refrigerator. It can be frozen for up to 3 months.

Serves 12 to 15

Carrot Parsnip Pudding

This is an old-fashioned steamed pudding very similar to a moist bread.

¼	cup butter	¼	cup milk
⅓	cup honey	1¼	cups whole wheat flour
1	teaspoon baking soda		
½	teaspoon ground cinnamon	1	cup raisins
		2½	cups grated combined carrots and parsnips*
½	teaspoon ground nutmeg		
½	teaspoon ground cloves		

Cream the butter until light and add the honey. Beat until thoroughly combined. Stir in the baking soda, cinnamon, nutmeg, cloves, and milk. Beat in the flour. Add the raisins, carrots, and parsnips.

Spoon the mixture into 2 buttered 1-pound coffee cans, and cover the tops with foil. The cans will be ⅓ full. Place a rack in the bottom of a deep pot, and stand the coffee tins on it. Pour boiling water halfway up the cans. Cover the pot. Simmer the water until the puddings are steamed, about 1½ hours. Add additional boiling water as needed.

Serve with my mother's Honey Cream Sauce (see page 211). The pudding can be served either hot or cold, but the sauce should be hot.

The pudding will keep for at least 1 week stored in a cool spot or in the refrigerator. It will keep for up to 3 months in the freezer.

*To grate with a food processor, use the shredding disk and then process again with the metal blade to cut the shreds.

Serves 6 to 8

Snacks and Beverages

On a per-ounce basis snacks are among the most expensive foods you can buy, so it's worth taking the time to put up a few favorites. Crackers and nut and seed mixtures are filling choices for moments when you crave a bit of junk food rather than a piece of fruit.

Seed and nut snacks also make good party fare and hostess gifts. In this chapter you'll find an unusual snack, Crunchy Chinese Cashews, served at a restaurant in Taiwan, as well as Honey Peanuts, Seed Snacks, and the Israeli chick-pea snack, Falafel.

You'll also find several cracker recipes in this chapter. I have 2 teen-age children who love cheese and crackers. At some point I noticed how much money we were spending on store-bought crackers, and I decided making crackers would probably be no more work than making pie crust. I've developed recipes for several kinds of crackers: firm crackers as a base for cheese; crumbly crackers to eat with soup; flavorful crackers to eat alone as snacks; and bland crackers to use with spicy dips. Once you start making crackers, I'm sure you'll see how easy it is to add and subtract spices and flours to create your own variations.

In my travels I became addicted to the fruit syrups sold in European markets: even the smallest grocery stores in France and Germany carry syrups such as raspberry, black currant, or apricot to use in beverages and desserts. The fruit syrup recipes I've developed make a wonderful base for nonalcoholic drinks. A spoonful of Ginger Syrup stirred into ice water or seltzer water is an ideal thirst quencher on a sweltering summer day.

Lately I've noticed more and more people drinking apple and other fruit juices rather than soft drinks. Fruit juices have become so popular that a local natural food store I know stocks several shelves filled with different brands of juice. You can choose a simple pear juice or head for apple-pineapple or even a pina colada pineapple-coconut combination.

But frankly, unless you have your own supply of fruit, canning fruit juices is prohibitively expensive. That's why I have given you instructions for only the most common juices: Grape Juice, Pear Juice, and Apple Cider. If you'd like to learn more, I suggest you buy Rodale's preserving book, *Stocking Up*, or one of the canning guides put out by the Ball or Kerr companies or the United States Department of Agriculture.

Crunchy Chinese Cashews

Nina Simonds used to munch these nuts at the Rong Shing restaurant in Taipei.

2 cups water	6 cups peanut, safflower,
¼ cup honey	or corn oil
½ pound raw cashews	

Place the water and honey in a saucepan. Stir to dissolve the honey. Add the cashews and heat the mixture until boiling. Lower the heat to medium, and cook, uncovered, for 15 minutes. Remove the cashews from the liquid, drain thoroughly, and place them on a tray to air dry for 1 hour. Turn them occasionally.

Heat a wok, add the oil, and heat the oil to 350°F. Add the cashews and deep fry over high heat, turning constantly for 1½ to 2 minutes, until the cashews are a dark golden brown. Watch them carefully because the color changes quickly once it begins, and they can get too dark. Remove the nuts with a long-handled strainer or slotted spoon, and spread them out on brown paper to drain. (If you use paper toweling, the nuts will stick.)

Cool the nuts completely, then store in a covered tin. The nuts will keep for several weeks if stored in a cool, dark spot.

Makes about 1½ cups

Savory Nut Mix

1½	cups chopped lightly toasted almonds	¼	teaspoon cumin powder
1	cup toasted sunflower seeds	2	tablespoons soy sauce
½	cup rolled oats	¼	teaspoon cayenne pepper
½	cup lightly toasted whole filberts	1	cup raisins
1	tablespoon vegetable oil		

Preheat the oven to 350°F.

Combine the almonds, sunflower seeds, rolled oats, and filberts in a shallow roasting pan. Sprinkle with the oil and cumin and combine thoroughly. Bake for 10 minutes.

Toss with the soy sauce, and bake for another 10 to 15 minutes, or until the mixture has dried out. While it's still warm, toss with the cayenne and raisins.

Cool the mixture and store in a cool place in a covered jar for up to 1 month.

Makes about 4 cups

Curried Pecans

The light dusting of curry powder accentuates the flavor of the roasted pecans. You can substitute cashews or peanuts for the pecans.

3	cups pecan halves	2	teaspoons good-quality curry powder (such as Spice Islands)
1	tablespoon vegetable oil		
½	teaspoon chili powder		

Preheat the oven to 300°F.

Place the pecans in a bowl, and toss with the oil to coat thoroughly. Sprinkle with chili powder and curry and stir until evenly distributed. Spread the pecans on a baking sheet, and bake for 20 to 25 minutes, or until evenly browned, tossing them occasionally.

Cool, and store in a glass jar on the pantry shelf, where the pecans will keep for up to 2 months.

Makes 3 cups

Lebanese Tahini Spread

Every once in a while it's pleasant to make a recipe that takes about 15 seconds. This spread is tasty on crackers. Make as much or as little spread as you wish; just remember to keep the proportions at 2 parts tahini to 1 part honey.

½   cup tahini (sesame
      seed paste)
¼   cup honey

Mix the tahini and honey together. Spoon into a container, and store at room temperature or in the refrigerator if you wish.

The spread keeps for several weeks in the refrigerator. Bring to room temperature before serving.

Makes about ¾ cup

Variation
• Add ⅓ cup finely chopped walnuts.

Honey Peanuts

The peanuts brown all at once, so check on them frequently during the last few minutes of cooking. These might be a bit sticky if you make them in hot weather.

½   cup water
2   tablespoons honey
¼   teaspoon Chinese
      five-spice powder

1   teaspoon soy sauce
1   pound blanched raw
      peanuts

Preheat the oven to 275°F.

Combine the water, honey, five-spice powder, and soy sauce in a small saucepan. Bring the liquid to a boil, and continue boiling until the honey is dissolved, about 2 minutes.

Pour into a bowl, add the peanuts, and toss until the peanuts are coated with the liquid.

Place the peanuts in a shallow ovenproof pan such as a roasting pan or a jelly-roll pan, and bake for about 1 hour, stirring every 10 minutes. Watch carefully for the last 15 minutes because the syrup cooks away and the nuts can burn. The peanuts are done when they turn a golden brown and are lightly coated with the honey.

Store in a covered container. The nuts will keep for several weeks.

Makes 1 pound

Seed Snacks

You can do all the shopping at a natural food store for this addictive snack developed by Alice Senturia.

1	pound raw hulled sunflower seeds	1	pound raw hulled pumpkin seeds
1½	tablespoons soy sauce	1	15-ounce box raisins
1½	tablespoons water		
¾	pound roasted soybeans		

Preheat the oven to 400°F.

Mix ½ the sunflower seeds with the soy sauce and water, and roast until lightly browned, 10 to 15 minutes. Cool.

Mix in the remaining sunflower seeds, soybeans, pumpkin seeds, and raisins. Store in a tightly covered jar in a cool place. The mixture will stay fresh for up to 6 weeks.

Makes 12 cups

Variation
• Seed Nut Mix: Add equal amounts of unsalted raw cashews, unsalted dry roasted cashews and almonds, and brazil nuts.

Falafel

These falafel have a softer texture than those sold as snacks in Israel. The amount of chick-peas varies depending upon whether you start with canned or cooked dried chick-peas. If the mixture thickens in storage, thin it out with lemon juice.

2¼ to 2½	cups cooked chick-peas (canned or cooked dried)	1	tablespoon tahini (sesame seed paste, optional)
1	cup chopped onions		freshly ground black pepper
2	cloves garlic, minced	1	tablespoon lemon juice
¾	teaspoon cumin powder	¼	cup whole wheat or chick-pea flour
¾	teaspoon ground coriander	1	egg
⅛	teaspoon cayenne pepper		peanut oil

Grind the chick-peas in a food processor or meat grinder. Do not use a blender, because it will destroy the texture. Add the onions, garlic, cumin, coriander, cayenne, tahini (if used), pepper, lemon juice, flour, and egg. Process until thoroughly combined.

Form the mixture into 1½-inch balls, and line them up on a piece of waxed paper on the counter.

Heat the peanut oil to 340°F in a deep skillet or fryer, and deep fry the falafel, a few at a time, until deep brown. Drain on paper bags. Serve with *Taratoor* (see page 251), chopped mint, chopped tomatoes, lettuce, and pita bread.

Store the uncooked falafel mixture in a covered glass jar in the refrigerator, where it will keep in good condition for at least 5 days.

Makes 25 falafel

Variations
• Add ½ cup chopped parsley or ¼ cup chopped mint just before shaping the balls.

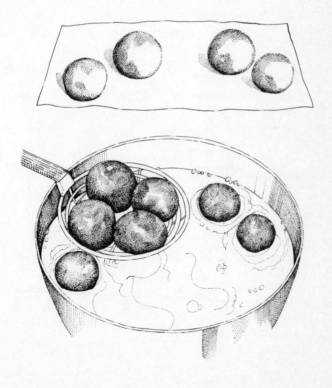

Making Crackers

Making crackers is easy and inexpensive. If you can make pie crust, you can make crackers.

I've given you a choice of several types of crackers. Some are savory snacks to be eaten alone and are often of too delicate a texture to hold up under a spread; others are designed to be served with cheeses or dips. My recipe notes indicate which are which.

The crackers I make have a more tender texture than commercial crackers because they are made with butter rather than shortening or oil. I prefer the taste and texture of butter; you may wish to substitute a light vegetable oil. Occasionally I add a little oil to vary the texture.

When you make crackers, work quickly and do not overmix the ingredients. (Overmixing makes crackers tough.) You'll notice I often suggest lightly kneading the ingredients in a plastic bag—a technique that helps prevent overmixing.

It's also important to roll out the crackers as thinly as possible. The first time you make crackers, measure the thickness with a ruler—from then on you'll be able to gauge with little difficulty.

Part of the fun of making crackers is varying the flours you use. Try the flours I suggest as a starting point for developing your own recipes. Barley flour is particularly good for adding a subtle flavor, while soy flour should be used with restraint, as it tends to overpower the other ingredients.

Also, watch like a hawk the last 1 or 2 minutes when the crackers are baking. Because they are so thin, the crackers tend to go from slightly underbaked to burned in just a moment.

Onion Crackers

1	onion	½	cup wheat germ
½	cup water	½	cup barley flour
1	cup whole wheat flour	½	teaspoon dry mustard
		½	cup butter

Purée the onion in a food processor or blender. Add the water and continue puréeing until the onion is almost liquified. Strain the onion liquid through coffee filters to obtain onion juice. You should end up with ⅜ cup juice. Discard any extra juice.

Mix together the whole wheat flour, wheat germ, barley flour, and mustard. Cut in the butter until it is amalgamated into fine particles. Add the onion juice, bit by bit, tossing constantly with a fork.

Pour the mixture into a plastic bag, and press together until it forms a ball. Knead lightly.

Preheat the oven to 400°F.

Divide the cracker dough into quarters, and roll out—¼ at a time—on a lightly floured board. The dough should be ¹⁄₁₆ to ⅛ inch thick (approximately 9 × 9 inches). Cut the dough into rounds with a biscuit cutter or a glass, and prick each dough round with a fork.

Place on ungreased baking sheets, and bake for 8 to 10 minutes. Cool on racks, then store in an airtight container. The crackers will keep in good condition for at least 1 week.

Makes about 38 crackers

Soy Crackers

These crackers are best with cheese.

⅓ cup soy flour	2 tablespoons brown rice flour
1 cup whole wheat flour	½ cup butter
⅓ cup rye flour	2 tablespoons vegetable oil
⅓ cup oat flour	½ cup buttermilk
2 tablespoons cornmeal	

Preheat the oven to 400°F.

Thoroughly combine the soy flour, whole wheat flour, rye flour, oat flour, cornmeal, and brown rice flour. Cut in the butter until it is incorporated in small particles. Mix together the oil and buttermilk, and add them to the flour mixture, bit by bit, tossing constantly with a fork.

Spoon the mixture into a plastic bag, and knead briefly until it forms a ball. Divide the dough into quarters. Roll out on a lightly floured board, ¼ at a time. The dough should be between ¹⁄₁₆ and ⅛ inch thick. Cut into rounds with a biscuit cutter or glass, and prick with a fork.

Bake for 13 to 15 minutes. Cool on a rack and store in a covered, airtight container. The crackers will stay in good condition for at least 1 week.

Makes about 50 crackers

Wheat Thin Crackers

1½	cups whole wheat flour	½	teaspoon dry mustard
½	cup barley flour	¾	cup butter
¼	teaspoon cayenne pepper	⅜ to ½	cup ice water

Combine the whole wheat flour, barley flour, cayenne, and mustard in a mixing bowl. Cut in the butter until the mixture resembles coarse crumbs. With a fork stir in ice water until the mixture barely holds together. Do not add too much water or the crackers will be tough.

Place the dough in a plastic bag, and knead a few times until the dough holds together.

Preheat the oven to 350°F. Butter a baking sheet.

Divide the dough into quarters, and roll it out, a section at a time, on a lightly floured surface. Try to roll the dough as thin as possible: ¹⁄₁₆ to ⅛ inch thick is best.

Cut into 1½-inch squares. Set aside any scraps to reroll later. Place the squares on the baking sheet, and prick them with a fork.

Bake for about 10 minutes, or until they are lightly browned. Watch closely because the crackers burn very quickly.

Cool on racks. Store in a covered tin, where the crackers will stay fresh for at least 2 weeks.

Makes about 136 crackers

Variation
• Sesame Seed Crackers: Add ¾ cup roasted sesame seeds to the dough. Lightly brush each cracker with sesame oil before baking.

Whey Crackers

If you peruse the ingredients listed on cracker packages at the supermarket, frequently you'll find dried whey included as an ingredient. I use the liquid whey by-product from Buttermilk Pot Cheese (see page 144) and find that whey gives a slight tang to the crackers. One caution: make up all the cracker dough in 1 day because the dough sours after a few days in the refrigerator. Of course, if you prefer, substitute ice water for the whey.

½	cup rye flour	½	cup butter
½	cup oat flour	⅜	cup whey
1	cup whole wheat flour		

Thoroughly combine the rye flour, oat flour, and whole wheat flour. Cut in the butter until it is incorporated in small particles. Add the whey, bit by bit, continuously tossing with a fork. The dough will be damp but should not stick together.

Preheat the oven to 400°F.

Place the dough in a plastic bag, and knead slightly until the dough forms a ball. Divide the dough into quarters, and roll out ¼ at a time on a lightly floured board. The dough should be ¹⁄₁₆ to ⅛ inch thick. Cut the dough into rounds with a biscuit cutter or glass. Prick the rounds with a fork.

Place the dough rounds on ungreased baking sheets, and bake for 8 to 10 minutes, or until cooked through but barely browned.

Cool on racks, and store in an airtight container. Treated this way, the crackers will hold in good condition for up to 1 week.

Makes about 40 crackers

Cheese Pennies

These rich, savory crackers are a tasty snack after a brisk fall walk. They also make an excellent hostess gift for a winter party.

⅜	cup butter	1	cup grated Cheddar cheese
2	tablespoons rye flakes		
¼	cup brown rice flour	¼	cup grated Parmesan cheese
½	cup whole wheat flour		sesame seeds
½	teaspoon dry mustard		

Cream the butter and combine with the rye flakes, brown rice flour, whole wheat flour, and mustard. Stir in the cheeses.

Place the dough on a lightly floured surface, and shape it into 2 cylinders about 1¼ inches in diameter. Roll the dough cylinders in the sesame seeds. Wrap the dough in waxed paper, and refrigerate it for at least 1 hour, or until firm.

Preheat the oven to 350°F. Butter a baking sheet.

Slice the dough into ¼-inch rounds, and place them about 1 inch apart on the baking sheet. Bake for 15 minutes, or until the "pennies" are cooked through. Remove them from the baking sheet immediately or they will stick. Cool on racks before storing.

If the pennies are stored in a tightly covered container, they should last for at least 1 week.

Makes about 50 crackers

Variations
• Substitute finely chopped pecans or walnuts for the sesame seeds.

Corn Crackers

These crackers are slightly crumbly but can be spread with soft cheeses or spreads. Enjoy them with soup or as a savory snack. The amount of water varies, depending upon the texture of the bran in the whole wheat flour.

1	cup cornmeal	½	teaspoon chili powder
⅓	cup brown rice flour	⅓	cup butter
⅔	cup whole wheat flour	1	teaspoon sesame oil
½	teaspoon dry mustard	2	tablespoons corn oil
¼	teaspoon curry powder	1	egg, beaten
		4 to 5	tablespoons ice water

In the bowl of a food processor, combine the cornmeal, brown rice flour, whole wheat flour, mustard, curry, and chili powder. Whirl the ingredients together until combined.

Cut the butter into ½-inch pieces, add to the bowl, and pulse on and off until the butter is incorporated. Add the sesame oil, corn oil, egg, and 4 tablespoons ice water. Pulse the mixture until the dough clumps together. You may need to add the remaining ice water.

Preheat the oven to 400°F.

Press the dough together and let it rest for 15 minutes. Divide the dough into quarters. Roll it out, ¼ at a time, on a lightly floured counter. The dough should be ⅛ inch thick. Cut the dough into circles with a 2½-inch-diameter jelly glass or biscuit cutter. Continue shaping the crackers until all the dough is used up.

Place the crackers on an ungreased baking sheet, and prick several times with the tines of a fork. Bake for about 10 minutes, or until cooked through. Do not let brown. Cool on a rack.

If the crackers are stored in an airtight container at room temperature, they will stay in good condition for up to 10 days.

Makes 44 to 50 crackers

Variation
• If you'd like a shorter-tasting, more crumbly version, omit the egg and use only 4 tablespoons water. Cut into miniature shapes with pastry cutters, and serve as party snacks.

Melba Toast

To make melba toast, remove the crusts from thinly sliced whole wheat bread. The bread should be sliced as thinly as possible. Diagonally cut the slices in half, and toast in a 325°F oven for 6 to 8 minutes on each side. Cool completely before storing in an airtight tin.

Another method must be used if the bread is already sliced in standard fashion rather than extra thin. Trim the crusts for evenly shaped pieces, then toast as you would normally to make toast. Pull each slice apart, using 2 forks, to form 2 thinner slices. Place each ½ slice, with the rough side up, on a baking sheet. Bake in the oven at 325°F until lightly browned, about 8 minutes. Cool completely before storing in an airtight tin.

Melba toast will keep for several months.

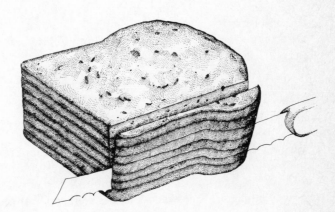

Fruit Syrups

Before sweetened carbonated drinks became the standard beverage for many Americans, homemade fruit syrups were a common pantry item. Cooks simmered a liquid fruit base with a sugar syrup and stored the syrup plain or combined it with brandy. When 2 or 3 tablespoons fruit syrup were mixed with water, the result was a cooling summer drink —or often was suggested as a pick-me-up for invalids.

Some of the most intriguing fruit syrups were devised in Louisiana, where Creole cooks made syrups or liquors using fruits such as bananas, apricots, cranberries, cherries, or lemons. Several such recipes are given in the *Picayune Cook Book*, first published in 1901, which is fascinating reading for anyone interested in experimenting with syrups or learning more about the food heritage in the United States. The book is available as a Dover Publications reprint.

The Shaker religious sect also excelled in the preparation of delicious syrups, many of which are included in Amy Bess Miller's book, *The Best of Shaker Cooking*.

It would be pleasant to conjecture that a century ago cooks used less sugar, but an addiction to sweets appears to be a long-standing American failing. Some of the old recipes called for phenomenal amounts of sugar—more than most cooks would use today.

Fruit syrups are equally delicious made with a honey base. However, when you replace the sugar in a recipe with a comparable amount of honey, the honey totally overpowers the fruit taste. And maple syrup has an even more distinctive flavor. I've found that slightly tart syrups retain the best fruit flavors.

Making your own syrups is easy to do and a delicious way to utilize a surplus crop of berries or stone fruit. Sometimes it works well to just cook the fruit with the honey. Most times, however, it is best to make a honey syrup and combine it with a fruit liquid base.

I'm giving you the basic procedure, but the amount of fruit and honey varies depending upon the type of fruit and how much syrup you desire. As a general rule I have found that 1 quart berries will yield about 1 cup fruit liquid and that 1 cup honey and 1 cup water cooked together will yield 1 cup of syrup.

To make a fruit base for syrups, start with absolutely ripe fruit. (Underripe fruit has more pectin that might jell the syrup.) Dice the fruit and crush it with a potato masher. Add ½ cup to 1 cup water, depending upon the type of fruit and how juicy it is. Stir well and heat the fruit just to a boil, stirring constantly. Boil the fruit slowly but watch carefully because if you cook the fruit too long, it will lose its fresh flavor. Five minutes is usually long enough.

Pour the hot fruit into a colander lined with cheesecloth or coffee filters, or place it in a jelly bag. Let the fruit juices drip into a bowl. After the pulp appears to have released all of its juice, press down on it to extract any extra juice. (This may make the syrup cloudy, so if you want it as clear as possible, skip this step.) Discard the pulp.

If you are working with raspberries or other fruits with large seeds, it is just as easy to let the juices drip through a colander first and then pour the liquid through a fine sieve to remove any remaining seeds and sediment.

Boil the honey and water together for about 5 minutes, or until the liquid is reduced and a syrup is formed.

Stir the honey syrup into the fruit liquid, and boil just long enough to combine the mixtures. The cooking time depends upon the strength of the fruit liquid and the honey syrup, but 5 to 10 minutes should suffice if you have started with sufficiently strong fruit liquid and syrup.

Pour the hot syrup into hot, sterilized jars, and seal. Store in a cool, dark place or in the refrigerator. The syrup should keep for several weeks. For longer storage leave a ½-inch headspace as you fill the jars. Then process the syrup for 20 minutes in a boiling water bath.

Ginger Syrup

The gingerroot gives the syrup a hot taste that dissipates when it is added to water to make gingerale. Use about 1 tablespoon syrup to 1 cup seltzer water.

½	pound gingerroot	1	cup honey
5	cups water	¼	cup strained lime juice

Finely chop the gingerroot. This is easiest to do in a food processor. Peel the gingerroot only if it is old. You should end up with about 1⅔ cups chopped gingerroot.

Place the gingerroot and 4 cups water in an enameled or stainless steel pan. Bring the water to a boil, then gently boil for 5 minutes. Cover the pan with a kitchen towel, and let the gingerroot steep in the water overnight.

Boil together the remaining water and the honey until a light honey syrup is formed. The mixture will reduce to 1 cup. This will take 5 to 10 minutes.

Strain the ginger liquid first through a colander, then through a fine sieve—or through coffee filters. Add the ginger liquid to the honey syrup. Boil it together for 5 minutes. Skim off any foam. Add the lime juice and cook for 2 minutes longer. Pour the syrup into a jar, seal the jar, and store it in the refrigerator.

The syrup will keep for several weeks in the refrigerator if kept tightly capped. It will keep in the freezer for up to 1 year. For easy thawing, freeze in ice cube trays and pop into a plastic bag when the cubes are frozen.

Makes about 3½ cups

Cherry Shrub

An authentic colonial American shrub would be made with brandy or rum. This version has vinegar added to help preserve the fruit liquid base. Mix 2 to 3 tablespoons shrub with 1 cup seltzer water or ice water for a refreshing summer beverage.

3½	pounds sweet cherries	½	cup strained lime juice
1	cup honey	¼	cup white vinegar
1	cup water		

Place the cherries in a large enameled or stainless steel pot, and mash them slightly with a potato masher. Add the honey and water and bring the mixture to a boil. Lower the heat and let the cherries gently boil for 10 to 15 minutes, or until they have released their juices. Strain the cherry pulp through a colander, pressing hard on the cherries to release their juices. You should end up with about 1½ cups cherry juice.

Place the cherry juice back in the pan, add the honey syrup, and boil for 2 to 3 minutes. Add the lime juice and vinegar and boil for just 1 minute longer.

Pour the mixture into a hot, sterilized jar. Cap, and store in the refrigerator.

The shrub mixture will keep for several weeks in the refrigerator. You can also freeze it for up to 1 year.

Makes about 2 cups

Variation
• Add 4 mashed peaches along with the cherries.

Raspberry Shrub

Use the raspberry liquid as a base for an old-fashioned raspberry cream soda. Add equal parts raspberry syrup and cream to a soda glass, fill it with seltzer water, and stir. Taste the shrub and adjust amounts. Or add 2 tablespoons syrup to a glass of seltzer water.

1	quart ripe raspberries	1	cup honey
2	cups water	¼	cup white vinegar

Place the raspberries and 1 cup water in a large enameled or stainless steel pan. Crush the berries with a potato masher. Bring the mixture to a boil, lower the heat, and gently boil for 5 to 10 minutes, or until the berries release their juices. Cool slightly.

Place the berries in a colander, and let the juices drip through. Then strain the juices through a fine sieve (or coffee filters) to remove any remaining seeds and pulp.

Meanwhile, boil the honey and the remaining water together for 10 to 15 minutes, or until a light syrup is formed.

Stir the raspberry juice and the honey syrup together, and boil for 1 or 2 minutes. Add the vinegar and boil for 1 minute longer. Pour into a hot, sterilized jar, and seal.

The raspberry shrub will keep for several weeks in the refrigerator if tightly capped. You can freeze it for up to 9 months.

Makes about 3¼ cups

Pear Juice

Grocery stores in France and Italy sell an addictive pear nectar that's really just pear juice made with absolutely ripe pears. Linda Gilbert, the product development manager at the Rodale Test Kitchen, makes a similar juice with the surplus fruit from her pear tree. She also uses the juice as a marinade for pork and poultry by seasoning it with star anise, cinnamon, and cloves. A refreshing sorbet can be made very easily by puréeing sweetened pear juice. This is how Linda makes pear juice.

Stem and core washed whole pears and place them in the top of a steamer-juicer. Steam the pears until soft and easily pierced with a knife. Mash the pears in the juicer, and continue cooking them until they have released all their juices, about 1½ hours. The time varies depending upon the size of the juicer and the quantity of pears.

Place the hot juice in hot, clean quart canning jars, leaving a ½-inch headspace. Process for 30 minutes in a boiling water bath. Cool the jars and store them in a dark, cool place where they will keep for up to 1 year.

15 pounds pears yield about 5 quarts

Variations
• Pear Apple Juice: Add apples along with the pears.
• Pear Syrup: Linda boils 6 quarts juice into a thick syrup, which she uses for glazes and for basting meats and poultry. The syrup keeps in the refrigerator, covered, for up to 1 year.

Apple Cider

At one time in rural New England, almost every home had its own press for making apple cider or perry—a pear cider. Today it's still common each fall to see signs posted for cider pressing along New England country roads. If you have a small apple crop, it's probably most economical to bring your apples to a local press, but if you have several trees, you may find it makes more sense to press your own cider. Many wine-making stores carry hand presses for cider, and there are mail-order catalogs, such as the one put out by Garden Way (Charlotte, VT 05445), from companies that stock larger presses.

Whether you have cider pressed or make your own, I think the best ciders are made from a mixture of apples. On a farm we once owned in Maine, we had old yellow transparent, russet, pear-apple trees. These trees were covered with dead limbs and suckers when we bought the property, but after a few years of judicious pruning and feeding with a deep leaf mulch, the trees produced fine apples once again.

The russets gave a depth of flavor to the cider that was unequaled by the single-crop ciders for sale at the local farm stands. Russets can be difficult to find; if you have no luck locating them, try for a mix of any good tart and sweet varieties.

It's fine to use misshapen apples, but don't use fruit with blemishes, which could contain bacteria that will destroy the cider. You want ripe apples because green apples have too much starch and too little sugar to produce good-tasting cider.

To begin, rinse off the apples and set them aside.

The apples have to be ground before being pressed. If a standard apple grinder is not available, a food processor or kitchen-type food grinder can be used, but the apples will have to be seeded first. Make sure to catch all the juice.

Place the ground pulp in the nylon mesh bag that comes with the press. Most presses can be filled ⅔ full. Fold the top of the bag over the pulp.

Assemble the press and place a scrupulously clean, small plastic waste basket or garbage can underneath it to hold the juice. Then press the apples, and the juice will begin to flow into the bucket. Don't try to extract every last drop.

Pour the apple juice into clean plastic jugs that have been rinsed very thoroughly and scrubbed with a bottle brush, or use sterilized glass bottles. If you'll be freezing the cider, leave a 2-inch headspace for gallon containers and ½ inch for quarts. Cover the jugs and store the cider in the refrigerator for up to 2 weeks, or freeze it for up to 9 months.

Grape Juice

Years ago, when I was visiting relatives in Washington state, Bernice Skinner gave me these instructions for making her delicious grape juice.

Use clean and well-ripened, but not overripe, grapes. Wash them thoroughly. Place the grapes in a stainless steel kettle, and barely cover them with water. Gently boil until the seeds are free. Strain the mixture through a cheesecloth bag without squeezing.

Measure the juice and add ¼ cup honey for each quart. Heat the juice to dissolve the honey. Fill hot, clean quart jars with the hot juice, leaving a ½-inch headspace. Process for 15 minutes in a boiling water bath.

The grape juice will keep for up to 9 months.

Cold Sauces and Salad Dressings

Cold sauces come into their own during the summer months. A bowl of Aioli or Catalonian Almond Garlic Sauce surrounded by steamed baby vegetables, or a spoonful of Cucumber Basil Sauce flanking a slice of poached fish, is an easy do-ahead solution for nights when you may not feel like cooking, but you feel like eating something special.

Unlike standard sauces made from stock and pan juices at the last minute, cold sauces can be made at leisure and stored in the refrigerator for days, usually improving in flavor as they sit.

I prefer uncomplicated cold sauces: Creamy Dill Horseradish Sauce, for example, requires only stirring together horseradish, yogurt, lemon juice, and dillweed, while the Middle Eastern *Taratoor* uses tahini as a base for a sauce that's delicious with fish or with chopped vegetables in a pita bread sandwich.

Despite the fact that the blender and the food processor have turned the making of salad dressings and mayonnaise into a matter of seconds, commercial dressings and mayonnaise continue to sell well. I have never understood why people will pay a premium for the privilege of shaking a bottle, rather than taking a moment longer to whip together a dressing. As many commercial dressings are loaded with preservatives and never taste fresh, you've got a compelling argument to make your own dressings.

During the summer, when there's a vast choice of delicate salad greens such as matchstick or oak leaf lettuce, I favor a green salad with minced fresh herbs, lightly coated with my mother's tart salad dressing. She steeps crushed garlic, a pinch of dry mustard, and freshly ground black pepper in vinegar for several hours. Just before serving, she strains out the garlic, stirs in a bit more oil than vinegar, and tosses the salad with the dressing. I never tire of this dressing but, unfortunately, it stores poorly.

For days when I want a change of pace, or during the winter when it's difficult to buy any lettuce but iceberg, I'll switch to one of the flavorful salad dressings in this chapter. All of the dressings keep for several days on the refrigerator shelf.

Mayonnaise, which is a staple at our house, is a much more versatile dressing than most people realize. It may be the ultimate sandwich spread, but its bland, smooth taste is also a good foil for different flavors. I'll add some chopped chives, a dash of Worcestershire sauce, and a touch of chili sauce and coat leftover diced vegetables with it for lunch. Or I'll combine it with minced watercress and herbs to make a green mayonnaise to accompany fish. When I add chunky ingredients such as diced hard boiled eggs, chopped onions, and shredded cheese, the mayonnaise becomes an excellent dressing for cold salads.

Mayonnaise Blender-Style

This mayonnaise is slightly thinner than the commercial variety when first made, but it thickens as it sits in the refrigerator.

2	tablespoons cider or wine vinegar	1	egg
½	teaspoon dry mustard	1	cup sunflower oil or combined safflower and sunflower oils

Place the vinegar, mustard, egg, and ¼ cup oil in a blender. Process, immediately pouring in the remaining oil in a slow, steady stream. The mayonnaise will not thicken until most of the oil is incorporated.

Store in the refrigerator for up to 2 weeks.

Makes 1¼ cups

Mayonnaise
Food-Processor–Style

1	tablespoon Dijon mustard	¼	cup lemon juice
1	egg	1	cup safflower oil
2	egg yolks	1	cup olive or vegetable oil

Place the mustard, egg, egg yolks, and lemon juice in a food processor. Process for 1 minute.

Keeping the motor running, drizzle in the safflower and olive or vegetable oils in a slow stream. The mayonnaise will thicken gradually.

Store the mayonnaise in a glass jar in the refrigerator, where it will keep for up to 3 weeks.

Makes about 2½ cups

Aioli or
Garlic Mayonnaise

In southern France and northern Spain aioli (eye ō′ lēē) often accompanies grilled or poached fish and vegetables; it is also stirred into hot fish soup. It's a potent dip (strictly for garlic lovers) and must be made with very fresh garlic with not a tinge of yellow or green — or it will have a bitter, disagreeable aftertaste. Couple it with Catalonian Almond Garlic Sauce (page 236), and serve them both with cooked fresh vegetables, or use it alone as a base for potato salad.

3	egg yolks	7	cloves garlic
1½	tablespoons lemon juice	1	cup vegetable oil
½	tablespoon Dijon mustard	½	cup finest quality olive oil

Place the egg yolks, lemon juice, mustard, and garlic in a food processor or blender, and process until smooth.

Keep the machine running, and add the vegetable and olive oils in a very, very slow, steady stream. Continue processing until the sauce is thick.

Place in a glass container, cover, and refrigerate. Aioli will stay in good condition for at least 2 weeks.

Makes about 2 cups

Walnut Garlic Mayonnaise

This thick mayonnaise was inspired by a walnut sauce we had in the southwest part of France, which was more of an emulsified oil sauce than a mayonnaise. Try this as a base for an apple and orange salad, thin it with lemon juice to use as a dip for julienne raw vegetables or hard cooked eggs, or serve it along with broiled fish or chicken. Garlic lovers will enjoy this spread on bread or crackers. Wait 1 day before serving, because the walnut and garlic flavors mature during storage.

¾ cup walnuts
1 tablespoon chopped
     garlic
2 eggs
2 tablespoons red wine
     vinegar

1 cup vegetable oil
     chopped parsley
     (optional)

In a food processor purée together the walnuts and garlic. Add the eggs, vinegar, and ¼ cup oil. Pulse for a moment to combine. With the motor running, slowly add the remaining oil. The mixture will thicken to a mayonnaise consistency. Add parsley to taste.

This sauce keeps for weeks stored in a covered jar in the refrigerator.

Makes about 1⅔ cups

Avocado Salad Dressing

Alice Senturia tosses escarole, Boston and romaine lettuce, scallions, cherry tomatoes, and sesame seeds with this dressing. She also adds 2 minced anchovy fillets.

¾ cup mayonnaise
⅛ cup lemon juice
½ clove garlic, minced
½ teaspoon Worcester-
     shire sauce

¼ teaspoon black pepper
     dash of hot pepper
     sauce
1 ripe avocado, mashed
1 teaspoon minced chives

Mix together the mayonnaise, lemon juice, garlic, Worcestershire sauce, pepper, hot pepper sauce, avocado, and chives. Store in a glass jar in the refrigerator. The dressing keeps for at least 1 week.

Makes 1½ to 2 cups

Catalonian Almond Garlic Sauce

At a rustic tavern in the hills high above Barcelona, we first tried this unusual almond sauce with a mayonnaise consistency. This specialty of Catalonia is usually served with grilled leeks, shellfish, or chicken, accompanied by a garlic mayonnaise. The diners at the restaurant dipped the leeks first into this sauce then into the garlic mayonnaise.

⅓	cup lightly toasted blanched almonds	1	teaspoon tomato paste or 1 ripe tomato, peeled, seeded, and finely chopped
1½	teaspoons finely chopped garlic		
¼	teaspoon cayenne pepper	1	cup almond* or olive oil
¼	cup red wine vinegar		

Purée the almonds and garlic together in a food processor or blender. Add the cayenne, vinegar, and tomato paste (or tomato), and whirl until all the ingredients are combined. Slowly beat in the oil, 1 tablespoon at a time. By the time ½ the oil has been beaten in, the sauce should look creamy. The sauce will hold its shape solidly in a spoon.

Store the sauce in a covered container in the refrigerator, where it will keep for up to 1 week.

*Almond oil, which is a mild, delicious oil low in saturated fats, is available through the California Almonds Growers Exchange, Sacramento, California 95808.

Makes about 1⅓ cups

Creamy Dill Horseradish Sauce

I prefer the flavor of the sour cream, but substitute yogurt if you wish. This is an excellent sauce with smoked whitefish, sturgeon, or chub. It's also good with baked potatoes.

3	tablespoons freshly grated horseradish	1	tablespoon chopped dillweed
1	cup sour cream or yogurt		freshly ground black pepper
2	tablespoons lemon or lime juice		hot pepper sauce

Stir together the horseradish, sour cream or yogurt, lemon or lime juice, and dillweed. Taste, and add pepper and hot pepper sauce. Chill before serving.

Store in a tightly covered container. The sauce will keep for up to 2 weeks in the refrigerator.

Makes about 1 cup

Cucumber Basil Sauce

This sauce is good with any poached or baked fish. The cucumbers soften slightly in storage, so if you're holding the sauce for any length of time, you might wish to add them just before serving. If you have any pan juices left from poaching a fish or from the fish terrine, reduce them to strengthen the flavor, then add 2 or 3 tablespoons to the sauce.

½	cup mayonnaise (preferably homemade)	2 to 3	tablespoons fish juices (optional)
1	cup sour cream	⅔	cup chopped peeled cucumber
1	teaspoon prepared horseradish	1	tablespoon minced basil (or dillweed)
1	teaspoon Dijon mustard		lemon juice

Beat together the mayonnaise, sour cream, horseradish, and mustard. Stir in the fish juices, if you wish, and the cucumber and basil or dillweed. Add lemon juice to taste.

Store the sauce in a covered jar in the refrigerator, where it will stay in good condition for up to 4 days.

Makes 2 cups

Blue Cheese Salad Dressing

My friend Alice Senturia keeps a supply of this dressing on hand at all times. She usually serves it with her garlic croutons (see page 43).

1	jumbo egg (about 2 ounces)	⅛	teaspoon ground sweet Hungarian paprika
⅓	cup lime juice		dash of cayenne pepper
⅓	cup Garlic Oil (safflower, see page 22)	2	ounces blue cheese (such as Roquefort)
1	teaspoon honey		
⅛	teaspoon black pepper		

In a mixing bowl combine the egg, lime juice, garlic oil, honey, pepper, paprika, and cayenne. Crumble the cheese and stir it in.

Store the dressing in a covered glass jar in the refrigerator, where it will keep for up to 10 days.

Makes about ⅔ cup

Spicy Lime Salad Dressing

This dressing peps up a raw zucchini or cucumber salad, a winter fruit salad of apples and pears, or sliced oranges. Try it also as a marinade for chicken or fish.

⅓	cup lime juice	½	teaspoon ground coriander
⅛	teaspoon cayenne pepper	½	teaspoon dry mustard
2	cloves garlic, minced	⅛	teaspoon ground sweet Hungarian paprika (optional)
	pinch of ground cardamom	½	teaspoon honey
½	teaspoon cumin powder	⅔	cup vegetable oil

Combine together in a glass jar the lime juice, cayenne, garlic, cardamom, cumin, coriander, mustard, paprika (if used), honey, and oil. Cover and shake. Store tightly covered in the refrigerator, where it will keep for at least 1 week.

Makes about 1 cup

Profile

Nitzi & Pat Rabin

Years ago, when I was writing an article about Cape Cod's best restaurants, I ate dinner at Chillingsworth in Brewster, Massachusetts. My meal, which was beautifully prepared and served, equaled any I had tasted in the Michelin-starred restaurants of France. This was no coincidence, I later discovered, because the young owners, Nitzi and Patricia Rabin, headed for France every spring to work with other chefs and share ideas.

When the Rabins bought Chillingsworth in 1975, it already had a reputation for good food. The original owner, Robert Stevenson, had recruited several excellent chefs and had hired James Beard as a menu collaborator.

During the summers while Nitzi was in graduate school, the Rabins worked at Chillingsworth. When Stevenson died in the midst of a busy summer season, Nitzi stepped in, ran the restaurant, and eventually bought it. At first the Rabins planned to cook only during the spring and fall seasons and bring in guest chefs during the summer. But the second year, when Nitzi overheard two well-recommended chefs discussing whether they could hold hollandaise sauce on a steam table, he decided enough was enough and took over as head chef; Pat became the pastry chef.

The foundation of Nitzi's cooking is his stocks, which he transforms into the sauces essential for the serious style of cooking for which the restaurant is known.

As stocks constitute a key element in pantry food cooking, I was curious to find out how Nitzi achieves such high-quality results. Stocks, he pointed out, are ideal pantry foods because they have to be prepared in advance and, when reduced, will last for several weeks in the refrigerator. (They can also be frozen.) "Making stocks is a great rainy day project because the stocks can simmer away while you wash the windows or watch a ball game. The ingredients for good stocks cost money, though, and the home cook must be willing to gather the ingredients that a restaurant chef has on hand as a matter of course," he told me.

"You have to be organized and learn how to use the equipment you have to best advantage. People say they don't have room on top of the stove to let a stock simmer for hours. Not all stocks have to be made on the stove top; I make many stocks in the oven.

"I always make turkey, lamb, pheasant, and venison stocks in the oven. I put a thick-bottom pan in the oven, get it hot, add the bones, and stir them around. It's important not to overload the pan, because then the pan cools off and the bones sweat rather than bake. Then I add the vegetables—carrots, onions, celery, leeks, garlic—and water. There's no need to peel the vegetables, as long as they are washed," he said.

Nitzi added, "The real secret to making a good stock is never to add more liquid than you need—that's particularly true with poultry stocks. You can't cook poultry stocks too long, for the longer you cook them, the less taste they have."

On the other hand, Nitzi cooks veal stocks on top of the stove for hours, with the liquid barely bubbling. (He doesn't bother making beef stock, because he prefers the lighter flavor of veal stock.) He plans on about 1 pound veal bones for each quart the pot holds. He browns the bones, deglazes the pan, adds the vegetables, and covers everything with cold water. Cold water is essential, he says, because hot water seals in the flavors, rather than letting them seep out into the water.

Then Nitzi slowly raises the heat and skims off the fat from time to time. He cooks the stock for about 6 hours. At this point the stock looks done, but Nitzi isn't finished.

"Now comes the important part that no one ever tells you. I strain the liquid, put it in a clean pan, and start all over again with fresh vegetables and meat trimmings to improve the flavor. I simmer this stock for about 2 hours, strain it, then reduce it to concentrate the flavor and viscosity," he said.

Even the leftover bones from the first cooking of the stock get utilized. Instead of tossing them out, Nitzi covers them with water and simmers them for 2 more hours to remove every last drop of flavor. He reduces this liquid, which he warns will look like dishwater, and ends up with a few cups of a stock that adds body and a light flavor to sauces.

In case this sounds like a lot of work, appropriate only for gourmet restaurant cooking, consider the end results. Although making stocks takes time, the actual work involved is minimal. You end up with an ample supply of stock, which you can also reduce into a concentrated *Glacé de Viande* (see page 264), as well as a light stock from the used bones.

Also, as Nitzi pointed out, "By using this method, it's possible to achieve a flavorful thickened sauce without using flour or cornstarch. The stock will have such a nice flavor of its own, you can easily turn it into sauces."

"For example, I'll sauté meat portions on top of the stove, deglaze the pan, and then add the stock. If the stock is heated, you can cook it at a high temperature to make a simple pan reduction sauce. Swirl it around with a spoon or a whip, and finish up with a walnut-size lump of butter for every 2 servings," he said.

Stocks are not the only item that the Rabins prepare ahead of time. Nitzi peels shallots, covers them with white wine, and stores them in covered jars in the refrigerator. (He thinks vinegar would work as well as wine.) Most of the herbs used at Chillingsworth come from the Rabins' garden: they wash the herbs, blot them with paper toweling, then roll the herbs in toweling and store them in plastic bags in the refrigerator for up to 12 days. Extra basil is turned into pesto and frozen.

As the chief pastry chef at the restaurant, Pat has developed several techniques to make sure good food doesn't go to waste. When she has leftover fruit, she'll often turn it into frozen sorbets. She'll freeze raspberries and blueberries whole and turn them into sauces when they're defrosted. Or she'll take fresh raspberries, purée them with honey and lemon juice, and store the sauce in the refrigerator, where it will keep for up to 1 week.

When the herb garden is in full production, she'll make herb sorbets out of tarragon or mint. Pat makes an essence by steeping 2 cups lightly packed leaves in 1½ cups hot water along with the juice of 2 lemons and ¼ cup honey. She freezes this essence, then defrosts it and adds a simple syrup; she then uses it as a sorbet base.

Even extra Pastry Cream (see page 258) isn't wasted. If, at the end of the evening, Pat has leftover *crème anglaise*, she converts it into ice cream. Pat places the pastry cream in the ice cream machine and adds about ⅓ cup heavy cream for each 2 cups *crème anglaise*. Once the mixture begins to set, she'll add flavorings, such as fresh peaches that have been cooked with a little honey and water until softened, and then freeze the mixture until solid.

She grinds leftover unfrosted cake trimmings or ladyfingers and nuts in the food processor, moistens the mixture with a ginger brandy and a fruit poaching syrup or honey, and uses the mixture to stuff poached pears or baked apples. Pat suggests a proportion of 2 parts cake to 1 part nuts.

At home the Rabins use little or no salt in their cooking. "However, when you start getting away from salt, you have to experiment with other things to fill the void. Salt gives an intensity to flavors. Herbs are an essential ingredient in salt-free cooking. I think sweet marjoram has far and away the best flavor. It never gets sour, as tarragon does when you add too much. Lovage is another great flavor. We also grow 3 kinds of basil and grill food with the dried *herbs de Provence*," Nitzi explained.

"A touch of good vinegar also helps compensate for the lack of salt," Pat added. "We use spices such as dried coriander and cardamom. These are hidden flavors, background seasonings . . . cardamom is so much more pungent than salt. Some flavors, such as saffron, however, only come through with salt, and curries need the balance of curry and salt."

The Rabins also cook with herb-flavored oils. "We'll macerate a bunch of basil in oil and then marinate fish in this oil before cooking it," Pat pointed out.

In this chapter you'll find directions for making some of the unusual sauces served at Chillingsworth. Nitzi has also shared his recipes for Scallop Terrine and Melon Soup, both of which you'll find elsewhere in the book (see page 126 and 51).

Mustard Green Sauce

Nitzi Rabin serves this sauce and Sweet Red Pepper Sauce (see page 244) flanking a mixed grill of vegetables and meats at his restaurant, Chillingsworth. He'll vary the grill, depending upon what's on hand, but he might include such items as sweet red peppers, small whole shallots, duck legs, lamb tenderloins, or chicken breasts cut into finger shapes. This is a beautiful green sauce with a sharp, piquant flavor.

1 egg	½ teaspoon white pepper
1½ cups tightly packed mustard-green leaves	1½ tablespoons red wine vinegar
1 teaspoon lemon juice	2 to 2¼ cups light vegetable oil

Place the egg, mustard greens, lemon juice, pepper, and vinegar in a food processor, and pulse it on and off until the mustard greens are chopped. With the machine running, add the oil very slowly until the sauce has a mayonnaise consistency.

If the sauce is covered and stored in a glass jar in the refrigerator, it should keep in good condition for at least 1 week.

Makes about 3½ cups

Seviche Sauce

This unusual sauce was invented by Nitzi and Pat Rabin to serve with marinated scallops tossed with dried sweet red pepper and a little avocado for color. The consistency is more like a frothy coating than a sauce. Like seviche this is strongly flavored with lime.

⅓	cup lime juice	2	tablespoons red wine vinegar
1	tablespoon ground coriander	¼	cup egg whites (from about 2 eggs)
2	tablespoons chopped coriander	2 to 2½	cups vegetable oil
1	teaspoon freshly ground white pepper		

Place the lime juice, all the coriander, the pepper, vinegar, and egg whites in a food processor. Process with on and off bursts for 15 seconds. Gradually add the oil in a slow, steady stream until the sauce has the consistency of slightly beaten egg whites.

If stored in a covered jar in the refrigerator, the sauce should keep for up to 10 days, although it may separate a little. If that happens, just whip it lightly to restore the texture.

Makes about 2 cups

Orange Basil Sauce

Nitzi Rabin says this sauce is terrific with a salad made with chicken, watercress, sliced oranges, and papayas or with a cold poached bass.

1	egg	⅓	cup basil
½	cup orange juice (or ¼ cup lime juice)	1	tablespoon red wine vinegar
1	mango or papaya, peeled and seeded	2½ to 3	cups vegetable oil

Place the egg in a food processor, and add the orange or lime juice, mango or papaya, basil, and vinegar. Process the mixture until combined. Then, with the machine running, add the oil in a slow, steady stream until the sauce is as smooth as you want it to be.

The sauce will keep for at least 1 week if stored in a covered glass jar in the refrigerator.

Makes about 4 cups

Variation
• For a thicker sauce substitute 2 egg yolks for the whole egg.

Sweet Red Pepper Sauce

At Chillingsworth restaurant, on Cape Cod, the Rabins often serve this sauce with brochettes of grilled scallops, shrimp, onions, and peppers. It would also be delicious with cold poached vegetables or grilled strips of chicken breasts. Nitzi roasts the sweet red peppers in a hot oven for about 30 minutes, turns them, sprinkles them with oil, and continues cooking them until the skins have become darkened and blistered in places but not blackened.

2	large sweet red peppers, roasted and cooled (do not peel)	1	tablespoon red wine vinegar
1	egg	½	teaspoon ground white pepper
1	egg white	2	cups light vegetable oil
½	tablespoon lemon juice	2 to 3	tablespoons finest quality olive oil

Pull the stems, and whatever seeds come with them, out of the sweet red peppers. Put the peppers, the egg, and the egg white in a food processor, and process for 1 minute, until puréed. Then add the lemon juice, vinegar, and pepper, and process until combined. With the machine running, slowly add the vegetable oil. The sauce will thicken to a thin mayonnaise consistency. Taste the sauce and correct the seasonings. Then, with the processor running, add the olive oil.

If this sauce is kept in a sealed glass jar in the refrigerator, it will keep for at least 1 week.

Makes about 4 cups

Variation
• Add 3 tablespoons chopped basil along with the lemon juice and vinegar.

Nitzi & Pat Rabin

Spicy Barbecue Sauce

Alice Senturia barbecues beef or pork with this sauce, sometimes adding a little tomato paste to bring out the flavor of pork.

1⅓	cups Beef Stock (see page 260)	1	teaspoon garlic powder
1	cup water	1	teaspoon chili powder
¾	cup Worcester-shire sauce	1	teaspoon hot pepper sauce
⅓	cup cider vinegar	1	bay leaf
⅓	cup vegetable oil	½	teaspoon ground paprika
½	tablespoon dry mustard		

Place the stock, water, Worcestershire sauce, vinegar, oil, mustard, garlic, chili powder, hot pepper sauce, bay leaf, and paprika in a saucepan. Bring the mixture to a boil, and cook for 5 minutes. Remove from the heat, and refrigerate for 12 hours before using, so that flavors can blend.

Store in glass jars in the refrigerator, where it will keep for several weeks if you boil it every 3 or 4 days, or for up to 2 weeks if you do not boil it. You can also freeze it for up to 1 year, or can it.

To can, pour the hot sauce into hot, clean pint canning jars, leaving a ½-inch headspace. Process for 15 minutes in a boiling water bath. Store for up to 1 year in a cool, dry place.

Makes about 4 pints

Chinese Dipping Sauce

Nina Simonds uses this sauce with steamed pork and cabbage dumplings.

½	cup soy sauce	1	tablespoon Chili Oil (see page 22)
2	tablespoons Chinese black vinegar or Worcestershire sauce		

Mix together the soy sauce, vinegar or Worcestershire sauce, and chili oil. Cover, and store in a cool spot. The sauce will keep for several months.

Makes ½ to ¾ cup

Variations
• Add 1 tablespoon shredded gingerroot or minced garlic.

Fresh Mint Sauce

Anyone who has tried commercial mint sauce, with its musty, unpleasant flavor, will find this sauce a revelation. The method here preserves mint's fresh, refreshing taste. Try this sauce with lamb, pork, or barbecued chicken. I like the delicate flavor of apple mint, but any culinary variety will work well.

½ cup white vinegar
¼ cup water
2 tablespoons honey

1 cup firmly packed chopped mint

Boil together the vinegar, water, and honey for a moment until the honey dissolves. Pour the hot mixture over the mint, and set the mixture aside for at least 1 hour.

Strain the liquid through a sieve, then squeeze the mint to extract any juices, much as you would squeeze blanched spinach.

As the syrup has a slight gray-green or brown-green color, I think the sauce looks best garnished with mint leaves.

If placed in a covered jar, the sauce will keep for at least 2 weeks in the refrigerator.

It can be frozen for up to 6 months. For small quantities, freeze in ice cube trays, and pop into plastic bags once frozen.

Makes about ¾ cup

Mint Garlic Sauce

This sauce was inspired by one of my friends, Marie Caratelli, who told me her mother served a similar sauce with polenta, the cornmeal specialty of the Piedmont region of northern Italy. It is also good as a marinade for vegetables, especially peas and beans, and for marinating lamb.

2 cups cider vinegar
½ cup mint
3 cloves garlic, chopped

Warm the vinegar. Add the mint and garlic. Cover, and let sit in a cool, dark place for at least 2 weeks before serving. Strain and rebottle for a mild sauce; leave as is for a stronger version.

This sauce will keep for several months if strained and stored in a sterilized jar in a cool place.

Makes about 2½ cups

Pesto

The northern Italians have made pesto a worldwide favorite. Who would imagine that chopped basil, oil, cheese, and pine nuts would combine into such an addictive combination? My garden always includes at least 15 basil plants to supply pesto for cold and hot pasta or as a seasoning for vegetable soups—but if you don't have a garden, many markets now carry fresh basil in a culinary herb section. I think the texture of the pesto is best if you make it in small batches.

2	cups tightly packed basil leaves (stripped from the stems and thoroughly washed and dried)	½ to ¾	cup olive oil
		¼	cup peanut oil
		¼	cup pine nuts
		½	cup grated Parmesan cheese
2	teaspoons chopped garlic	1 to 2	tablespoons grated Romano cheese

Place the basil and garlic in a food processor or blender, and process for a few seconds. Add the olive oil, peanut oil, pine nuts, and the cheeses. Process the ingredients just long enough to chop the pine nuts and combine all the ingredients. (Do this at 1 time because if the chopped basil sits around uncovered, it darkens.)

If the pesto is placed in a glass jar in the refrigerator and sealed with olive oil, it will keep in good condition for at least 1 month.

Freeze the pesto base for longer storage, up to 9 months. To freeze pesto, process just the basil, garlic, and oil. Freeze this base—then add the remaining ingredients once the pesto base thaws. For convenience freeze the pesto in ice cube trays, and pop into a plastic bag once frozen. When thawing, do so in the refrigerator rather than at room temperature, so the pesto base doesn't lose its vibrant green color.

Makes about 1½ cups

Garlic Yogurt Sauce

Serve this with Gyros (see page 110) or lamb kabobs. Do not use a food processor to mix the garlic and yogurt, because it thins out the yogurt too much.

½ tablespoon finely
    minced garlic
1½ cups yogurt

Crush the garlic with the back of a knife or with a mortar and pestle until it is puréed. Combine with the yogurt, making sure it is well blended. Chill before serving.

Makes 1½ cups

Variation
• Stir in 1 tablespoon finely chopped mint along with the garlic.

Pear Mustard Sauce

This unusual pear sauce is attractive served hot or cold in a glass compote, garnished with fresh mint, as an accompaniment to roast pork, lamb, or veal. Adjust the amount of mustard to suit your taste.

4 cups diced peeled ripe
    pears (about 2½
    pounds)
1 cup water

1 tablespoon honey
⅓ cup white vinegar
⅓ to ½ cup Dijon mustard

Cook the pears in the water until soft, stirring frequently to prevent the pears from burning. Drain, and cool slightly. Add the honey, vinegar, and mustard, and purée in a food processor until smooth.

Store in a covered glass dish in the refrigerator, where it will keep for at least 1½ weeks.

Makes 3 to 4 cups

Cranberry Sauce

½ to ¾   cup honey
    ¾   cup water

⅓   cup lemon juice
1   quart cranberries*

Bring the honey, water, and lemon juice to a boil in a medium-size saucepan. Lower the heat and simmer until the honey dissolves, about 2 minutes. Stir in the cranberries and gently boil for 10 minutes, stirring frequently. Remove from the heat and cool.

Stored in a covered jar in the refrigerator, the sauce will keep for up to 1 month. You can also freeze it for up to 1 year.

*Frozen cranberries can be used but be sure they boil for the full 10 minutes.

Makes 2¼ cups

Eastern European Plum Sauce

1½   cups water
1½   pounds plums
 2   tablespoons finely
      chopped coriander
      leaves

    1   clove garlic, chopped
2 to 3   tablespoons lemon
       juice

Boil the water and plums together for 3 minutes. Remove from the heat, and set aside for 15 minutes, then bring back to a boil over high heat. Cook for another 15 minutes, or until the plums are cooked through and tender. Pour through a sieve, and set the liquid aside.

Discard the plum pits and combine the plums, coriander, and garlic in a blender. Pour in ½ cup of the reserved plum liquid, and blend at high speed. Gradually add the remaining plum liquid.

Transfer the sauce to a saucepan, and bring the mixture to a boil. Cook for 2 minutes. Remove from the heat, stir in the lemon juice, and let cool before serving.

This sauce is good served with pork or poultry or as a spread for bread. It will keep in good condition for up to 2 weeks in the refrigerator.

Makes about 2 cups

Mango Strawberry Sauce

This is a fresh-tasting, unusual sauce for ice cream or egg custard.

3 cups chopped mangoes (about 3)	⅔ cup lime juice (about 8 limes)
3 cups sliced strawberries (about 1 quart whole)	1 cup honey

Combine 2 cups mangoes, the strawberries, lime juice, and the honey in a heavy enameled or stainless steel saucepan. Bring the fruits to a boil, stirring constantly until they release their juices, about 12 minutes. Lower the heat, skim off any foam, and simmer for 10 minutes more. Stir in the remaining mangoes and continue cooking over medium-low heat for another 10 to 15 minutes, or until the sauce thickens. Stir frequently so the sauce won't stick to the bottom of the pan.

The sauce will keep in good condition for up to 2 weeks in the refrigerator if stored in a covered container. Or freeze for up to 9 months.

If you wish, can the sauce, using the boiling water bath method. Pour it hot into hot, clean pint or ½-pint jars, leaving a ½-inch headspace. Process for 15 minutes.

Makes 7½ cups

Strawberry Cantaloupe Sauce

This attractive sauce is quick to make.

4 cups sliced strawberries	½ cup fresh orange juice
2 cups diced cantaloupe	
1 cup honey	

Stir together the strawberries, cantaloupe, honey, and orange juice in a large stainless steel or enameled pan such as a stockpot or preserving kettle. Bring the mixture to a slow boil, and boil until the fruits are cooked and the sauce reduces and thickens. This will take 10 to 15 minutes, depending upon how much juice the strawberries have.

Remove from the heat, and immediately bottle in hot, sterilized jars. Seal, and store the sauce in a jar in the refrigerator, where it will keep for several weeks.

Makes about 3 cups

Taratoor or Sesame Sauce

Serve this sauce with baked fish or with raw vegetables in a pita bread sandwich. Or mix it with an equal amount of mashed cooked chick-peas to make *hummus*.

2	cloves garlic, minced	¾	cup lemon juice
1	cup tahini (sesame seed paste)	about ½	cup cold water

Mash the garlic into a paste with a mortar and pestle, or use the back of a knife. Place in a mixing bowl or food processor and add the tahini. Process until the garlic is thoroughly incorporated. Add the lemon juice first, then the cold water, a little at a time. (The lemon juice thickens the sauce; the cold water thins it.) The sauce should end up with the consistency of a thick mayonnaise.

This sauce will keep for at least 1 week placed in a covered jar in the refrigerator.

Makes 2 cups

Variation
• Toast 3 tablespoons sesame seeds, and stir into the sauce just before serving. The seeds absorb moisture from the sauce and soften, so if you are planning to hold the *taratoor* for a few days, add the seeds as needed.

Basics

Basic recipes and techniques never sound intriguing, but they're important: once you know how to can preserves and relishes, make stocks, or preserve herbs, you'll have mastered several elements of fine cooking that will make your cooking easier yet better tasting.

But it isn't enough to be a good cook and to prepare a backlog of pantry foods, because if you don't store them correctly, all your work is wasted. In this chapter I've included a great deal of storage information, as well as instructions on basic canning techniques.

Anyone who's ever had a garden knows the satisfaction of converting surplus fruit and produce into colorful and flavorful preserves and relishes. Yet, since I first started canning 20 years ago, home economists have changed their minds about the ways preserving should be done.

The latest thinking from the United States Department of Agriculture and other food researchers is that the open kettle method, used for years for putting up preserves and jams, is no longer recommended. Instead, they advise using the boiling water bath method. This may affect the flavor a bit, giving more of a cooked taste to your preserves, but it's a small price to pay for safely canned foods. I've given you instructions for canning with the boiling water bath method in the pages that follow.

This chapter also includes basic information on drying fruits and herbs (one of the oldest preserving methods known) and freezing certain specialty items. This is not a freezing book, but some pantry foods freeze so well that I wanted to include the information here.

Stocks, one of the foundations of good cooking, are ideal pantry foods because they form the basis for thousands of recipes. Simmering bones, meat, and vegetables for hours sounds tedious, but an ample supply of flavorful stocks can make it possible to give extra flavor to soups and casseroles and to produce a delicious meal in minutes.

If you have chicken, beef, veal, or fish stock in the freezer, you can make a quick sauce or gravy at the last minute just by using the pan juices and the stock you've prepared in advance. Anyone who works out of the house all day should make up a supply of stocks for just such moments.

I've given you recipes for making stocks from scratch, but you can also simmer any leftover meat or poultry bones in water with onions (and maybe garlic) to make flavored broths, which can then be used for soups or be reduced for sauces.

I've also included instructions for such specialty items as a flavored butter, Baked Garlic Cloves, and Duxelles, a concentrated mushroom mixture. These are handy cooking aids and take but a minute to prepare. Restaurant chefs prepare a supply of flavored butters to dot on fish or meats just before serving. If you slice butters before freezing them or storing them in the refrigerator, you need only pry each serving loose with a fork when you need it. A spoonful of puréed garlic or concentrated mushrooms in a sauce or soup adds flavor without last-minute work.

Many of the classic sauces, such as mayonnaise, are included in the Cold Sauces and Salad Dressings chapter. Here, however, you'll find a recipe for Hollandaise Sauce Food-Processor–Style because hollandaise sauce is one of the prime sauces of French cooking and the basis for other sauces. Fold in whipped cream, and you have a Mousseline Sauce.

These recipes, as well as others that don't fit into any special category, can be found in this chapter. Take a moment to thumb through the pages that follow, so you'll remember where to locate these pantry food staples.

Herb Garlic Butter

Herb butters give color and flavor to broiled fish or poultry. Many restaurant chefs keep them on hand to use as needed. I like to make up several rolls of butter in late fall, freeze them, and have the illusion of fresh herbs throughout the winter. This particular herb butter is one of my favorites.

1	pound butter, softened	1	tablespoon finely chopped chives
½	teaspoon dry mustard		
2	cloves garlic, minced	¼	cup finely chopped shallots
¼	cup finely chopped parsley		
1	tablespoon finely chopped lovage (optional)		

Beat the butter and mustard together. Stir in the garlic, parsley, lovage (if used), chives, and shallots. Store in a covered bowl or jar in the refrigerator.

Or fashion the butter into a roll, using foil, for refrigerator or freezer storage. Line a wide strip of foil with waxed paper. Using a spatula, shape a long cylinder of butter about 1½ inches in diameter. Fold the foil partially over the butter, then roll up the remaining foil to enclose the butter. Twist the foil ends in opposite directions. The butter is now ready to be refrigerated or frozen. Slice into pieces to top cooked fish, poultry, vegetables, or pasta.

The butter will keep for at least 2 weeks in the refrigerator and for up to 3 months in the freezer.

Makes 2 cups

Clarified Butter — Two Ways

Both the French and the Indians clarify butter, but the techniques are different. The French clarified butter is made by straining the clear melted butter off the milky residue on the bottom of the pot, while the Indian version simmers a long time to allow the moisture in the milk solids to evaporate, giving it a nutty flavor.

French-Style Clarified Butter

Slice 1 pound (unsalted) butter, and place it in a heavy saucepan. Melt over medium heat, then slowly boil. When the white solids on the surface of the butter have sunk, the butter is done. The milky residue will be on the bottom of the pan.

Strain off the clear liquid on top, and store in a covered glass jar in the refrigerator, where it will keep for several weeks; freeze for up to 6 months.

Makes about 1½ cups

Indian-Style *Ghee* (gē)

Cut 1 pound butter into small pieces, and slowly heat it in a heavy saucepan over low heat. Once the butter has completely melted, raise the heat to medium. As the layer of foam appears on the top, the butter will make a crackling noise; this is the moisture being released from the milk solids. Let it simmer for about 10 minutes.

Once the crackling stops and the foam subsides, start stirring constantly. The moment the solids turn brown, remove the pan from the heat, and let the brown residue settle to the bottom.

Cool for a few minutes, then pour the clear liquid on top into a jar. Cool the ghee completely, then cover the jar. The ghee will keep for several weeks in the refrigerator; freeze for up to 6 months.

Makes about 1½ cups

Roux

Roux is a basic ingredient in Louisiana Cajun cooking. Usually it's made with shortening, but Susan Harnett's version uses sesame oil.

1	cup sesame oil
2 to 2¼	cups whole wheat pastry flour

Stir the oil and flour together in a large, heavy saucepan. Cook over very low heat, stirring constantly, for 25 minutes. The roux will turn a dark golden brown and have the consistency of heavy cream.

Cool the roux and store in a tightly covered jar in the refrigerator, where it will keep in good condition for several months.

Makes about 2¾ cups

Hollandaise Sauce
Food-Processor–Style

The food processor produces a thinner, lighter hollandaise than the traditional version made by hand, with an emulsified texture that allows the sauce to be reheated. It's important, however, that when you reheat the sauce in a double boiler, you whisk it constantly and reheat the sauce only to lukewarm—otherwise it will separate. It's also essential that the eggs be at room temperature and that the butter be top quality. If you want a thicker sauce, add a generous pinch of salt.

3	egg yolks	2	teaspoons lemon juice
1	teaspoon Dijon mustard		cayenne pepper or hot pepper sauce (optional)
¼	teaspoon dry mustard		
1	tablespoon boiling water		
½	pound butter (1 cup), heated to near boiling		

Place the egg yolks, Dijon mustard, and dry mustard in the container of a food processor, and pulse it for 1 or 2 seconds to combine the ingredients. Turn on the machine and, while the machine is running, add the boiling water. Run the machine for about 1 minute.

Slowly add the butter, almost dribbling it in. After the hollandaise has thickened, add the lemon juice. Taste, and add cayenne or hot pepper sauce only if necessary.

Serve warm or store in a covered glass jar in the refrigerator, where it will keep for at least 1 week.

Makes 1½ cups

Variation
• Mousseline Sauce: Fold ½ cup whipped heavy cream into the sauce just before serving.

Crème Fraîche

French crème fraîche has a slightly acidic and nutty flavor American heavy cream lacks. I tried several approximations before ending up with this easy recipe. Converted into crème fraîche, heavy cream will keep for days without spoiling and also can be boiled without curdling. Do not use ultra-pasteurized cream; the recipe will not work if you do.

2	cups heavy cream	1	tablespoon sour cream
2	tablespoons buttermilk		

Heat the cream to 100°F. Do not overheat or you will destroy the fermenting agents. Remove the cream from the heat, and stir in the buttermilk and sour cream.

Pour the mixture into a glass container, partially cover, and let stand at room temperature until it is the consistency of yogurt. The length of time the crème fraîche takes to thicken depends upon the room temperature. An ideal temperature is 70 to 75°F. In cold weather, if you have a gas stove, placing the jar above the pilot light on top of the stove works well.

Chill for at least 24 hours before serving, to allow the flavor to develop.

Crème fraîche keeps for at least 10 days in a covered jar in the refrigerator.

Makes about 2 cups

Baked Garlic Cloves

Use the cloves of garlic to make garlic bread, season mashed potatoes, or pep up homemade mayonnaise. A few of the puréed cloves stirred into sauces will give them an elusive flavor.

large bulbs garlic,   olive or safflower oil
    unpeeled

Trim the garlic roots but keep the bulbs unpeeled. Coat each garlic bulb with 1 tablespoon oil, wrap them together in foil, and bake in a preheated 300°F oven for 1½ to 2 hours, or until the cloves are easily pierced with a fork.

Cool the garlic and separate the cloves. Squeeze the pulp out of the skins, and store the pulp (which by now has almost a puréed texture) in a clean glass container. Cover with oil.

The garlic will keep for several weeks in the refrigerator.

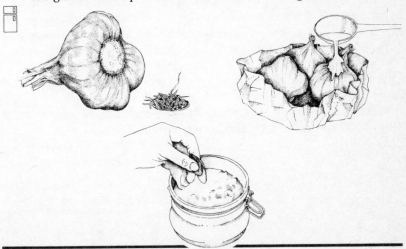

Pastry Cream

Unlike a standard pastry cream, which is based on eggs, sugar, milk, and flour, this recipe calls for cornstarch, which stabilizes the pastry cream while producing a delicately flavored custard impossible with whole wheat flour. It is essential to continuously stir the custard after returning it to the stove, or else the cornstarch will lump. (Should this happen, just put it through a fine sieve, and no one will be the wiser.) Also, use a heavy-bottom stainless steel or enameled pan; aluminum will give a gray coloration to the cream.

Use the pastry cream to fill banana or coconut cream pies, cream puffs—or tarts, made with either of the puff pastry recipes (see page 187 and 188). Bake a puff pastry shell and coat the bottom with a thin layer of strained apricot preserves or red-currant jelly. Fill the pastry with chilled pastry cream, and top it with fresh golden or red raspberries, blackberries, blueberries, sliced peaches, poached pears, or strawberries.

7	egg yolks	1	tablespoon vanilla extract
⅓	cup honey		
¼	cup plus 1 tablespoon cornstarch	1	tablespoon butter (optional)
3	cups milk		

Beat together the egg yolks, honey, and cornstarch in a large mixing bowl. Check to make sure that the cornstarch has been incorporated smoothly and that no lumps remain.

Meanwhile, in a heavy stainless steel or enameled pot, heat the milk until it is hot. (If you test with your finger, the milk should feel hot but not scalding.) Slowly beat the hot milk into the egg yolk mixture.

Pour the mixture back into the pot, and place it over medium heat. Immediately start stirring with a whisk or heavy wooden spoon as rapidly as you can. All of a sudden the cornstarch will start to lump, but if you are constantly stirring, it will smooth out. Once the mixture comes to a boil, let it boil, stirring constantly, for about 1 minute until it is smooth. Stir in the vanilla and let the cream cool before storing it.

If you wish, dot the surface with the butter to prevent a skin from forming. Store, covered, in the refrigerator, where the pastry cream will keep for at least 1 week. The custard may weep slightly in storage, but it won't affect the flavor. Just drain before serving.

Makes about 4 cups

Variation

• Frangipane (frŏn' jă păhn) Cream: Stir in ½ cup finely ground almonds (or filberts) after you add the vanilla. Use as the base for a fresh pear tart made with ground nuts in the crust.

Vegetable Marinade

Marinate blanched vegetables in this for 2 to 3 days before serving them. Good choices would be baby carrots, peeled but with 1 inch of the stems left on for color; cauliflower florets; pickling onions; baby green beans; 2-inch-long baby zucchini or pattypan or yellow summer squash; red pepper strips; diagonally sliced Florence fennel; or baby leeks or scallions. I always make this with chicken stock, but vegetarians may prefer using water and increasing the amount of lemon juice to ¾ cup.

1	quart Chicken Stock (see page 262) or water		bouquet garni of 1 celery stalk, 3 parsley sprigs, 1 thyme sprig, and 1 bay leaf
½	cup olive oil		
⅓ to ¾	cup lemon juice		
2	cloves garlic, sliced	½	teaspoon dried thyme
8	peppercorns		
8	coriander seeds		

Place the stock or water, oil, lemon juice, garlic, peppercorns, coriander seeds, bouquet garni, and thyme in an enameled or stainless steel saucepan. Bring the mixture to a boil, lower the heat, partially cover the pan, and simmer the marinade for 30 minutes.

Strain the liquid and store in the refrigerator in a covered glass jar. The marinade should keep for at least 1 week if you boil it every 3 days. Freeze for longer storage.

When you are ready to marinate the vegetables, reheat the marinade and pour it over the warm vegetables. Cool the vegetables and store in the refrigerator for at least 3 days, turning them in the marinade occasionally.

Makes about 4 cups

Variation
• Add ½ teaspoon aniseed during the last 15 minutes of simmering the marinade.

Duxelles

Duxelles (deuhk sell') is a concentrate of minced mushrooms. Just a spoonful gives a mushroom flavor to sauces, stuffings, or gravies. In Boston the open-air markets often reduce the price of mushrooms just before closing. When that happens, I buy a batch and make Pickled Mushrooms (see page 57) out of the caps and duxelles out of the stems. Using a food processor turns mincing the mushrooms from an onerous chore into a speedy procedure of a matter of seconds. Be careful not to overprocess, or the mushrooms will turn to paste.

2¼   pounds mushrooms
⅜   cup butter

Finely mince the mushrooms and put them in a large bowl. Place a handful of mushrooms into the center of a clean kitchen towel. Twist the towel around the mushrooms and gently squeeze to extract the mushroom juices. Continue squeezing the remaining mushrooms, a handful at a time. You should end up with a scant cup of mushroom juice from 2¼ pounds mushrooms. Save the juice for braising a pot roast or swiss steaks.

Melt the butter in an enameled or stainless steel frying pan and add the mushrooms. Sauté quickly over high heat, stirring frequently, for 10 minutes. At this point any moisture left in the mushrooms should have evaporated and the mushroom pieces will have separated and will be lightly browned.

Let the mixture cool, then pack in a covered glass jar, and store in the refrigerator. Treated this way, the duxelles will keep for several weeks.

Makes about 2½ cups

Beef Stock

Beef stock or broth is the liquid that remains after you simmer meat and vegetables in water for several hours, to extract the flavor, and then strain it. If you have access to an inexpensive supply of beef cuts, shin beef makes a flavorful broth. All you have to do is simmer 3 pounds of meaty shin beef in water for 3 or 4 hours, and you have a beef essence for soups or stews with almost no work. Otherwise, it's best to extract flavor from a mixture of beef (or veal) bones and vegetables.

The stone soup adage applies to stocks more than any other basic cooking item: you cannot dump a few bones and limp old vegetables into a pot, add some water, and expect them to miraculously turn into a wonderful, flavorful stock. A stock made from bones alone will be gelatinous, but it will lack flavor unless you include some meat. You will end up with a flavorful stock only if you use a sufficient amount of meaty bones and vegetables. Stockpile bones and meat scraps in the freezer, and when you have a sufficient quantity, turn them into a stock. Make sure knuckle and other solid bones are cracked before you start.

5 to 6	pounds meaty beef bones (such as shin or shank), cut into 3-inch sections	6	peppercorns
		6 to 8	parsley sprigs
		1	tomato (optional)
3	large carrots, thickly sliced	2	leeks, white parts only, quartered
2	large onions, quartered	2	cloves garlic, unpeeled

Preheat the oven to 450°F.

Brown the beef, carrots, and onions for 15 to 20 minutes. Do not crowd the pan or the bones will sweat rather than brown. Do not let the vegetables burn. When the meat and vegetables have browned, place them in a deep, heavy pot, and cover with at least 4 quarts cold water.

Add some water to the baking pan, scrape the bottom, and bring the mixture to a boil. Boil for 1 minute, until all the browned bits on the bottom of the pan have been incorporated into the liquid, and set aside.

Slowly bring the water in the stock pot to a rapid simmer, lower the heat, and skim any scum off the surface. Add the liquid from the baking pan.

Stir in the peppercorns, parsley, tomato (if used), leeks, and garlic. Partially cover the pot and simmer the stock for 4 to 5 hours, or until the meat has released all its flavor. Add additional cold water as needed and skim the stock occasionally. Strain the stock and cool it, uncovered. You should have 2 to 3 quarts stock.

Remove the fat from the surface, and refrigerate the stock for up to 4 days. If you wish to store it longer, boil it every 2 to 3 days to keep it from spoiling. Or freeze the stock in ½-cup or 1-cup amounts.

If you wish, reduce the stock before freezing, to concentrate the flavor further, or make a *Glacé de Viande* (see page 264).

Makes 2 to 3 quarts, depending upon the concentration of flavor

Variation
• Veal (or White) Stock: Substitute 4 pounds veal bones and 1 to 2 pounds veal meat for the beef bones, and add 1 teaspoon dried thyme along with the other ingredients.

Chicken Stock

More often than not when I need chicken stock, I'll simmer a 4-pound chicken (or backs, necks, and gizzards saved in the freezer and defrosted) in water, along with a halved onion, some celery and parsley leaves, and 4 or 5 peppercorns. After 1 hour I'll remove the meat, set it aside for another recipe, and put the skin and bones back in the broth to cook for another 1½ hours. Then I'll strain the stock, cool it, and refrigerate it so I can lift off the fat. Once the stock is degreased, I'll boil it down to concentrate the flavor, then store it. This method works well for recipes that need a delicate chicken flavor.

The recipe below is a little more complicated, but it produces a stock with a full, rich flavor that's excellent for sauces. A few tablespoons will add flavor to casseroles as well.

1	6-pound fowl, cut into pieces	6	stems parsley or 2 stems lovage
3	stalks celery, chopped	2	thyme sprigs (about 1 teaspoon leaves)
3	carrots, chopped		
2	leeks, white parts only, quartered	4	cloves garlic, unpeeled (optional)
1	large onion, halved	½	bay leaf

Place the fowl, celery, carrots, leeks, onion, parsley or lovage, thyme, garlic, and bay leaf in a large, heavy pot, and cover with cold water. Slowly bring the water to a simmer, and simmer for 3 to 3½ hours, occasionally skimming the scum and fat from the surface.

Pour the stock through a colander into a large bowl and cool it immediately, uncovered. (If the stock is covered while it cools, it might sour.)

Place the stock in a large container, and store it in the refrigerator until the fat congeals on the surface. Remove the fat. If a stronger flavored stock is desired, boil the stock down until it reduces to 2 quarts or has the concentration of flavor you wish.

Store the stock in the refrigerator for up to 4 days, or freeze the stock in ½-cup amounts. The stock should keep in good condition in the freezer for up to 6 months.

Makes 2 to 3 quarts

Variation
• Make the stock in the oven while you are cooking a casserole. In a large roasting pan brown the ingredients, cover with water, and cook in the oven at 350°F for 3 to 4 hours. Strain, cool, and degrease.

Fish Stock

A flavorful stock is a must for fish sauces or as a base for chowders or fish soups. I like to make stock with fish heads and trimmings from any non-oily white fleshed fish such as halibut or haddock. If you're using fish heads, be sure to remove the eyes and gills, or they'll give an off taste to the stock.

2½ pounds fish trimmings and bones
1 large carrot, thinly sliced
1 large onion, thinly sliced

herbs (including 2 to 3 parsley sprigs, lovage, and thyme)
4 peppercorns

Place the fish trimmings and bones in a large stainless steel or enameled pan, and cover with water. Add the carrots, onions, herbs, and peppercorns and partially cover the pan. Bring the water to a boil, lower the heat, and simmer for 35 to 40 minutes, skimming off any scum that rises to the surface.

Pour the liquid through a fine sieve, then reduce the liquid by boiling rapidly until it has the strength you desire. How much the stock has to be reduced really depends upon how fleshy the bones were: I usually end up with a reduction of about half. Strain the stock through a colander lined with coffee filters.

Cool the stock and store it in the refrigerator for up to 3 days. For longer storage keep it in the freezer for up to 6 months.

Makes 2 to 3 quarts

Variation
• Add a strip of orange zest and ¼ teaspoon aniseed along with the vegetables.

Clarified Stock

Use this method to clarify stock for consommé or aspic. Degrease the stock and strain it through coffee filters before you clarify it.

2	quarts stock	4	egg shells, in pieces
4	egg whites, beaten until frothy		

Bring the stock to a boil, and stir in the egg whites and shells. Lower the heat and stir constantly for 2 minutes. Then let the stock gently simmer for 15 minutes.

Place a colander in a large bowl, and line it with a linen or flour-sacking dish towel that's been dampened and wrung dry. Slowly pour the stock into the colander. Any impurities will be removed by the egg whites and shells, which stay in the colander while the clear stock drains through.

Makes about 2 quarts

Glacé de Viande

Glacé de viande is the French phrase for a meat glaze produced by slowly reducing stock until it becomes a syrupy glaze. It's important to start with a fat-free, clear stock. If you are a purist, remove the sediment that forms on the sides of the pan as the stock reduces; this will result in a clearer glaze. I usually reduce beef stock, but you can also make a chicken stock glaze using the same technique. This glaze adds flavor to casseroles and sauces.

10   cups beef or veal stock

Place the stock in a large pan, bring it to a boil, and immediately lower the heat. Simmer the stock until it forms a syrupy glaze that's about 1/10 the original volume. Skim off any foam or skum on the surface.

The reduction time varies depending upon the strength of the stock. I've reduced small amounts of stock (about 4 cups) in 40 minutes. The important aspect is the syrupy consistency of the glaze—not the reduction time.

Cool the glaze at room temperature, uncovered, and place in a clean glass jar in the refrigerator, where it will keep for at least 1 month. Or freeze the glaze in ice cube trays, and store the cubes in plastic bags in the freezer, where they will keep for at least 5 months.

Makes 1 cup

Granola

Susan Harnett makes this granola for her 3 children. She cautions that it's important to use rolled oats, because oatmeal has been steamed and the bran and germ have been removed.

⅓	cup safflower oil	½	cup chopped dates
⅓	cup honey	½	cup chopped dried
3	cups rolled oats		apples
1	cup hulled sunflower	1	cup raisins
	seeds		
½	cup slivered almonds		
½	cup unsalted raw		
	peanuts (or any of		
	your favorite nuts)		

Preheat the oven to 350°F.

Beat together the oil and honey until thoroughly combined. Stir in the rolled oats, sunflower seeds, almonds, and peanuts or other nuts. Spread the mixture out on a baking sheet or roasting pan. Roast until crunchy and brown, about 45 minutes, stirring frequently.

Cool the mixture and add the dates, apples, and raisins. Store in a covered glass jar, and keep in a cool, dark spot.

The mixture will keep for several weeks, as long as it is tightly covered and dry. A small amount of dry milk wrapped in a cheesecloth bag and kept in the granola storage container will extend the storage time.

Makes about 7 cups

Quatre Épices

The French spice mixture used for pâtés varies from cook to cook. This is my version. Try it also in meat loaves or in stews or sausage.

2	teaspoons ground cinnamon	2	teaspoons ground nutmeg
1	tablespoon plus 1 teaspoon ground allspice	3	teaspoons ground coriander
½ to ¾	teaspoon ground cloves	½	teaspoon ground ginger

Mix together the cinnamon, allspice, cloves, nutmeg, coriander, and ginger. Store in a tightly covered jar.

The spice mixture is best used up within 1 month, but it will last for up to 3 months, at which point it should be tossed out.

Makes about ⅓ cup

Cider Syrup

Years ago my mother picked up a cider syrup in Vermont that was delicious on pancakes, for poaching fresh apples or pears, or for basting roast pork; it had a wonderfully intense apple flavor. This is my version.

1	gallon fresh cider	1	cinnamon stick
1	cup honey		grated nutmeg
3	cloves		

Boil the cider in an enameled or stainless steel pan until it reduces to 1 quart. Add the honey, cloves, cinnamon, and nutmeg. Boil over medium heat until it is reduced again to 1 quart. I like a thin syrup but if you prefer a thicker version, continue boiling until the syrup has the consistency you want.

Pour boiling hot into 2 hot, sterilized pint containers, seal immediately, and store in the refrigerator, where it will keep for several months if kept tightly capped. Or process for 15 minutes in a boiling water bath to store for up to 1 year.

Makes about 2 pints

Fresh Tomato Sauce

Before I had a garden, I always made tomato sauce with canned tomatoes, grated carrots, chopped onions and garlic, red wine, and chicken stock. These ingredients produced a robust sauce we enjoyed—but somewhere along the way, the fresh tomato flavor disappeared. Now, I go out to the garden, pick absolutely ripe plum tomatoes, use as few ingredients as possible, and end up with a delicate sauce that's the essence of tomatoes. During the season I make several batches and stock the freezer so we can enjoy the sauce throughout the winter. It's important to cook the sauce rapidly; a temperature halfway between a simmer and a slow boil is best because the longer tomatoes cook, the more acidic they become and the more they lose their fresh garden taste.

4	pounds ripe plum tomatoes	3	tablespoons chopped basil or combined basil and sweet marjoram
3	tablespoons olive oil		
3	cups chopped onions		
2	cloves garlic, minced		

Peel, seed, and chop the tomatoes and set aside. Heat the oil in a heavy stainless steel or enameled pan and add the onions and garlic. Cook, stirring frequently, for 10 to 15 minutes, or until the onions are soft but not browned.

Add the tomatoes, bring to a boil, and boil until the juices are released, 3 to 4 minutes. Lower the heat to a rapid simmer, and cook, stirring frequently, for 30 minutes. At this point the sauce should have thickened; if it has not, cook for 10 to 15 minutes longer. Stir in the basil and sweet marjoram (if used), and cook for 2 to 3 minutes.

Cool the sauce and store in the refrigerator in a covered glass bowl. The sauce should keep for up to 1 week. It will also keep in the freezer for up to 10 months.

Makes about 5½ cups

Tomato Sauce

This is a good recipe when you only have canned tomatoes on hand. The carrots sweeten the slightly acidic taste of the tomatoes.

¼	cup olive oil		freshly ground black
2	cups chopped onions		pepper
¼	cup grated carrots	2	teaspoons chopped
1	teaspoon finely minced		sweet marjoram or
	garlic		oregano
4	cups chopped seeded	2 to 3	tablespoons chopped
	canned tomatoes		basil

Heat the oil in a large saucepan, and add the onions, carrots, and garlic. Cook, stirring constantly, until the vegetables are cooked through and are starting to brown. Add the tomatoes and a generous sprinkling of pepper.

Partially cover the pan and simmer for 15 minutes. Sieve the sauce, or process for a few seconds in a food processor. Return the sauce to the stove, and add the sweet marjoram or oregano and basil. Partially cover the pan and simmer for 25 minutes longer, or until the liquids have reduced and the sauce is the consistency you prefer.

If stored in the refrigerator, the sauce will stay in good condition for at least 1 week. Freeze the sauce for up to 1 year.

Makes 3½ to 4 cups

Sun-Dried Tomatoes

Sun-dried Italian plum tomatoes are currently among the trendy items in many gourmet food shops, retailing at more than $10 per small jar. They're delicious as snacks with homemade white cheese, thinly sliced in antipasto salads, or as special ingredients in sandwiches. These tomatoes, which originated as peasant food in southern Italy, are fun to make if you have tomatoes from the garden. I've had limited success drying tomatoes in the humid Northeast, but if you live in a climate with hot, dry summer days, you should have more luck.

Halve meaty plum tomatoes crosswise; Roma or San Marzano varieties work well. Dry them in the sun, protected by screening. (Follow the general drying instructions starting on page 271.) You want the tomatoes to slowly dehydrate and become slightly chewy. This could take up to 4 days.

Lightly brush the cut halves with vinegar, and layer them in sterilized jars, adding a little olive oil to each layer and then topping each jar with olive oil. Cover the jars and store them in the refrigerator, where the tomatoes will keep for several months. Be sure that the tomatoes are covered with oil at all times.

Variations
• Place several peeled cloves of garlic or basil or tarragon sprigs (or both garlic and herbs) in each jar.

Freezing Tomatoes

As many of the new tomato varieties are less acidic than those of the past, I think it is risky to can tomatoes without adjusting the acidity with vinegar or lemon juice. Instead, I freeze them whole and find it an equally convenient way to preserve my surplus harvest.

I wash and dry the tomatoes and spread them out on a baking sheet, then pop them into the freezer. Once the tomatoes are frozen solid, I pour them into plastic freezer bags and seal the tops. The tomatoes stay in good condition for at least 6 months.

When it's time to use the tomatoes, I remove them from the freezer, place them in a colander, and run them under the hot water tap while they are still frozen. The skins peel right off, leaving the pulp. As the tomatoes defrost, the tomato juices separate out from the pulp and can be drained off.

Canning Preserves and Relishes

No one wants to become ill from poorly canned food or to go to all that work only to have the food have a disappointing taste or look—or worse, spoil. Using the right kind of equipment and some commonsense canning rules will prevent these occurrences from ever happening.

Your most expensive purchase, and certainly the most important one, is a deep, heavy stainless steel preserving pot. When you are cooking with sugar, you can get away with a light pot, but honey can burn as preserves or relishes thicken, so a pot that's heavy enough to evenly distribute the heat is essential. My pot, which I use almost every day, cost $55 at a restaurant supply store. You could also use this pot as a canning kettle by placing a rack on the bottom of the pot and following the general boiling water bath directions that follow. (Mine also makes a fine stockpot.)

If you want a separate canning kettle, you should be able to find one for less than $20. Canning kettles in good condition often come up for sale at yard or estate sales for even less. Be sure to buy a large kettle, deep enough so that the canning jars can be covered with at least 2 inches of water. Unless you're sure you'll always be canning pints, make sure the kettle will be deep enough for quart jars, too.

I use jars made expressly for canning, store them every year, and inspect them each summer for chips that would interfere with the canning process. I reuse canning bands, but I buy new lids every year.

A wire basket that fits inside the kettle and is used for blanching vegetables and dipping tomatoes or fruits into boiling water to loosen their skins is handy: I own 2 baskets purchased at yard sales for less than $0.50 apiece.

After groping around in my kettle with tongs to retrieve hot jars, I finally broke down and bought a jar lifter, which is certainly not a necessity but is very helpful and much safer than using the awkward tongs.

Some people swear by a steam pressure canner. I don't can vegetables, meats, nor fish, so I have never bought one. None of the recipes in this book call for the use of a steam pressure canner, but if you're canning low-acid foods, it's a necessity.

There are 2 basic methods for canning high-acid foods: the open kettle method and the boiling water bath method. The open kettle method was traditionally used to process many more foods than it is used for today. The United States Department of Agriculture and other canning authorities used to recommend it for canning fruit preserves and for recipes high in vinegar, but they have since found that it does not always heat food hot enough to prevent the possibility of spoilage. The people at the Ball Corporation, manufacturers of canning jars, refer to open kettle canning in their canning guide, *The Blue Book*, as "an old style method . . . no longer considered safe . . . for any food but jellies." The Department of Agriculture agrees.

I used to can relishes and preserves with the open kettle method, but now I'm much more cautious and use the boiling water method for most foods. It's the only canning method used throughout this book.

The Boiling Water Bath Method

While you are preparing the food, get the canning kettle ready. Place the rack in the kettle, and fill the kettle about ½ full with hot water. Wash your canning jars. Then put the kettle on the stove, add the canning jars, and start heating the water. The jars don't need to be sterilized, so they can come out of the kettle before the water boils; all you want is for them to be hot when you fill them. Also prepare a tea kettle of hot water to add to the canning kettle once you're ready to start processing the jars.

Fill the hot jars, leaving the headspace specified in the recipe. Run a clean knife inside the jars, pressing against the food to release any air bubbles. Wipe the jar rims clean, and top with clean, new lids and clean bands. Screw on the bands as tightly as you can, and place the jars in the hot, not boiling, water in the canning kettle, making sure the jars don't touch the sides of the kettle nor each other.

When all the jars are in the kettle, pour in enough hot water from the tea kettle to cover the jars by at least 2 inches. Cover the canning kettle, bring the water to a gentle boil, and the minute the water starts boiling, start timing for processing. A gentle boil is sufficient for canning. Process for the amount of time indicated in the recipe you're using.

When the food is processed, lift the jars from the canner with a jar lifter or with tongs. Place the jars, spaced apart, on a rack away from drafts: a blast of air from an air conditioner, for example, could crack your jars. Do not retighten the bands, because this might break the seal that forms as the food cools. After 12 to 24 hours, check the lids to make sure you have a good seal; they should be slightly depressed in the center. If you do not, then reprocess the food, or store it in the refrigerator and use it within 1 week or so.

Store the jars in a cool, dark, dry spot. Refrigerate all jars once you've opened them.

Drying Fruits

Drying foods is one of the oldest preserving methods known to mankind. If you have a number of fruit trees or access to large quantities of fruits, you may wish to dry the surplus. Dried apples, apricots, pears, and other fruits make delicious snacks—or quick pick-me-ups when camping or hiking.

I will give you basic instructions for drying fruits. You can use the same techniques for drying vegetables: plum tomatoes, hot peppers, beans, and corn work out well, but for many vegetables freezing or canning is a better solution.

Sun drying is an excellent choice if you live in a hot, dry climate. I've had only occasional luck with sun drying, because when it's hot in Boston, it's usually humid as well, so I have better results with the oven drying method. You could also build a food dehydrator: Rodale's *Stocking Up*, *Home Food Systems*, or the *Solar Food Dryer* give instructions on how to build a dryer at home, as well as suggestions on how to pick a commercial dryer.

How you prepare fruit for drying is important. When you're making fruit desserts or sauces, you can sometimes get away with fruit in less than perfect condition, but fruit for drying must be top quality, because any bruises can cause the fruit to spoil. Wash the fruit thoroughly, and if you are cutting it, do so with a stainless steel knife. Keep the slices uniform so the pieces of fruit dry at the same speed.

If you are drying apples, pears, or peaches—or other fruit that discolors when exposed to the air—drop them into a solution of acidulated water, then let them stand for at least 5 minutes. Acidulated water is merely water to which an acid such as lemon or lime juice is added. I usually use 2 tablespoons lemon juice to every 6 cups water. Pour off the water and place the fruit on absorbent toweling to drain.

Firm-textured fruits such as apples and pears benefit from a short preliminary steaming (blanching, not cooking), which will soften the interiors, making it easier to dry the fruits successfully.

When you are planning to dry large quantities of fruit, I would recommend buying a vegetable steamer at a restaurant supply store. My steamer, which I use almost daily to cook vegetables, cost less than $25. For smaller quantities you could use a simple vegetable steamer that sells for under $5.

Place 1½ inches of water in the bottom of your steamer, and bring the water to a boil. Arrange the fruit on the perforated metal insert, drop it into the pot, and cover the steamer. Medium-size slices of pears and plums should steam for only 2 minutes, while apples and apricots of the same size will need 4 or 5 minutes. The texture of the fruit is the key to the amount of steaming time: buttery soft fruit such as figs would not need steaming at all, while apples definitely benefit from this treatment. Use your judgment, and do a test batch if you're in doubt. These times are only suggestions, because different varieties of fruit contain different amounts of water. Compare, for example, the juiciness of a Rome apple to a McIntosh. Place the fruit on kitchen towels to cool off while you load the trays.

Arrange the fruit on drying trays in a single layer. The trays need be no fancier than stainless steel hardware cloth fastened with a staple gun onto a square or rectangular frame made of pitch-free lumber. The screening allows the air to circulate around the fruit. (Do not use galvanized, fiber glass, vinyl, or copper screening. I've used baking sheets and once— following instructions in a drying book—stretched cheesecloth directly on the oven racks. I managed to burn my hands, and ½ the fruit fell onto the oven floor, but if you're more coordinated than I was, perhaps this is the method for you.)

As you're arranging the fruit on the trays, remember that the air should be freely circulating around it and that to crowd the trays to save time will only end up taking longer in the end, because the fruit will not dry properly.

The preferred temperature for drying foods is 140°F. If your oven can't go that low, it's best to concentrate on sun drying, freezing, or canning. Prop open the door with a block of wood or a stick so the moist air escapes. Check the fruit and move it around about every 45 minutes so it dries evenly.

Most fruits will dry in 6 to 14 hours. To check whether they're ready, let them cool before testing. Dried fruits will be leathery and chewy and will show no moisture when you cut into them.

Cool the fruit, then place it in a mixing bowl loosely covered with a kitchen towel, and let it sit at room temperature for 3 to 4 days. Stir it occasionally so any moisture left in the fruit can evaporate.

Put the fruit in capped jars or plastic bags, and store it in a cool, dark spot. (Light will fade the colors of the fruit.) The fruit should stay in good condition for several months.

Making Fruit Leathers

Around here the fruits in greatest supply to make fruit leathers with are peaches, nectarines, apples, and pears. If I had access to really ripe apricots, though, they would be my first choice. If you are starting with a firm-textured fruit such as apples or pears, it's easiest to coarsely chop or grind the peeled and seeded fruit in a food processor or food mill and cook it with just enough water or juice to keep the fruit from burning. For example, 6 pounds apples would take from ¾ to 1¼ cups apple juice.

Place the apples and liquid in an enameled or stainless steel pan, and slowly bring the mixture to a boil. Cook it, stirring frequently, until the mixture is soft and resembles applesauce. Then add honey to taste, remembering that the fruit purée will dry out and it should not be too sweet. Sweet apples will need very little honey—no more than ½ cup to every 6 pounds fruit.

Cook the mixture for a few minutes longer until it is very thick, and then cool it slightly. Then process it until it's puréed, and cook it again until thickened.

(Softer-textured fruits, such as peaches, should also be chopped and cooked, but you may wish to drain the purée before drying it, to speed up the process.)

Spread the pulp on oiled jelly-roll pans (or baking sheets with sides), or line the pans with oiled waxed paper. Remember that the thicker you spread the leather, the longer it will take to dry: ¼ to ½ inch thick is best.

Dry the purée in a low oven set at about 140°F, in a food dryer, or in the sun. (If you are sun drying the purée, protect it with cheesecloth stretched across the top so yellow jackets and other insects are deterred.) Leave the oven door ajar, and make sure the temperature doesn't creep up. Rotate the pans occasionally. The leather usually will dry in 8 to 12 hours.

When the leather is cooked, remove it from the pans and place it on racks to dry further. If you wish, dust the leather with cornstarch before stacking it in layers and storing it in a box in the pantry, or loosely roll it up into a jelly-roll shape.

The leather will keep in good condition for several months if stored in a cool, dark place. Or freeze it for up to 1 year.

Drying Hot Peppers

In New Mexico and Arizona you can frequently find long strands of dried red chili peppers for sale at farmer's markets. Aside from their usefulness for cooking, the peppers make an attractive wall decoration. If you have a source for long, tapered hot peppers, try drying your own. The technique is simple.

Start with mature red peppers of a hot pepper variety such as Anaheim. The peppers should be about 5 to 7 inches long. Wash and dry the peppers.

Take a heavy strand of twine and tie the stems close together onto the twine, creating a clustered effect. You can make the strand as long or short as you wish. Tie an end of the twine over a nail in a dry area with good air circulation.

After a few weeks the hot peppers will dry out and their skins will turn a dark red shade. At this point the peppers are ready for cooking or decoration. If you keep them in a relatively dry spot, the peppers should stay in good condition for months, ready to be used in Chinese or Mexican cooking or for recipes such as Dried Hot Pepper Sauce (see page 21).

Preserving Grape Leaves

Grape leaves are traditionally preserved in a brine solution, but it's easy to freeze them instead.

Pick young, tender grape leaves (usually found at the ends of the vines). Trim and wash the leaves. Blanch them in a large pot of boiling water for 3 to 4 minutes. Immediately run cold water over the leaves to stop the cooking process, then drain them.

Place the leaves, a few at a time, between 2 kitchen towels, and gently press down to extract some of the water.

Stack the leaves, shiny side up, and place them in plastic freezing bags. I like to freeze 16 per bag, which gives me 4 grape leaves to be stuffed for each member of the family, but adjust the amount to suit your needs. Freeze the leaves.

Defrost at room temperature or in the refrigerator. For quick defrosting just place the plastic bags containing the leaves in a bowl of warm water until they thaw.

The leaves will keep in the freezer for at least 6 months.

Stuffing for Grape Leaves

When stuffed grape leaves are to be served cold, they're usually filled with a vegetarian rice mixture. I like a mixture of brown rice, chopped onions, mint, parsley, ground cinnamon, and ground allspice, all moistened with lemon juice and olive oil. Brown Rice–Sweet Pepper Appetizer Salad (see page 47) is also a good stuffing mixture.

Preserving Herbs

I prefer cooking with fresh herbs and have designed my large herb garden so it keeps me supplied from April through November. Out of season I use a few dried or frozen herbs, but because I feel many herbs lose so much of their essence when dried or frozen, I am more likely to flavor foods with concentrations of vegetables, onions, garlic, and spices.

Certain herbs do freeze and dry adequately, however, so it's worth taking some time in the fall to stock up your freezer or pantry. But be selective: even though herb packagers have promoted every conceivable form of dried herb, not every herb preserves well.

My suggestions come from 20 years' experience growing and preserving herbs. Even so, I know that not everyone will agree with me. I once mentioned in my *Horticulture* magazine food column that I thought chives tasted like grass when dried, only to get an irate letter from a reader in Maine, who said she always dried chives and liked the flavor. That's fine. So much of cooking with herbs is a matter of personal taste. Take my list as a starting-off point, and use the general freezing and drying instructions to put up your own favorites.

To dry herbs, harvest them when they have the highest concentration of oils, which is just before the flower buds open. Put them in an airy, dry, dark spot. You can also tie the stems together and place them inside a large brown paper bag; pull the mouth of the bag around the stems and tie it, leaving a loop of string so that the bag may be hung from a hook. Make sure that the leaves do not touch the sides or bottom of the bag. Once the herbs have dried, strip off the leaves, crumble them, and store them in an airtight container in a dark place. Don't expect the herbs to retain a fresh aroma and taste for longer than 3 to 6 months.

To freeze herbs, chop them and place them on a baking sheet in the freezer. Once they are frozen, tightly pack them in freezer bags or cartons, and enjoy them in stews and soups all winter long. Or freeze chopped herbs in water or stock to flavor casseroles. Ice cube trays are particularly good for this. Frozen herbs usually last for 4 to 6 months.

Basil

I prefer to keep fresh basil under olive oil in a wide jar. Basil will darken in oil, but the flavor is fine. Just wash and dry the leaves, and layer them in a canning jar, dribbling a little olive oil on each layer. When the jar is full, pour in additional oil to cover the leaves so no air can reach them. You should end up with about 1 inch of oil above the top of the leaves. The basil (and the basil scented oil) can be used in casseroles and other recipes all winter. As you use the basil and oil, replace the oil if necessary. Basil will keep this way for up to 7 months.

You can also chop the basil in a food processor or blender, add just enough oil to moisten it, and place the basil in a jar. Press down on the basil and cover it with oil to seal off the air.

Sometimes I freeze chopped basil in ice cube trays. I also make Pesto (see page 247) out of most of my end-of-season basil. Or I just freeze the sprigs to preserve as much of the flavor as possible. I think drying basil is the least preferable preserving method because the basil oils dissipate.

Chervil

Chervil, one of the classic French cooking herbs, has a subtle flavor, midway between parsley and anise, that is lost when it is dried. For best results chop chervil leaves and stems and store them in the freezer.

Chives

When chives are frozen, the flavor becomes stronger and the texture is affected, but they're all right for some cooked dishes. I prefer to keep a pot of chives growing on my sunny kitchen counter all winter so that I can cut fresh chives whenever I need them. I still think dried chives taste like stalks of grass and would never recommend drying them.

Coriander (Cilantro)

Coriander leaves do not freeze or dry well, but you can let the plants go to seed in the fall and dry the seeds. Dried coriander seeds have an aromatic flavor with a slightly bitter tinge that's wonderful in homemade vinegars, marinades, and curries.

Dill

I do not like the flavor of either dried or frozen dillweed. But I think dill heads freeze adequately, and as dill never seems to head when you need it for pickling, it's worth picking the dill heads, popping them into plastic bags, and freezing them whole. When you make pickles, you need only put the frozen heads in the pickling solution.

Dillseed dries well: let the seeds ripen on the plants, harvest and dry them, and store them in a jar on your pantry shelf, or place the ripe seeds in hot vinegar to make dill vinegar.

Lovage

Lovage dries poorly but freezes adequately, although the flavor will never be the same as fresh. I will occasionally chop lovage, place it in ice cube trays, add water, and freeze it for a convenient seasoning for winter soups or stews. Lovage seeds dry well, and a few are good to flavor casseroles. In old English cookbooks you will sometimes see recipes for cakes with dried lovage seeds.

Mint

Although mint dries well, I think the oils are lost in the drying process, and I use it dried only for mint tea. Otherwise I use it fresh. Middle Eastern cooks, however, use dried mint all the time. I do not like frozen mint, although mint syrup freezes nicely.

Parsley

Parsley dries poorly, losing most of its flavor and color. Although it freezes adequately, you can buy parsley year round in the market or grow it on a sunny window sill. I think fresh parsley is worth the expenditure, especially in the winter when your fresh herb options are limited.

Rosemary
Rosemary dries well, but I think the flavor becomes too strong when it is frozen.

Sage
Only use sage fresh, when it is delicious stuffed into the cavity of a chicken with some sprigs of rosemary and thyme, some cloves of garlic, and peppercorns. In Northern Italy the grocery stores sell roast chicken stuffed with this herb mixture. I think dried sage has an unpleasant, musty aftertaste and should be used sparingly for cooking; frozen sage has too strong a flavor for my taste.

Summer Savory
I grow summer savory to use with beans (the Germans call it the bean herb) because its peppery flavor contrasts nicely with the beans (also with cabbage and rutabaga). Summer savory dries well and is often hung from the ceiling in sprays as a decorative accent in a country kitchen. By the way, I don't grow winter savory because summer savory has a far better flavor. Do not freeze summer savory.

Sweet Cicely
This unusual herb, with its delicate anise flavor, is best fresh in salads and soups, but it freezes adequately. Dried, sweet cicely loses its delicate flavor.

Sweet Marjoram
Sweet marjoram dries and freezes well and is, in my opinion, a far better dried cooking choice than basil.

Tarragon
I like to flavor olive oil with sprigs of tarragon, which can then be used in stews and vegetable dishes. Tarragon also keeps well stored in vinegar:

Stuff a sterilized jar with tarragon leaves, cover them with hot vinegar, seal the jar, and keep it on the pantry shelf. The vinegar flavored leaves are good in dishes such as chicken tarragon, vinaigrettes, reduced butter sauces, and béarnaise sauces. As you use the tarragon, add more vinegar. Tarragon also dries well and freezes adequately, although I think either preserving it in oil or vinegar or drying it is preferable.

Thyme
Thyme dries well, but I think it becomes too strongly flavored when frozen.

Index

Index

Index

Rodale Press, Inc., publishes PREVENTION®, the better health magazine.
For information on how to order your subscription,
write to PREVENTION®, Emmaus, PA 18049.